REGIONAL CHANGE IN INDUSTRIALIZING ASIA

Regional Change in Industrializing Asia

Regional and local responses to changing competitiveness

Edited by
LEO VAN GRUNSVEN
Utrecht University, The Netherlands

Routledge
Taylor & Francis Group

LONDON AND NEW YORK

First published 1998 by Ashgate Publishing

Reissued 2018 by Routledge
2 Park Square, Milton Park, Abingdon, Oxon, OX14 4RN
711 Third Avenue, New York, NY 10017, USA

Routledge is an imprint of the Taylor & Francis Group, an informa business

A Library of Congress record exists under LC control number: 98070979

Typeset by Leo van Grunsven Utrecht University

ISBN 13: 978-0-367-00039-4 (hbk)
ISBN 13: 978-0-429-44484-5 (ebk)

Contents

List of Figures

List of Tables

Contributors

Claes G. Alvstam, Professor of Economic Geography, Helsinki School of Economics and Business Administration, P.O. Box 479, FIN-00101, Helsinki, Finland and Department of Human and Economic Geography, School of Economics and Commercial Law, Gothenburg University, Vasagatan 1, S-41180 Göteborg, Sweden.

John Friedmann, Adjunct Professor, Department of Planning, Policy and Land scape, Royal Melbourne Institute of Technology and Professor emiritus, Department of Urban Planning, University of California, Los Angeles. 18 A Loch Street, St. Kilda, Victoria 3182, Australia.

Carl Grundy-Warr, Senior Lecturer, Department of Geography, National University of Singapore, Kent Ridge, Singapore 119260.

Bo Terje Kalsaas, Senior Lecturer, Department of Town and Regional Planning, Norwegian University of Science and Technology, 7034 Trondheim, Norway.

Erja Kettunen, Research Associate, Department of Economic Geography, Helsinki School of Economics and Business Administration, P.O. Box 479, FIN-00101, Helsinki, Finland.

John McKay, Director, Monash Asia Institute, Monash University, Clayton, Victoria 3168, Australia.

Geoff Missen, Senior Lecturer, Department of Geography, University of Melbourne, Parkville, Victoria 3052, Australia.

Sam Ock Park , Professor, Department of Geography, Seoul National University, Seoul 151-742, South Korea.

Sang-Chul Park, Fellow, Department of Human and Economic Geography, School of Economics and Commercial Law, Gothenburg University, Vasagatan 1, S-41180 Göteborg, Sweden.

Martin Perry, Senior Lecturer, Department of Geography, National University of Singapore, Kent Ridge, Singapore 119260.

Leo van Grunsven, Assistant Professor, Section International Economics and Economic Geography and Institute of Development Studies Utrecht, Faculty of Geographical Sciences, Utrecht University, P.O. Box 80.115, 3508 TC Utrecht, The Netherlands.

Chung-Tong Wu, Professor and Dean, Faculty of the Built Environment, The University of New South Wales, Sydney 2052, Australia.

Preface and acknowledgements

This volume has its origins in the annual Residential Conference of the International Geographical Union Commission on the 'Organization of Industrial Space', held in Seoul in August 1995. It includes a number of the papers presented at the Conference, in substantially revised form, as well as some invited contributions. At the time of writing this preface (in the stage of final completion of the book), a 'financial crisis' appears to be emerging which may engender significant changes in industrializing Asia. Though the extent and implications of what is currently evolving in the region are still by no means clear (at the moment new facts surface and are reported in the press daily), it will certainly impinge on what constitutes the central theme of this volume. However, understandably there is no possibility of addressing this development here.

The editor would like to thank the authors for their contribution and participation in this publication. Sergio Conti, Ed Malecki and Sam Ock Park from the Commission's Executive gave advice and encouragement throughout the project, which helped to persevere when original arrangements for the preparation of this volume did not materialize.

Thanks are due to the Cartographic Laboratory of the Faculty of Geographical Sciences, Utrecht University, for the preparation of the figures. At various stages in the preparation of the manuscript, Paula van Duivenvoorde, at the Institute of Development Studies Utrecht, provided assistance with word-processing. Special thanks go to Gina Rozario, who provided much editorial and typesetting assistance at the final stage of preparation of the text and tables to the camera-ready state.

Leo van Grunsven
Utrecht University

Abbreviations

AEM	Asean Economic Ministers' Meeting
AFTA	Asian Free Trade Association
AIC	Asean Industrial Complementation
AIJV	Asean Industrial Joint Ventures
AIP	Asean Industrial Projects
ANIC	Asian Newly Industrialized Country
APEC	Asia Pacific Economic Cooperation
ARF	Asean Regional Forum
ASEAN	Association of Southeast Asian Nations
ASIC	Application Specific Integrated Circuit
CEPT	Common Effective Preferential Tariff
DPRK	Democratic People's Republic of Korea
DRAM	Dynamic Random Access Memory
EAEC	East Asian Economic Causus
EC	European Community
ECU	European Currency Unit
EU	European Union
ERSO	Electronics Research and Service Organization (Taiwan)
FDI	Foreign Direct Investment
GATT	General Agreement on Tariffs and Trade
GNP	Gross National Product
GDP	Gross Domestic Product
IC	Integrated Circuit
IMF	International Monetary Fund
JIT	Just In Time
KMT	Kuomintang state in Taiwan
MITI	Ministry of International Trade and Industry (Japan)
MNC	Multinational Corporation
NAFTA	North American Free Trade Agreement

NET	New Economic Territory
NIC	Newly Industrialized Country
NID	New Industrial Districts
NIE	Newly Industrialized Economy
NMC	Nissan Motor Corporation
OEM	Original Equipment Manufacturing
OHQ	Operational Headquarter
PBEC	Pacific Basin Economic Council
PCB	Printed Circuit Board
PECC	Pacific Economic Cooperation Conference
PRC	People's Republic of China
PTA	Preferential Trading Arrangements
REZ	Regional Economic Zone
R&D	Research and Development
SEOM	Asean Senior Officials Meeting
SEZ	Special Economic Zone
SIJORI	Singapore-Johor-Riau Growth Triangle
SITC	Standard International Trade Classification
SLORC	State Law and Order Restoration Committee (Myanmar)
TEDA	Tumen Economic Development Area
TMC	Toyota Motor Corporation
TNC	Transnational Corporation
TREDA	Tumen River Economic Development Area
TSMC	Taiwan Semiconductor Manufactruing Corporation
UMC	United Micro-electronics Company (Taiwan)
UNCTAD	United Nations Conference on Trade and Development
UNDP	United Nations Development Programme
WH	Western Hemisphere
WTO	World Trade Organization

1 Introduction: Regional Change in Industrializing Asia

Leo van Grunsven

Already for some time, the Asian Pacific Rim, defined as East and Southeast Asia, is the most dynamic macro-region in the world economy. This area, designated in this volume as industrializing Asia, comprises 16 countries (after the return of Hong Kong to China; incl. Japan) with a total population of some two billion. Already for more than a decade, the most striking developmental characteristics of this subregion — as expressed in exceptionally high growth rates of national economies, rapid industrialization, increasingly intense participation in the world economy related to the role of globalization and outward orientation — are receiving much scholarly attention.

To date a range of interpretations of these developmental characteristics have been forwarded, showing how they are connected to processes in the global economy. Notwithstanding the mountain of academic research into many facets of the development of industrializing Asia in the context of global economic change, the 'quest' to apprehend the 'reality' of the region continues. This is hardly surprising. The region continues to display extraordinary economic dynamism, as a result of which the 'reality' of the region, portrayed in an endless stream of publications in the 1970s and a large part of the 1980s, now may be viewed as a phase in the evolution of the region. As the 'reality' of the region almost continuously changes, new constructs of the region become necessary and are being devised, in the attempt to capture the forces shaping that new reality. By way of introduction to the theme of this volume, it is useful to consider some of these constructs.

The first concerns industrializing Asia as a sub-global region, though more often this construct is applied to the entire Pacific Rim, rather than to the Asian Pacific Rim (McGee and Watters, 1997). While the idea of the Pacific Rim as a sub-global system is based to a significant extent on the fact that the countries have been drawn closer together through increased trade, investment, communication and population movement, the same applies to the Asian Pacific Rim. We will return to this point below. It is becoming a cliché to observe that over the last quarter of the century there has been a significant shift of economic power to industrializing Asia. This is revealed first of all in the aspect of its position in total world trade. According to IMF statistical data, the current share of the region in world trade amounts to 25 percent. Until the 1970s this trade showed a pattern of serving colonial interests (with the exception of Japan) and was based on the supply of raw materials to European industry. While primary commodities still constitute a not insignificant share of trade (especially exports from Southeast Asia), currently the region is a major world producer and supplier of manufactured goods such as consumer electronics, electronic components, personal computers and peripheral equipment, voice and datacommunication equipment, textiles and garments, shoes, toys and cars.

Initially, this trade was dominated by Japan. The ANICs, some ASEAN countries and South China have gradually assumed a large role. Nowadays, these economies are used by Japanese firms as third-country export platforms. Not only the composition and volume, but also the direction of trade has changed substantially. The relationships of the Asian Pacific Rim with Europe have expanded, with the region developing a trade surplus. However, the expansion of trans-Pacific trade (i.e., with North America, or more precisely NAFTA) has been much more significant. Despite the increase of imports from NAFTA, the result has been that in 1994 the trade balance showed a surplus of more than US$100 billion, in favour of the Asian Pacific Rim. This all the more demonstrates the strength of the economies of industrializing Asia. Notwithstanding GATT and WTO agreements on the further liberalization of world trade, the trade deficit with the Asian Pacific Rim has led both the EU and NAFTA to take protectionist measures.

The position of industrializing Asia in the world economy can also be derived from trends in foreign direct investments. According to the UNCTAD, the share of developing countries in worldwide foreign direct investments increased from a 21 percent annual average in the period 1988-1992 to 35 percent, 39 percent and 32 percent in 1993, 1994 and 1995 respectively. But the regional trend is uneven, in favour of industrializing Asia (excl. Japan), whose share in foreign investments in developing countries increased from 37 percent between 1981 and 1985 to 57 percent in 1992 and over 60 percent in 1995. As a corollary, Africa and Latin America saw a decline in foreign investments (UNCTAD, 1996). These trends reflect the differences in competitiveness or comparative advantages. In turn, these relate to a host of factors, of which state policies is only one. With the large volume of FDI attracted to industrializing Asia, and — as will be referred to later — increasingly flowing within the region (incl. Japan), the region ranks very high in terms of the presence of affiliates of multinational corporations. In addition, there is a substantial involvement of local firms in international subcontracting, a second major form of incorporation of the region in international production.

The idea of industrializing Asia as a sub-global system also partly derives from the notion of the 'East Asian Growth Model' and Confucian values underpinning the model, reinforcing the idea of a common regional identity (e.g. World Bank 1993).

2

The roles played in the region by FDI and global sourcing through international subcontracting bring us to a second construct, that of industrialization and development under globalization. From the 1950s, the process of industrialization has been the engine of the dynamic growth of the region, progressing through the region in different phases and, as far as individual countries are concerned, progressing through different (not always identical) stages. After reconstruction immediately following the Second World War, and a phase of concentration on heavy industry, in the course of the 1970s the Japanese export industry started to conquer the world, especially its consumer electronics and automotive industries. From the end of the 1960s, industrialization occurred very rapidly in what are now known as the Asian Newly Industrialized Countries (ANICs): Hong Kong, Singapore, Taiwan and South Korea. Export manufacturing assumed a prominent position. In Singapore this occurred under the aegis of international capital. In the other three 'Tigers', domestic capital has been of greater importance (e.g. in South Korea the large domestic conglomerates, the *chaebol*, have played a pivotal role). Since the mid-1980s the regional pattern has been evolving rapidly, with the rapid emergence of a second generation of economies as 'global export manufacturing platforms'. These include the ASEAN countries of Malaysia, Thailand and Indonesia. In the first half of the 1990s, a third generation has been emerging, South China and more recently Vietnam.

As regards industrialization, the continuous transfer of production to the region from other regions partly underlies the idea of development under globalization (or internationalization, a term with a somewhat different meaning). In this idea, the way globalization is seen to impact the region is, as McGee and Watters (1997, p.5) put it, through an 'international steamroller' effect with growing transnational corporate dominance and power (and also by means of cultural convergence and the globalization of consumption practices). Since the second half of the 1980s, the development under globalization idea has assumed new dimensions. To a very significant degree the emergence of the second and third generation countries as 'global export manufacturing platforms' can be linked to the internationalization of both Asian and non-Asian capital *within* the region, Japan and the four 'Tigers' constituting the origins (see e.g. Nomura Research Institute & ISEAS, 1995). As far as Japan is concerned, the *endeka* (appreciation of the yen after 1985) triggered several waves of large volumes of foreign investment in other parts of the region (see e.g. Rimmer, 1997a). In the second half of the 1980s, the changing local environment, affecting competitiveness, made it imperative for the ANIC states and firms operating in these economies to engage in industrial restructuring (Clark & Kim, 1995), leading to significant flows of outward investment, in large part directed to elsewhere in the region.

The above-mentioned view of globalization is reinforced as export-oriented industrialization under the influence of cross-border flows of capital evolves in the Asian Pacific Rim as a process, incorporating — or spreading to — a next group of countries after the (initial) stage marked by labour-intensive low value-added production has become difficult to maintain in the ANICS. The 'flying geese' have

3

become the metaphor to depict this process. An integral element of the process is also the functional upgrading in the 'early group', which moves to the next higher stage. The developmental 'escalator' has become the rather awkward metaphor to depict this feature of the process.

The increasing role of intra-regional investment and trade constitutes one of the core elements in a third construct, that of an inter-linked region through integration and cooperation. This construct substitutes the ideas of separateness and fragmentation for homogeneity and integration, the latter are both market-driven and government-driven (for references to these ideas, see e.g. Cook et al., 1996; Forbes, 1997; Le Heron and Park, 1995; Rumley et al., 1996). The idea of homogeneity is also partly based on the notion referred to earlier of the 'East Asian Growth Model' and Confucian values underpinning the model, reinforcing the idea of a common regional identity. Forbes (1997) identifies four elements in the evolution of industrializing Asia into a region of interaction and connectivity: economic linkages (investment and trade), international population movements; information and communications, and institution building.

As to the first element, reflecting the increased interlinkage of the economies in the region, intra-regional trade in industrializing Asia has increased significantly over the past fifteen years. Firstly, the trade between Japan and the ANICs may illustrate the point: in 1980 the value of Japan's commodity exports to the ANICs amounted to US$19 billion, while its commodity imports from the ANICs amounted to US$7 billion. In 1994 these trade flows amounted to US$93 billion and US$31 billion respectively. In 1980, ASEAN exports to other countries in the region were valued at US$30 billion (two-thirds of which were directed to Japan and one-third to the ANICs). In 1994 these exports amounted to US$77 billion (US$32 billion of which was directed to Japan, US$41 billion to the ANICs and US$4 billion to China). During the period referred to, intra-regional trade increased five-fold to some 45 percent of total trade (Flüchter, 1996).

Though there are important historical antecedents (as expressed in the significant Chinese and Indian diasporas in Southeast Asia), international population movements in the region have increased substantially since the 1970s, especially labour migration between labour deficit and labour surplus countries (both legal and illegal flows). The rapid integration of the region through information flows and communications links reflects substantial infrastructure improvements, especially telecommunications. This is a significant facilitator of the growing economic links. Not only have information flows increased rapidly, so too have flows of goods and people, as reflected in the tremendous growth during the last decade of sea and air transport. In tandem, sea and air transport infrastructure have expanded rapidly throughout the region (Rimmer, 1996, 1997b).

As to institution building, the willingness to spread growth further is indicated by new (political) arrangements at the supra-national level, such as APEC and more recently the extension of ASEAN (the Association of Southeast Asian Nations) to nine members (the new members are Laos and Myanmar; Cambodia was not admitted yet due to the political events in the country immediately before the

ASEAN meeting held in June 1997). This is aided by national differences in comparative advantages, which can bring about increased investment and trade. At a sub-regional level, a new arrangement achieving or aiming at similar outcomes has evolved and is now widely propagated, namely cross-border regional economic zones (see e.g. Thant et al., 1994).

Institutional change and new arrangements are not just a matter of government-driven integration. Government initiatives may in part be perceived as inspired by and responding to market-driven integration, in which private actors, particularly MNCs, play a dominant role. In the course of time, the composition of these MNCs has changed substantially, not only in terms of origin (e.g. the increased role of Japanese and, recently, of ANIC MNCs), but also in terms of sector/branch (manufacturing versus the financial, service and commerce sectors), investment motives (cost-driven versus market-driven), functional position (e.g. main firms versus dependent firms), etc. Also, the scale of operation, the production strategies/organization and operational structure/characteristics of many large industrial MNCs operating in the region have undergone substantial modification. A few of the significant outcomes have been the emergence of regionally organized corporate networks and locally as well as regionally embedded production and supply networks. Networking indeed has become a major phenomenon in the region and constitutes an important aspect of increased interaction and connectivity. There are many forms, often linked to specific actors, operating at different geographical scales (see e.g., Park, 1997). In addition to the ones referred to above, recently attention has been directed to the operation of overseas Chinese networks which Cho-Oon Khong (1996) suggests provide the 'glue' of regional identity, rather than institutional arrangements.

The elements indicated above signal, in Forbes' terminology, the 'new geographies' of the region. These are alternatively referred to as the changing contours of human and economic geographies of the region, or as the visible changes to the spatial structures and linkages which determine the way in which the region is organized and are shaped by the uneven processes of economic growth accelerated economic integration (Forbes, 1997, p.13-14). The developments which forge changes in the geographical configuration of the region, according to Forbes (1997, p.26):

demonstrate the need for a rethinking of the approach taken to understanding the dynamics of this region. Increasingly, scholars will need to be better attuned to the great complexity of interaction and less fettered by traditional expectations of the significance of national boundaries.

A fourth construct concerns the interpretation of the economic dynamics and changes in the spatial patterning of the region as outcomes of responses at different levels (from the regional to the local) by different actors to changing global and regional forces. Thus, central in this construct is the concept of the global-local dialectic. Instead of a view of globalization as an 'international steamroller', local forces in a variety of political, regional and cultural forms are always negotiating with the global, in an attempt to forge specific outcomes (McGee and Watters, 1997). The shaping and production of firm behaviour and strategies, the behaviour and strategies of states, changes in industries and economic sectors, as well as changes in the characteristics of spaces can thus be understood from the interaction between the global and the local, and the negotiation involved. Negotiation may be directed to achieving different aims by different actors, or by the same actor at a different stage of engagement to the global. Local-global interaction may thus revolve around offering resistance to global elements, becoming incorporated in global elements, changing the form of incorporation in global elements, or providing global elements a regional or local distinctiveness. As the interaction and negotiation take place in local or regional spaces, these impinge on the role of specific spaces with respect to the global. The dynamics of interaction between the global and the local provides a useful framework for an understanding of the region as a 'mosaic', or, in dynamic terms, 'kaleidoscope' of spaces.

Key themes in this book

The main theme of this book builds on some of the constructs outlined above, especially the third and fourth construct. It is necessary to state first of all that we perceive the 'reality' of the region as a 'kaleidoscope' which operates under a range of internal and external forces. The dynamics of the region and the behavioural changes of actors (be it national and local states, multinational corporations, local firms, labour or consumers), in response to changing internal and external forces, have given rise to and is constantly giving rise to alterations in the patterns of growth, new characteristics or trends. By focusing on regional change, understood as changes to existing or new forms of spatial organization (in the vein of 'new geographies'), the volume places the spatial aspect of the kaleidoscopic picture of the region in the forefront. It is inspired by the observation that, from a geographical perspective, the dynamics and behavioural changes referred to above are expressed in the reconstruction of spatial organization.

As to the forces underlying regional change, this volume emphasizes the imperatives of dynamic comparative advantage, changing global or regional competitiveness, and regional competition, faced by different actors, entities and/or units of analysis (including territorial units at different scale levels, supranational, national and subnational) as important forces shaping regional change, i.e. the local or regional responses to these imperatives. Many of the changes and new phenomena in the spatial organization and 'tendencies in places' in the region can be interpreted from this perspective.

Over the past decade, the forces referred to above have evoked regional and local responses by multiple actors — individuals, entrepreneurs, firms (ranging from the small local firm to the large multinational corporation), national and subnational regional and local states — in differential geographical settings. One response to the challenges of increased global or regional competition and the struggle of firms to maintain or gain competitiveness has been the development of business networks already referred to above, in tandem with increased internationalization. Within the spectrum of emerging networks, those shaped by strategic firm behaviour in response to dynamic local, regional and global conditions, external and internal to firms, include the intra-firm inter-establishment networks. These tend to be highly dynamic, associated with changing locational strategies of firms. Next, in large part to cope with problems of competitiveness, cooperative strategies are developed or reconfigured by firms focusing on several kinds of inter-firm relations (supplier networks, producer networks, customer networks and technology cooperation networks). The geographical patterning of the intra-firm and extra-firm structure of network linkages 'contains' many of the manifestations constituting regional change. In cases where inter-firm relations and cooperation have been intensified or de-intensified *locally*, the outcome has been increased or decreased networking of firms within industrial complexes or districts, rapidly changing the character of such complexes or districts. *Non-local* inter-firm cooperation and inter-establishment intra-firm links imply that such networks may and do develop or change across regional and national boundaries (Park, 1997). The increasing role of overseas Chinese entrepreneurship in business development in specific parts of the region, demonstrates that business networks differ substantially in nature and functions. The broadening of the spectrum of (international) business networks has been an important element in spatial reorganization in the region over the past decade.

Business networks are not unconnected to the dynamic comparative advantages of places. Many industrializing areas which have experienced rapid growth during the last two decades contend with serious problems such as higher costs, shortages of production workers and an ever more competitive environment. As 'new' states and regions which have placed themselves in a rival position *vis-à-vis* longer established industrializing states (the ANICs) and regions have captured comparative advantage, a spatial shift of foreign investment, associated with the locational strategies of firms, has occurred. This has led the ANICs to initiate a state-led process of (spatial) restructuring for survival. In this process existing types of production and forms of organization have been shedded and 'niche' strategies have been adopted, based on 'new' comparative advantage fashioned by the state for higher value-added activities across value chains (Clark and Kim, 1995). As the role assigned to the longer established industrializing 'places' in globally and emerging regionally organized commodity chains (Gereffi and Korzeniewicz, 1994) has altered, the strategic and organizational responses by major actors are manifested also in 'newer' intra-regional divisions of labour at several levels (see e.g., Dobson and Chia, 1997; Nomura Research Institute and ISEAS, 1995). Linked manifestations are the regionalization tendency, as well as the realignment of the global-regional-local divide in the operation of firms (associated with spatial reorganization of production in the process of maintaining and reconfiguring competitiveness) as well as in production systems within industries and production

7

complexes. Increases in intra-regional trade, with a significant contribution of intrafirm trade, and foreign direct investment emanating from the ANICs are part and parcel of this process.

New economic arrangements and territorial configurations which have emerged from the micro level up to the macro level in the process of adjustment to changing global and regional competitiveness, dynamic comparative advantage and intensified competition between places, are at a meso level also manifested in the phenomenon of the New Economic Territories (NETs), alternatively designated as Regional Economic Zones (REZs) or Growth Triangles (Forbes, 1997; Thant et al., 1994). Apart from providing a unique Asian solution to problems of regional integration among countries marked by different socio-economic systems, these constitute one of the spaces within which the regionalization of firms and industries (away from the ANICs) and intra-regional division of labour have taken shape. Within industrializing Asia, economic production environments are still highly differentiated, both at the national and the sub-national levels. Actors make use of these differences, especially where regions with different endowments and comparative advantages are located cross-border but adjacent to each other. The well-known examples, the Singapore-Johor-Riau Triangle, the Northern Triangle (comprising Northwest Peninsular Malaysia, Southern Thailand and the region of Medan in Sumatra, Indonesia), and the Greater South China REZ (comprising South China, Hong Kong and Taiwan) are frequently cited to illustrate the point.

At the macro level, new institutional arrangements such as APEC, an extended ASEAN, and the ASEAN Free Trade Area (AFTA), while heralded as instruments or facilitators of intensified regional cooperation and integration, are at the same time responses to increased global and regional competition. The fear of ASEAN (with the exception of Singapore) of losing out to China in attracting foreign direct investment illustrates the point. It may be noted here that competition between (sets of) economies in the region may heighten regional rivalry (alongside regional cooperation, spurred on by increasing global protection or rivalry between/of global sub-regions). In addition, regional diversity of comparative advantages presents opportunities but poses problems as well. In this respect, it is perhaps worthwhile to note that the fluidity of development in the region does not guarantee that cooperation always leads to win-win situations. During economic recession, patterns of domination and dependence can become more clear, and win-win situations of today may well be win-lose situations tomorrow. In the 'global and regional game', players cooperate and compete at the same time. As the volume edited by Cook et al. (1996) suggests, this may lead to a scenario of future development, revolving around fragmentation and disintegration rather than increased interaction, interlinkage and integration. Another possible scenario is one, which combines these opposite tendencies.

An element to take into account as to the foregoing, concerns competition between places at yet another level. As with everywhere in the developing world, urbanization is increasing in industrializing Asia. Limiting ourselves to the two largest countries in terms of population, in 1975 17 percent of China's population lived in cities, in the case of Indonesia's population, this amounted to 19 percent. It is forecasted that in the year 2000 these percentages will reach 34 percent and 40 percent respectively. The urbanization process is marked by a concentration of urban population in large metropolitan areas. In the year 2000, Tokyo will have 25 million inhabitants, Shanghai 13.5 million, Seoul 10.9 million, Jakarta 9.2 million, Manila 8.0 million, etc. (UNCHS, 1996, pp. 16-7, 440). New representations and configurations of the metropolis have emerged in industrializing Asia: the 'desakota' (extended metropolitan region), the mega-urban region, the new economic territories, the World City and the international urban corridor. Common to these five concepts is the idea of the integration of the metropolis in industrializing Asia into the global economy, and the determining impact of globalization processes on spatial structures (Lo and Yeung, 1996).

Urbanization and concentration in mega-urban regions are part of the process of economic change. This reflects the position of mega-urban regions as the 'containers' of economic dynamism, where a large part of national GDP is generated. McGee (1997, p. 37) states that:

.. the states (of industrializing Asia) are openly embracing the forces of globalisation which emphasise the concentration of population and economic activity in large mega-urban regions. Both global and national investment find these areas ideal 'investment sinks' in which to locate manufacturing of consumption goods, invest in the built environment and create the landscape of global consumption.

The process described by McGee is reinforced as competition for investment among the mega-urban regions has increased, leading to attempts to outbid each other by offering even more attractive incentives, or rather concessions. Thus, the interrelationship between (the spatial pattern of) economic change and the development of mega-urban regions is very much a mutual one (Lo and Yeung, 1996). Concentration and the implications of rivalry among urban regions have recently led to more attention being devoted to the questions of uneven development, from social and geographical perspectives (see e.g., Dragsbaek Schmidt et al., 1997; Dixon and Drakakis-Smith, 1997) and sustainability (see e.g. McGee, 1997; UNCHS, 1996). These are highly relevant questions from the perspective of a possible future scenario of fragmentation and disintegration.

In the above, an intriguing question, namely the interaction between state and market, has been implicitly addressed. This question still generates a lively debate. Another debate, which also revolves around the state, has originated from the reconfiguration of the economic and institutional landscapes in the region over the past decade. The emergence of new economic territories and the establishment of new institutional arrangements such as APEC and AFTA have invoked the question of the implications of the current and future position or role of different actors/ agents, particularly the nation state, in further shaping the new economic reality in the region and, as a corollary, its positioning in the global economic order. Central in the current debate are two opposing views about the fate of the nation state as a functional entity. One pronounces the end of the nation state, propagating region states as more suitable units of governance (Ohmae, 1995) or supra-national institutions as vehicles for regulation. The other considers declarations about the end of the nation state as both premature and foolhardy. Institutions at the level of the nation state still constitute a crucial force in shaping and regulating the nature, pace and attributes of (localized) growth processes (Gertler, 1997).

The contributions in this volume set out with objectives to provide further illumination, contextualization and interpretation of the spatiality of the economic reality in industrializing Asia, as expressed in contemporary regional change, as well as the role played by, and the implications for, different actors in this process. The set of contributions reflect the argument that regional change is not one singular process with one singular outcome at one spatial scale level, but a composite of responses driven by the government and the market involving different actors or agents, with many interconnected manifestations at different levels and spatial scales (from the macro to the micro), linked to both agents and territorial units. The volume examines the (sub)regional and local responses as well as the range of manifestations as to regional change (as an outcome) from the perspective of their interconnectedness and internal logic as well as the global-local relationships (and shifts in the global-regional-local divide) implied in them. Thus, the perspective adopted here builds and elaborates on the global-local construct of the region, emphasizing local and regional responses to the forces indicated above. As many of the observations made above fit the direction of increased interconnectedness, interaction, integration and cooperation, it also builds and elaborates on the interlinked region construct. At the same time, the possibility of fragmentation and disintegration is illustrated.

Structure of the book

Over the past decade, geographers have contributed significantly to the scientific enquiry in many areas related to the dynamics of industrializing Asia. As developments in the region evolve, new lines of scientific enquiry are opened up almost continuously, not only outside but also inside the field of geography. This volume brings together some of the work of geographers related to the changing 'reality' of the region.

Chapter two starts the enquiry at the macro level and considers the phenomena of regional economic integration and regionalization, as part of the economic dynamism and emerging new economic reality in industrializing Asia, which, as noted above, are currently receiving substantial attention, the more so in view of the government-driven institution of organizations of regional cooperation (e.g., APEC and the EAEC initiative). Marking a partial move away from regional rivalry in the face of increasing global rivalry between states and regions, as well as global competitive struggles of enterprises, Geoff Missen and John McKay

10

address this particular type of regional response, the underlying motives and internal logic against the background of rival interpretations of newly emerging economic relationships at a macro level in the region. Examining the economic rhetoric behind APEC and the EAEC initiative in the light of the constructions of the economic reality of industrializing Asia from two theoretical perspectives, it is concluded that processes evolving in the region are far less simple than orthodox views suggest.

In chapter three, Erja Kettunen considers the same theme of regional economic integration in the context of the Association of Southeast Asian Nations (ASEAN) countries. In particular, this chapter addresses the establishment of the ASEAN Free Trade Area (AFTA) in the 1990s. Originally, ASEAN was formed in the 1960s to promote regional economic cooperation and fostered by regional security concerns. Currently it comprises Indonesia, Laos, Malaysia, Myanmar, the Philippines, Singapore, Thailand, Brunei, and Vietnam. Despite the modest performance in intra-regional trade, the original ASEAN countries (the ASEAN-6) agreed to establish a free trade area in 1993. However, trade among the ASEAN has remained modest, and the countries seem not to aim at increasing intra-trade, hence contradicting the basic explanations for setting up a free trade area. Thus, the case of AFTA challenges the mainstream theorizing of economic integration. This chapter looks at the reasons for the formation of AFTA and discusses the relevance of integration theorizing considering the case at hand. First, ASEAN's formation and institutionalization is examined. Second, the aims of the ASEAN Free Trade Area are presented against the backdrop of the international politico-economic developments of the 1990s. Finally, prospects for ASEAN and AFTA are discussed, by deliberating the particular integrative and disintegrative factors prevailing within the Association. As a conclusion, some suggestions are presented concerning the basic theorizing on economic integration.

In chapter four, Claes Alvstam and Sang-Chul Park consider intra-regional division of labour and industrial change in East Asia, focusing on the case of the emerging high-technology interaction between Korea and Taiwan. In the process of industrial change in the ANICs, strong domestic firms in high technology industries have gradually emerged, particularly in Taiwan and Korea. These firms and the industries in which they are embedded have adopted internationalization, upgrading, specialization and niche production strategies to adjust to changing comparative advantage. After a phase of orientation towards the Old Industrial Core, the time lag in the transition process observed in the different countries has produced tendencies towards product differentiation in a regional market, opening up new avenues for intra-regional division of labour and contacts. This is reflected in increasing intra-regional trade connections in high-technology and knowledge-intensive goods and services. Set within the theoretical debate on intra-regional competition versus complementarity, this chapter is concerned with assessing the conditions for further change, thus contributing to the theoretical debate on how to interpret present and future developments.

In chapter five, Chung-Tong Wu adds new insights into the operation of overseas Chinese business networks. The author observes that most of the existing studies are chiefly concerned with the inner workings of Chinese businesses and enterprises, their business methods and the multiple linkages and networks that emerge around groups of families and the enterprises they control. Much of the interest is either political or sociological in that the researchers are mostly concerned with the political and social implications of these ethnic businesses in a political environment largely controlled by non-Chinese ethnic groups. However, none of the studies on Southeast Asian businesses deal explicitly with the spatial or regional impacts of their investments. By considering the regional impact of diaspora investments in China, comparing South Korean investments with overseas Chinese investments, the motivations and modes of operation of such investments are revealed. The data from China indicate that investors from the NIEs, at least during the initial investment stage, have strong location preferences. This is due partly to the ethnic and kinship links that the investors perceive to provide advantages for their initial investments, to ease the way, to gain a better bargaining position, and to obtain special assistance. The data from Hong Kong indicate that investors do move away from the beach-heads they established once they gain experience with investing in an environment that is largely unknown and, to them, full of uncertainties. Both the overseas Chinese and the ethnic Korean investors have shown similar tendencies in China. The literature on ethnic businesses and business networks does not specifically deal with the spatial implications. It is the argument of this contribution that by understanding where the diaspora capital may tend to first invest, we could understand better the development of regions that may be expected to attract large diaspora capital.

Chapters six, seven and eight focus on the dynamics of firm and industry behaviour as well as of industrial complexes, related to competitiveness and changing comparative advantage, and related pressures of restructuring. The emphasis here is on the territorial reconfiguration or evolution of industrial networks and the production system in which they are embedded as elements of regional change. In chapter six, Leo van Grunsven provides additional insights into industrial restructuring in the Asian NICs and the associated dynamics of local production systems in industries. The local responses at the micro level by both TNC establishments and local firms — associated with restructuring efforts in the ANICs — in order to maintain competitiveness are manifested in significant alterations in the production systems in a range of industry branches, especially those dominated by TNCs. This chapter considers the changing local production systems in Singapore, focusing on a very dynamic industry branch, the production of audio equipment. Empirical investigation reveals a shift in the main producer segment towards concentration on the final stage of assembly while the manufacturing of lower end products is shifted to other locations in the region. While subcontracting has been increased, in the supply segment a gradual de-localization of the supply structures, which developed before the onset of restructuring, can be observed. In terms of actual manufacturing and flows of components a more regionalized structure seems to be in the making. Thus, in the process of restructuring, patterns of production organization and the geography of the production system appear to be reshaped significantly. The territorial structure of production systems seems to be expanding significantly, reflecting shifts in the regional patterning of comparative advantage of 'places' and the efforts of firms to maintain competitiveness in the face of these shifts. The insights contained in this chapter add to the body of theory on the global-regional-local divide in industrial organization.

In chapter seven, Bo Terje Kalsaas analyzes the paths of development in the Japanese automotive industry, focusing on the implications of changing competitiveness for the Just-in-Time system and procurement patterns. This chapter addresses the development of Just-in-Time — as a specific form of production organization and regulation — in the Japanese automotive industry in a period in which the industry faces increased regional and global competition and has to struggle with the appreciation of the yen, undermining comparative advantage. Drawing on the regulation approach, emphasizing the contradiction between internal and external flexibility regarding labour, analysis of the path of development, subcontractor-final assembler relationships, competitive strategy, time compression in production chains and locational aspects, reveal the implications for production arrangements and the geographical structure of production organization. The responses adopted by firms point towards increasing pressure on the Just-in-Time system which has been a significant feature of the industry for a considerable time, resulting in significant regional change.

In chapter eight, Sam Ock Park considers the local-global networks of high-technology industrial districts in Korea. He discusses the implications of restructuring for the spatial organization of industrial activities from the point of view of localities, i.e. industrial districts. Set within the theoretical debate on issues of globalization and localization, related to 'new industrial districts', the nature of and changes in industrial networks and embeddedness of firms in industrial districts in Korea are analyzed using empirical data. The notions underlying the analysis concern the importance of both non-local and localized networks and embeddedness as elements to be considered in regional change at the level of territorial industrial complexes or districts, as well as the role of small firms — besides large firms — as agents. In the case of Korea, increasingly the remaking of comparative advantage and enhancement of the global and regional competitiveness of firms and of the industrial districts in which they are located, derive from the coexistence of both non-local and local networks and embeddedness.

In chapter nine, John Friedmann takes up the issues of concentration of development in metropolitan areas and competition for investment among mega-urban regions. He discusses emerging world cities and the role of urban and regional policies in the Asia Pacific region. The chapter first considers the growth of mega-urban regions, in both theoretical and policy terms and evaluates the world city concept within recent trends in the development of global capitalism. After examining the spatial dynamics of world city formation, Friedmann proceeds by looking at a series of policy issues facing planners in the Asia Pacific region, notably spatial organization, regional governance, social and environmental sustainability, the question of migrant workers or citizens, the rise of civil society, and intercity networks. He observes that in many ways current urban policies, which have been adopted in order not to lose out in city competition, are based on misguided premises and principles. Contrary to current planning practices, the nearsightedness of public policies that concentrate exclusively on economic issues and a natural tendency towards 'out-of-control' competition which, in effect, leads cities to forfeit part of their future to transnational capital whose primary concern is, after all, nothing more ambitious than the prospect of super-profits, he argues the case for intercity cooperation to balance the above-mentioned tendency. In addition, the principle — that cities are for the people who live in them, and that a city's inhabitants must be assured a way of flourishing in the new economic order — should explicitly guide planning. The life space of urban inhabitants must be defended against developments that tend to favour the few over the many; public services must be provided in adequate measure to everyone regardless of their ability to pay for them; and the conditions of the environment from city core to far periphery must be protected and enhanced. Adequate planning may require a substantial overhaul of the system of governance. Without all this, failure rather than success in city competition will be likely.

In chapter ten, Carl Grundy-Warr and Martin Perry examine the issue of the future position and role of the nation state in the framework of the changing economic landscape in Southeast Asia. It takes up the proposition of declining national sovereignty and discusses the status of the nation state. The starting point for this discussion is the view that a clear understanding of political processes needs to underpin claims about the advent of globalization. With this in mind, the chapter begins by outlining definitions of national sovereignty, integration and interdependence. From the discussion follows the argument that greater economic interdependence, or even limited economic integration, may dilute state sovereignty, but they do not necessarily signal the beginning of the demise of nation states. Sovereignty is an elastic concept as 'the frontiers of national sovereignty' are being moved, modified or changed based on deliberately taken alterations in state policies and actions. The authors subsequently examine this proposition through an analysis of the recent history of the Association of Southeast Asian Nations (ASEAN), including its promotion of regionalization amongst the nation states of Southeast Asia, competing regional economic groupings, and the development of sub-regional forms of cooperation amongst certain ASEAN member states. As to the latter, the discussion addresses the question of the applicability or validity of the features of a region state, as proposed by Ohmae, global-local tensions, issues of distribution, substitution and power, complementarity or competition, social tensions, and political relations and national security issues. In the assessment of the claims about the loss of national sovereignty and drift towards a globalized world economy in the context of regionalization initiatives promoted by or within ASEAN, the authors argue that claims about such a trend have tended to indiscriminately label processes producing different outcomes. In practice, in the case of ASEAN, it is possible to encourage this form of economic integration without significant loss of of sovereignty. As to sub-regional economic zones, the authors conclude that the blanket application of terms such as 'interdependence', 'borderless economies', 'region states' and 'integrated borderlands' tends to mask the contradictions produced by globalization as well as the segmentation and internal differentiation that often exist in any territory, particularly borderlands. They also suggest that whilst the sub-regional economic zones have certain 'transnational' characteristics, they are favoured forms of interaction by states precisely because levels of integration can be largely restricted to specific functions and activities. Furthermore, growth triangles involve little change in national and institutional arrangements and may even operate without formal treaties or changes in domestic regulations.

This volume endeavours to present different facets of intellectual enquiry on industrializing Asia that embody regional development issues. The contributions explore the ways in which regional development processes are taking place under a range of forces, and the spatial structures which are emerging and reconstituted, both of which escape preconceptions of Western principles of capitalism. A common denominator of the contributions is the opening up of new exciting fields of research. They all present challenges for geography.

References

Clark, G.L. and Kim, W.B. (eds) (1995), *Asian NIEs and the Global Economy:Industrial Restructuring and Corporate Strategy in the 1990s*, The Johns Hopkins University Press: Baltimore.

Cook, I.G., Doel, M.A. and Li, R. (eds) (1996), *Fragmented Asia: Regional Integration and National Disintegration in Pacific Asia*, Avebury: Aldershot.

Dixon, C. and Drakakis-Smith, D. (eds) (1997), *Uneven Development in Southeast Asia*, Ashgate: Aldershot.

Dobson, W. and Chia, S.Y. (eds) (1997), *Multinationals and East Asian Integration*, International Development Research Centre/Institute of Southeast Asian Studies: Ottawa and Singapore.

Schmidt, J.D., Hersh, J. and Fold, N. (eds) (1997), *Social Change in Southeast Asia*, Addison Wesley Longman Ltd.: Harlow.

Flüchter, W. (1996), 'Bedeutung und Einfluss Japans in Ost- und Südostasien', *Geographische Rundschau*, Vol. 48, pp. 702-709.

Forbes, D. (1997), 'Regional Integration, Internationalisation and New Geographies of the Pacific Rim', in Watters, R. & McGee, T. (eds), *Asia Pacific: New Geographies of the Pacific Rim*, Hurst & Co. (Publishers) Ltd: London, pp. 13-28.

Gereffi, G. and Korzeniewicz, M. (eds) (1994), *Commodity Chains and Global Capitalism*, Praeger Publishers: Westport, Connecticut.

Gertler, M.S. (1997), 'Globality and Locality: The Future of 'Geography' and the Nation State', in Rimmer, P.J. (ed.), *Pacific Rim Development: Integration and Globalisation in the Asia-Pacific Economy*, Allen and Unwin Australia Pte Ltd:

15

Sydney, pp. 12-33.

Khong, C.O. (1996), 'Pacific Asia As a Region: A View from Business', in Cook, I.G., Doel, M.A. and Li, R. (eds), *Fragmented Asia: Regional Integration and National Disintegration in Pacific Asia*, Avebury: Aldershot, pp. 167-80.

Le Heron, R. and Park, S.O. (eds) (1995), *The Asian Pacific Rim and Globalization. Enterprise, Governance and Territoriality*, Avebury: Aldershot.

Lo, F.C. and Yeung, Y.M. (eds) (1996), *Emerging World Cities in Pacific Asia*, United Nations University Press: Tokyo.

McGee, T.G. (1997), 'Globalisation, Urbanisation and the Emergence of Subglo bal Regions: A Case Study of the Asia-Pacific Region', in Watters, R. & McGee, T. (eds), *Asia Pacific: New Geographies of the Pacific Rim*, Hurst & Co. (Publishers) Ltd: London, pp. 29-45.

Ohmae, K. (1995), *The End of the Nation State. The Rise of Regional Economies*, The Free Press: New York.

Nomura Research Institute and Institute of Southeast Asian Studies (1995), *The New Wave of Foreign Direct Investment in Asia*, ISEAS: Singapore.

Park, S.O. (1997), 'Rethinking the Pacific Rim', *Journal of Economic and Social Geography (TESG)*, Vol. 88, pp.425-38.

Rimmer, P. (1996), 'International Transport and Communications Interactions Between Pacific Asia's Emerging World Cities', in Lo, F.C. and Yeung Y. M. (eds), *Emerging World Cities in Pacific Asia*, United Nations University Press: Tokyo, pp. 48-97.

Rimmer, P. (1997a), 'Trans-Pacific Oceanic Economy Revisited', *Journal of Economic and Social Geography (TESG)*, Vol. 88, pp.439-56.

Rimmer, P. (1997b), 'Japan's Foreign Direct Investment in the Pacific Rim, 1985-1993', in Watters, R. & McGee, T. (eds), *Asia Pacific: New Geographies of the Pacific Rim*, Hurst & Co. (Publishers) Ltd: London, pp. 113-32.

Rumley, D., Chiba, T., Takagi, A., and Fukushima, Y. (eds) (1996), *Global Geopolitical Change and the Asia-Pacific*, Avebury: Aldershot.

Thant, M., Tang, M. and Kazaku, H. (eds) (1994), *Growth Triangles in Asia. A New Approach to Regional Economic Cooperation*, Oxford University Press: Hong Kong.

The World Bank (1993), *The East Asian Miracle. Economic Growth and Public Policy*, Oxford University Press: Oxford.

United Nations Centre for Human Settlements (1996), *An Urbanizing World: Global Report on Human Settlements*. UNHCS/Oxford University Press: Oxford.

United Nations Conference on Trade and Development (1996), *World Investment Report 1996. Investment, Trade and International Policy Arrangements*. UNCTAD/United Nations: New York.

Watters, R. & McGee, T. (eds) (1997), *Asia Pacific: New Geographies of the Pacific Rim*, Hurst & Co. (Publishers) Ltd: London.

2 Asia Pacific Regionalization: Reality and Rhetoric

Geoff Missen and John McKay

Introduction

It seems everybody is talking about East Asia these days. The talk is not simply about the dynamism of the major industrial countries in this part of the world — Japan and the four ANICs — but also about a seemingly contagious spread of industrial export production to nearby countries — to China and a number of states in the South of East Asia. With so many dragons and tigers out and about, or miracles happening, the region itself, not just the countries within it, appears to have a distinctive dynamic.

So the talk is also about regionalization. Part of this is academic discourse, part of it is directed at instituting regional organizations. Two organizations, formal expressions of regionalism, have been promoted — APEC (Asia Pacific Economic Cooperation) and EAEC (East Asian Economic Caucus). APEC, the larger body, embraces non-Asian Pacific Rim countries (including the USA, Canada, Australia and New Zealand) but its clear basis for existence is East Asia. The other body, or rather the idea for such a body, has been activated by Dr. Mahathir, Malaysia's Prime Minister, and is exclusively East Asian.

The appearance of these two institutions of cooperation, the expansion of the long established ASEAN organization (ASEAN-6) to include Vietnam (and more recently Laos and Myanmar), as well as the development and plans of incorporating parts of different states into a production triangle suggest that a regional consciousness is emerging among these Asian states. If so, this cannot be considered a precursor to an economic community like Europe's. There are at present simply too many differences between states, not just the cultural and ethnic ones but economic differences, not to say rivalry in some instances, to take that conceptual leap. But the very differences raise the question central to this chapter: what is the logic behind these institutions of cooperation among states with so many differences?

We begin (section 2) by outlining the main organizations involved in the regional discourse, concentrating on the two that are nominally concerned with economic integration, APEC and EAEC. We argue here that political and strategic considerations buttress support for these organizations in a number of cases, even though economic arguments are stressed. As far as the economic rhetoric is concerned, free trade advantages flowing from regional organizations dominate the discourse, but in an uneven way: while all states engage in free trade talk, the air is far thicker with this talk when the USA or Australia has the floor and less so when Asian states are speaking; and EAEC is less a vehicle for free trade promotion than APEC is.

Sections 3 and 4 are more about economic reality in the East Asian region, or rather the constructions of that reality from two broad theoretical perspectives. The first perspective is the dominant one and underpins the arguments of the free trade proponents. This says that the spread of industrial production in the region follows product cycle, 'flying geese', patterns where a leading country (e.g. Japan) advances to newer products as factors change and gives up production of older established products to less advanced countries (e.g. Malaysia). Development is seen as an orderly progression ruled by changing prices of factors and comparative advantage and processed by free trade of goods and investment capital between the nation states.

The second perspective (section 4) disputes this flying geese notion. It sees the East Asian region as a production unit exporting to other parts of the world and internally interconnected, not through reciprocal trade, but by firm networks of production crossing national borders. This is a more hierarchical scenario, where parent firms sit above subsidiaries and subcontractors in other countries, and where some states sit above other, largely by occupying and defending their more advanced technological positions. It is also a less ordered and more unpredictable scenario, because interdependence between states is unequal (if mutually advantageous), and competition and rivalry between states can be fierce. We find this perspective of an exporting East Asian region of production networks closer to reality that images of flying geese.

In the last section we re-examine APEC and EAEC in the light of these perspectives. EAEC in some ways is more in line with the second perspective. It can be interpreted as accepting hierarchical order of states but organizationally is directed to relieving the incipient tensions that hierarchies, unequal interdependence and technological rivalry imply. APEC, at least as it is viewed by US and Australian interests in the East Asian market place, appears to be more in line with the first perspective, but whether their stress on freeing up trade amongst the nation states is in line with what is really happening in the East Asian region itself is another matter.

Regional discourse in the Asia-Pacific: aspirations and hidden motives

At the end of the APEC Heads of Government Meeting in Bogor, there was widespread satisfaction that so many leaders from so many diverse *countries* in the

Asia-Pacific region had agreed on a broad programme, and *even a general timetable*, for trade liberalization and facilitation in the region. Indeed, many commentators argued that the mere fact that the leaders even met, let alone discussed trade and a range of other issues, was remarkable enough. With some persuasion from President Suharto of Indonesia, the host of the meeting, even Dr. Mahathir of Malaysia, a notable absentee from the earlier summit in Seattle, was present. However, it has long been clear that the various governments have quite different reasons for giving at least token support to the APEC process, and are pushing quite different agendas and timetables. In some cases, these differences have become even more apparent since Bogor, and have made the next meetings somewhat problematic. However, for a variety of reasons, all governments are going with the process, for the moment at least, albeit for widely varying reasons. APEC is, of course, not the only game in town. Dr. Mahathir continues to favour his original EAEC formula, which should include the ASEAN countries, China, Japan and South Korea, in an Asian grouping: in what has been called 'a caucus without Caucasians'. Indeed, the founding of the ASEAN Free Trade Area (AFTA) as an extension of ASEAN, and the acceptance of Vietnam (and more recently Laos and Myanmar) into this grouping has given new life to this older regional organization, which ironically had as its original impetus the opposition to communist expansion in the region. What is clear is that the rhetoric of APEC, articulated most clearly in the Bogor Declaration, hides a range of hidden agendas and a diversity of aspirations, and the future of the APEC process will depend upon whether these diverse motives can be incorporated within a single grouping or whether some quite separate groupings will emerge.

The development of APEC

There is considerable debate about the origins of APEC, and indeed the acceptance of an 'official' version of its antecedents is part of the legitimation process for the entire institution. In the heretical version, the idea of an East Asian trade group was the brainchild of a number of influential officials in the Japanese Ministry of International Trade and Industry (MITI). The idea was talked about and refined over a number of years, but it was realized that the concept had little chance of acceptance if it was seen as a Japanese initiative — too many critics would quickly make analogies with the Greater East Asian Co-prosperity Sphere. It was important that the idea be seen as the initiative of a less powerful and threatening nation, hence it was quietly and subtly suggested to Australian Prime Minister Bob Hawke that the idea was a good one and he might like to put it forward as an Australian initiative. The 'official' view, including that repeated by the next Prime Minister Paul Keating, is that the idea was initiated in the Australian Department of Foreign Affairs and Trade, with the assistance of a number of academics from the Australian National University (for some quite contrasting views on the origins of APEC, see for example Mount, 1994, and Soesatro, 1994).

Whichever version of history one chooses to accept, the first public airing of the actual APEC proposal was made by Prime Minister Hawke in a speech in Seoul. He proposed the formation of an inter-governmental forum, to extend the idea of Pacific cooperation to an inter-governmental level and eventually to a set of regular meetings of heads of governments. There has been much speculation on the reasons why, in the initial invitation list to attend the first APEC summit in Canberra issued by the Australian government, the United States was not included. Some have suggested that this was a mere oversight, explainable by the extreme haste of the process, although it is difficult to understand how a Department of Foreign Affairs could simply overlook the United States. Others, more plausibly, have argued that Australia saw the process as a major avenue for greater integration into the dynamic Asian region and wanted an 'Asians only' association. Still others have suggested that Canberra feared that the United States would be lukewarm to the idea, and since they desperately wanted Washington to be involved the best way of achieving this would be to leave them out of the original list. Either way, Washington quickly protested about its exclusion and was very quickly added to the group of original members, comprising six ASEAN countries, Australia, Canada, Japan, Korea, New Zealand and the United States. Since then the group has been enlarged to include China, Hong Kong, Taiwan, Mexico, Papua New Guinea and Chile. United States support for the idea was highlighted in June 1989, when Secretary of state James Baker endorsed the Hawke initiative, and in July 1993 when President Clinton announced his support for the APEC Heads of Government meeting in Seattle, stressing the importance of APEC principles to United States policy in the region, and announcing the birth of a 'new Pacific community'. This momentum was taken a stage further at the 1994 APEC meeting in Bogor, Indonesia, when a broad timetable for trade liberalization was announced: it was agreed that free trade would be achieved by completely liberalizing the markets of all the 'industrialized' members by 2010 and of the 'developing' members by 2020.

Alternative visions of APEC

It is clear, then, that at least in certain quarters the APEC process has built up a considerable head of steam. But it is also apparent that there is no single vision of APEC which is accepted by all the current members, and some have been persuaded (or bullied) to become partners in a process with which they are far from happy. What are these alternative agendas for APEC, and what are the major divergent interests of the member economies?

The first thing that must be said is that although the process is government-driven, there are other forces and actors at work leading towards greater economic integration in the Asia-Pacific region. The rapid growth taking place in many of the regional economies leads automatically to greater levels of trade and interaction. From this viewpoint, governments are merely recognizing the reality of the situation or, more correctly, are attempting to build an institutional framework to deal with and regulate the already substantial economic interaction that is taking place in the region (Harris, 1993). To an extent, then, the existing activities of the private sector are helping to drive the process, although there is considerable anecdotal evidence to suggest that many business leaders are quite cynical about the ability of the politicians to achieve positive outcomes for them in the APEC negotiations as they are currently structured. There is also a significant degree of 'second-tier diplomacy' taking place in support of APEC and related organizations, such as the Pacific Economic Cooperation Conference (PECC) and the Pacific Basin Economic Council (PBEC). There is a strong network of APEC enthusiasts in the universities in particular, holding regular conference and making regular inputs into the policy formulation process. This group is also well-represented, along with government officials, in the ten working groups of APEC concerned with specific areas of regional cooperation, such as human resource development, energy, transport and tourism. The establishment in each economy of a APEC Studies Centre, designed to create both national centres for research and teaching in the area, and an international network of collaborating research centres, will add considerable weight to this process as well as, hopefully, a more critical appraisal of the whole process.

Some authors have suggested that the very special character of the APEC process has generated widespread support from a wide range of governments and private interest groups or at least has managed to avoid alienating any powerful actor. Bonnor (1995), for example, has argued that there are seven very special features which have given APEC a particular character. These are:

1   A gradualist approach to cooperation, dealing only with relatively non-controversial issues.
2   A consensus-based approach to all decisions.
3   Apart from a small secretariat, APEC has remained quite unstructured and unbureaucratic.
4   A focus on issues of benefit to all countries in the region.
5   An inclusive approach, involving all the major players in the region.
6   The system of rotating leadership avoids, to some extent, issues of domination.
7   The involvement of the heads of government (except for Taiwan) in regular meetings.

In spite of these special features, and the activities of these various support networks, it must be recognized that there are considerable structural differences between APEC members which colour their attitudes to both the form and pace of economic integration which is acceptable. As noted at the very start of this chapter, this is a region of considerable and rapid change, and few if any of the countries in the region expect that this progress will slow in the near future. No nation can be regarded as accepting the status quo, hence all are faced with particular problems of transition to their next desired stage of development. In all cases, too, the economic rhetoric of APEC masks a more complex and multifaceted set of ambitions that also include political, social and strategic goals.

It is particularly important to recognize that strategic concerns, which are rarely mentioned in official APEC documents, are probably crucial to much of the thinking behind the grouping. Mount (1994, p. 1) has argued, for example, that 'APEC, like ASEAN is economic in tone, but strategic in conception'. Similarly, Bonnor (1995, p. 1) has argued that:

> Although the members of the Asia-Pacific Economic Cooperation (APEC) forum would be reluctant to acknowledge it, APEC has taken on a security enhancing role. While the agenda for the recent APEC Leaders' Meeting at Bogor in Indonesia was focused on economic issues, the very fact that the meeting took place at all had implicit value for regional security. APEC's contribution to regional security — and the current low level debate which officials in member countries are having about whether that contribution should be formalized and expanded — has been all but neglected by academic commentators.

Space does not permit us to consider in any detail the particular national issues which are of particular concern to each APEC member and which have a major influence on attitudes to proposals for regional cooperation: rather, we must confine ourselves to some examples to illustrate the general point.

For Japan, involvement in the Asia-Pacific region as a leader rather than as a mere player, is problematic. Japan's economic growth has made it a major player, but even in the economic sphere Japan appears to be faltering. In terms of political leadership, and in particular in attempting to define a strategic role commensurate with its economic power, Japan has extreme difficulty. Rix (1994) has suggested that Japan faces particular problems in defining some acceptable concept of leadership. The nature of United States-Japan competition in trade and economic development is affecting a long-standing relationship on which many Japanese had come to rely. The recent growth of the Newly Industrialized Countries has created new conditions and expectations. Historical links, and in particular the memories of the Second World War, complicate regional ties. Internal political struggles and instabilities limit the capacity for leadership. The 'Japanese model' is seen by many as too pragmatic to produce the firm policy stances that are needed for true leadership. The result is that Japan sees its foreign aid programme as the most visible and easily controlled form of leadership. Thus the APEC agenda put forward by Japan has been dominated by economic cooperation priorities, giving rise to visions of an Asia-Pacific 'Partnership for Progress'. In part, this also reflects a desire to divert attention away from politically sensitive market access issues, and some commentators see the encouragement of an aid programme as just the first step in the establishment of Japanese economic and technological hegemony in areas such as Indo-China but the desire to 'lead from behind' is a distinctive feature of Japan's vision of APEC (Rix, 1984; Preston, 1995).

The United States is particularly ambivalent about APEC. The global gaze of the only superpower must necessarily take in Europe and the rest of the world as well as Asia, but the development of NAFTA and the narrow vision of the controllers of Capitol Hill encourage a more local concern. Many commentators doubt that the United States really understands Asia or feels at home with the need to develop an Asian policy. Incipient instability in the region, and in particular the demands of an emergent China, add to this discomfort (Betts, 1993). The victors of the Cold War are non-suited to the spirit of multilateralism on which APEC is based, and in any tight situation their instinct is to move into a bilateral mode in which their superior weight can be used. At the same time, the complexities of modern Asia defy the comfortable preconceptions of the Clinton administration. As a number of commentators have noted, there is a United States tendency to assume that 'all good things go together'. A 'democratic' nation by definition is peace-loving, God-fearing and supports the superior moral values of the free market. The fact that the very definition of democracy is so contested in Asia, and that there is very little evidence to support the neat unity of the package, is a severe complication in dealing with both APEC and its member economies. Yet the Asian economies remain crucial to the United States and its future. Trade across the Pacific is now 50 percent larger than that across the Atlantic, and by the turn of the century could be double the trans-Atlantic figure. Investment in Asia, especially in the expanding and liberalizing services sector, is also seen as a major economic prospect for the United States.

Australia has been using APEC as a major vehicle to redefine its position in the world. Like Japan, Australia is very anxious to maintain United States involvement in the region, but sees its future as being tied up with Asia. The special relationship with the United States is over, yet there are real problems in persuading Asian nations that Australia is integral to Asia's future. Gareth Evans has been at pains to develop an intellectual framework for Australia's engagement with the region. In one speech, he argued that Australia should be seen as part of a new 'East Asian hemisphere':

> Given our geography, our current and prospective economic and security needs, and the way in which the demography and culture of our own country is changing — and given, on the other side of the coin, the history of neglect and worse in our less recent relationships with the countries to our north — I think there may be a case for another, rather larger, sub-group within the Asia Pacific, and that is East Asia (Evans, 1995).

The trade disputes between Japan and the United States highlighted the extent to which Australia's interest lies predominantly in Asia but, like the United States, Australia also has a tendency to believe that all good things cluster together. However, in the Australian case it is free trade rather than democracy or human rights that is the primary source of all virtue, and this is clearly reflected in most Australian rhetoric about APEC at both government and business levels.

Taiwan and Korea have their own particular transition which they are attempting to make, from an industrializing to a mature and technologically advanced economy. Both are obsessed with the need to develop new technology and to build a human resource skill base capable of sustaining and advancing this technology. Both, too, have pressing security concerns, and both feel themselves hemmed in by the larger powers in the region. For Korea, APEC offers a forum for the development of a larger, international, role more commensurate with its expanding strength, and sees the medium-sized powers of APEC (notably Australia) as its natural allies in this endeavour. For Taiwan, the unique attraction of APEC is that this is the only international forum in which it has been able to gain a place, but Taiwan's view is dominated by the presence of the emerging superior in the region, China. Indeed, although China is a member of APEC, there is a strong body of opinion in APEC, as well as in ASEAN, that China poses the major threat in the coming decades. Increasingly, even the United States seems to regard the containment of China as the major policy imperative for the region. At the start of the East Asian 'economic miracle' a major driving force was preferential access to the United States market. Both Taiwan and Korea have been attempting to diversify their markets, and for both countries China is of rapidly increasing importance in terms of both trade and investment, but the United States market remains crucial especially at the higher end of the product range.

In summary, while there are different priorities and competing agendas, most nations see some positive value in the APEC process. It is really only Dr. Mahathir, the Prime Minister of Malaysia, who has strongly argued for an alternative framework for regional cooperation, and it is to this alternative proposal that we now turn.

Dr. Mahathir's dissent: the East Asian Economic Caucus

The original proposal to create an East Asian economic grouping was first made by Dr. Mahathir in December 1990, when the term 'Group' was suggested in the name. The term 'Caucus' was introduced later in an attempt to divert criticisms of the concept. and to emphasize the consultative nature of the proposed association. Subsequently, Dr. Mahathir has been at pains to emphasize that this would be a very loose arrangement for discussion by an informal group of economies within APEC (Mahathir, 1995). Yet behind the concept there are a number of features which underline Mahathir's desire to form an 'Asians only' grouping.

One is the belief that East Asia has a set of cultural, political and social norms which set it aside from the West. If the United States has a tendency to expect that 'all good things go together', Dr. Mahathir sees following Western values as a course that will destroy his nation. At various times he has blamed 'excessive democracy' for causing homosexuality, economic decline, moral decay, racial intolerance and one-parent families (*South China Morning Post*, 16 April 1995). Secondly, success in East Asia led many commentators and especially politicians to argue that the 'Asian way' or the 'Asian ethic' is superior to the worn-out and decadent procedures of the West. This view, shared by former Prime Minister Lee Kuan Yew of Singapore, has found a recent, eloquent champion in Kishore Mahbubani (1995, p. 105):

> The twenty-first century will see a struggle between an Atlantic impulse and a Pacific impulse. For the past few centuries, the Atlantic impulse has determined the course of world history. If my assumptions are right and the Pacific impulse takes centre stage over the Atlantic impulse, then Eurocentric strategic analysts will have to rethink their concepts and assumptions to understand the future flow of history.

Asians, Mahbubani (1995, p. 106) argues, have discovered a simple formula for success, and most Europeans are:

> ... blind to the biggest tidal wave to hit East Asia, which is the fundamental reason for the region's economic dynamism: the tidal wave of common sense and confidence. Over the past decade or two an immense psychological revolution has occurred and is continuing in most East Asian minds: increasing numbers realize that they have wasted centuries trying to make it in the modern world. They can no longer afford to do so. After centuries, their moment has come.

These statements of Asian 'solidarity' have worried both the United States and Japan, but for different reasons. The United States, keen to remain in the markets of the world's most dynamic region, fears that it will be excluded on essentially ethnic and cultural grounds. For example. Manning and Stern (1994) argue that much of the American rhetoric about the 'Pacific Community' is groundless in the face of a real Asian belief in a coherent Asian identity, value system and institutional system. These sorts of fears have not been helped by the wave of controversy surrounding Samuel Huntington's arguments on the coming 'clash of civilizations' (Huntington, 1993). Similar warnings have been made to Australians that the single most important economic truth about Asia is that Chinese from different parts of China like to deal with each other (Byrnes, 1994). For these sorts of reasons, the United States has always stressed that APEC must be the major (if not the only) vehicle for integration in the region, and that all major decision-making groups must be de-ethnicized by including countries such as Australia and New Zealand. For his part, Dr. Mahathir has stressed that he welcomes United States investments in Malaysia and is, of course, anxious to retain Malaysian access to United States markets, but he is wary of United States political and cultural domination.

For its part, Japan is also wary of 'ethnicizing' the process of economic integration, reflecting Japan's own fundamental ambivalence about its own Asian identity. In many ways, Japan prefers to regard itself as 'Western', and it is of course dependent on the United States market and defence support. Japan also fears that the rest of Asia is expecting too much of it in terms of improved access to Japanese markets. Dr. Mahathir, while on the one hand being worried about Japanese domination (Jomo, 1994), regards Japan as an essential partner in the continued development of the small and poor nations of Southeast Asia. In his appeal to Japan to join the EAEC, Mahathir suggested it would be 'more meaningful than 1,000 apologies for Japan's wartime atrocities' for Japan to participate (*South China Morning Post*, 27 April 1995).

Behind this confidence in an Asian future lurks a fear, at least in the short term, about the ability of Asian countries to obtain and deploy the technology needed to move their economic miracles to the next stage. In this regard, Malaysia's agenda is not too different from those of Korea or Taiwan, and similarly Malaysia is not convinced that the unaided forces of the free market, as currently enshrined in most of the APEC rhetoric, can deliver that transition. The need to retain the central role of the state as an initiator, coordinator and guarantor of continued industrial development is at the heart of Malaysia's problems with the APEC concept, and as such the EAEC proposal strikes at the central theoretical tenets of the APEC process. There is also a fear, despite the completion of the Uruguay Round, and all the rhetoric about 'open regionalism', APEC and similar bodies may not be able to prevent the world economy from breaking into three competing blocs, based in Europe, North America and Asia. In such a situation, Mahathir is desperate to ensure that Japan is more closely economically integrated into its own region and that Asian solidarity and joint action is ensured, but within a framework that avoids the domination of the small and medium powers of the region.

Orthodox construction of reality: trade, FDI and regionalism

Accepting that economic considerations, in one way or another, dominate the discourse on APEC and EAEC, the next question is whether this economic interest somehow reflects new economic patterns that have been emerging in East Asia.

A good deal of literature on the question of trading blocs, economic integration, and regionalization has appeared in recent years. Statistical material on changing trade and investment patterns in various regions is housed in this literature. We need to be aware, however, that there are considerable problems in assembling these data and in interpretation. First, there are no agreed criteria for measuring economic regions. All rest on some form of intra-regional contact and most rely on trade and investment data. But international trade theory is especially weak on intra-regional flows (Grant et. al., 1993).

Second, there is the problem of the regional boundary and defining the region's members. Apart from the fact that there exists a considerable diversity of groupings, making comparison of findings in the literature hazardous, intra-regional trade shares can be strongly influenced by the number of members and by the trading size of member countries. Third, regions are dynamic and a country

26

may well be outside an economic orbit at one time and well within that orbit a few years later.

The last two problems are especially apparent in the case of Asia. East Asia may embrace (as we do here) Japan, the four ANICs (South Korea, Taiwan, Hong Kong, Singapore), ASEAN-7 less Singapore (or the ASEAN-6: Brunei, Indonesia, Malaysia, the Philippines, Thailand and Vietnam) and China, but sometimes China is excluded (Franker, 1994) and sometimes Australia and New Zealand are included (e.g. Grant et al., 1993), and often East Asia is hidden in the wider APEC grouping. Any meaningful grip on trade and investment connections in East Asia would now have to speak of China, but five years ago this was not so.

Assuming agreement on the regional boundary and on an interest in intra-regional trade, there remain descriptive-interpretative problems. A focus on the trade amongst the region's states may lead to quite different interpretations from a focus on intra-firm trade within the region (as we shall detail below). In dynamic regions, increases in the measures of intra-regional trade may say nothing about changing trade behaviour but simply reflect increased size of countries as rapid growth occurs (Franker, 1994). Faster growth of intra-regional trade than of extra-regional trade does not necessary reflect the origins of the trade growth: the faster growth of intra-regional trade can be caused by exogenous trade growth triggering off input-output linkages within the region (Grant et. al., 1993, p. 61).

For our purposes, we have assembled the evidence alongside two broad interpretative arguments. The first, more orthodox (certainly more popular) school is dealt with in this section. This view examines intra- and extra-regional trade and investment based on units of national states, looks for evidence of trade liberalization or restrictions and of trading blocs, and is theoretically buttressed by orthodox theories of international trade, flying geese, product cycles, and comparative advantage.

The share of intra-regional trade in a region's total trade is frequently cited as a sign of rising economic integration and regionalization. Thus East Asia's intra-regional share increased from 23 to 39 percent between 1980 and 1990; the EC's share rose much faster (47 percent) over the same period (Franker, 1994). The share approach is misleading, however. First, the share is affected by the number of countries in a region, the larger the number of countries in a region the more likely the trade share will be larger. Second, the value of a country's trade affects the share figure; regions containing a large trader will have an inflated share relative to a region without such a country (Anderson and Norheim, 1994).

Two regional trade concepts that are considered more useful than simple share figures are the gravity and trade intensity approaches. The intensity of trade method considers each country's total imports and exports as given and measures bilateral trade in terms of the strength of obstacles between other trading pairs in the world (Drysdale and Garnaut 1994, p. 32). An intensity measure shows that trade within East Asia grows less rapidly than trade shares and very much less rapidly than the intensity index for intra-EC trade (Franker 1994, p. 228). The gravity model tries to explain the level of trade only by the characteristics of two countries and the obstacles between them. We cite here an example of each of these approaches, respectively Petri (1994) and Frankel (1994).

Petri (1994) examined intensity indexes for a number of East Asian countries in the colonial and post-colonial period and found variation over time. Trade intensities were high in the pre-war and immediate post-war periods, but then declined till the mid-1980s and then rose somewhat.

The remarkable trend is the decline in the regional trade bias for the major part of the post-war period when the economies grew apace in the region. Equally remarkable for Petri is the decline in this period of the variation of intensity of trade across an East Asian country's different trade partners:

> In effect, each country's bilateral trade pattern came to look more and more like the world's trade pattern .... [and] country-specific bias became less and less important ... (p. 117).

Petri provides three reasons for this homogenization tendency in East Asian trade till 1985: rounds of successful trade negotiations and improved transport and communications pulled all countries, including those in East Asia, toward more global sourcing and marketing; the growth in East Asian overall trade, a function of economic expansion, provided the scale and communication linkages; and the similarity of East Asian development patterns (the so-called 'flying geese') contributed to competition rather than cooperation between economies which therefore looked for extra-regional rather than intra-regional markets (Petri, 1994, pp. 117-118).

As the high index of intensity before the war was associated with what Petri calls the historical 'accident' of imperialist connectivities (both European and Japanese), so the rise in the intensity indexes since the mid-1980s is associated with the 'accident' (some might say 'historical conjuncture') of the currency appreciations, wage rises and other forces occurring in Japan, Korea and Taiwan at this time that threatened the competitive positions of these exporting economies. Currency appreciation and competitive risk had two trade integration effects. First, Petri notes, the rise in intra-regional trade intensity after 1985 was partly a result of the staggered timing of the currency appreciations in the region. For a few years after the yen appreciated following the 1985 Plaza Agreement, other East Asian countries whose currencies had yet to adjust became more competitive in both the United States and Japanese markets. Exports from these East Asian countries to Japan accelerated and their trade surpluses rose during 1985-1988. By the late eighties, however, their exchange rates had been adjusted and the gap between their currencies and the yen narrowed and Japanese imports slowed.

Petri sees a second effect as more important in the rise of intra-regional trade after 1985. This was a marked increase in FDI, first from Japan and in the late 1980s (and the early 1990s) from Korea and Taiwan especially. Industrialization in Thailand, Malaysia, Indonesia (and in the 1990s in Vietnam and China) received a substantial boost from these flows. Associated with the rise in intra-regional investment is a rise in intra-regional trade: along with the FDI flows went exports of technologies and components and (more arguable) exports of assembled products from the new industrializers back to the countries supplying the FDI. For the proponents of APEC who want to see an historical rise in economic integration in the region, Petri's evidence is disappointing: there is no long term rise (quite the opposite) post-war and the rise since 1985 is a cautious statement of direction rather than a confident statement of further integration to come.

Using a gravity approach, Frankel (1994) has assembled a number of different regions in the world — EC, Western Hemisphere (WH), ASEAN, EAEC (excluding China), Asia-Pacific, APEC and Pacific Rim — and calculated coefficients of intra-regional trade for different times between 1980 and 1990, seeking controls on size of economies and, in the case of EAEC, the openness of the entrepôt states of Hong Kong and Singapore. He also looks at investment flows from Japan. His general conclusions relevant here (pp. 236, 237, 245) are:

1 The level of trade in East Asia, and in the EC and the WH, is biased toward intra-regional trade more than can be explained by distance.
2 Despite the increased weight of Japan and other East Asian countries in world output and trade, there is no trend toward an intra-regional bias of trade and FDI in East Asia.
3 By contrast, the intra-regional trade bias increased in the EC, in the WH and in the APEC region in the 1980s.
4 The APEC trade grouping appears to be the world's strongest, with the United States and Canada 'being in the enviable position of belonging to both of the world's strongest groupings'.
5 The EAEC grouping is rather less strong than APEC and has declined in intra-regional trade intensity terms during the 1980s, especially if one allows for the openness of its economies.
6 There is no evidence that Japan has established or come to dominate a trading bloc in East Asia.

The results of Frankel's construction of reality, and those of other orthodox exercises, support the APEC rhetoric. For Frankel, 'APEC appears to be the correct place to draw the [trading region] boundary' (p. 233). Soogil Young (1994) comes to much the same conclusion. In assessing these sorts of exercises, we need to keep in mind, however, that the search for reality normally involves assembling data in a way that demonstrates, or at least does not contradict, an established point of view. The orthodox economic regionalization school is no exception to this generalization. Garnaut and Drysdale, the editors of a recent collection of readings on Asia-Pacific Regionalism (including that of Frankel above) are quite clear what they are looking for: economic integration is defined as 'movement toward one price for any piece of merchandize, service or factor of production ... Disintegration persists because of barriers, or resistance, to trade' (quoted by Arndt in Garnaut and Drysdale, 1994). We would prefer to call this 'trade integration' and treat the word 'economic' in the communally acceptable broad way and not put the interpretive cart before the descriptive horse. But in terms of trade models, the Asia-Pacific region is highlighted as the important region with EAEC as a nesting within it.

Not all of this analysis, we should note, has passed without comment from within the orthodox school. For example, Lawrence (1993) in a comment on Frankel's (1994) paper, raises some serious concerns about the units in this sort of analysis: trade, the quantity of trade, and nation states. 'We should,' he says, 'really be evaluating the precise nature rather than simply the quantity of Asian economic integration' and, while applauding Frankel's paper as a first-step, claims that 'we need to move beyond simply examining trade flows, toward examining institutional and industrial practices' (p. 86). These sentiments anticipate Section 4 and the paper by Bernard and Ravenhill (1995). But outside these misgivings there is a body of theory that supports the trade-investment studies of the orthodox school, and to these we now briefly turn.

Orthodox theory and regional integration

Amongst theorists of international cooperation and conflict there are disagreements about the mechanisms and rationales that drive cooperative and competitive behaviour. Many 'realist' theorists have argued that states tend to pursue relative gains (doing better than the competition) rather than competition induced absolute gains in welfare. On the other hand, the 'neo-liberal' school has argued that states are indifferent to the gains that others make so long as their own gains from transactions are maximized (see, for example Higgott, 1993). The thinking of this latter underpins, at least implicitly, much of the theorizing and policy advice of neo-liberal economists. These proponents of free-market ideas have, however, had to face some distinctive features of Asia-Pacific economic interdependence with important political implications. Whole industrial sectors, often long established in particular regions, have been cleaned out by more competitive East Asian industries (Ruggie, 1993), for example. This is, of course, behind the frequent United States demands that Japan reach agreement for managed trade within particular sectors. The United States response to its trade deficit problem with the region is to resort to bilateral trade deals in which its sheer muscle is likely to prevail. Most countries in the region fear the domination of both the United States and Japan and are searching for a framework to promote multilateral rather than bilateral resolutions to trade disputes. The smaller powers fear the 'hub and spoke' structure of trade negotiations preferred by the United States in particular. There is, to use the phrases of Higgott et al. (1993), a desperate search for a theoretical and political basis to overcome the 'patronage' and bilateralism of the past by developing a system of 'assimilation' and 'similarity' (pp. 320-24). The search has been for a theory which can hold out the prospect of similar outcomes and successful assimilation into a broader and more prosperous future.

To a remarkable degree the 'flying geese' model has provided such a framework. Originally put forward by the Japanese economist Akamatsu Kaname in the 1930s, the theory has been refined and combined with other, related, perspectives, notably the theory of comparative advantage and the theory of product cycles. Most of the empirical verification for this model has come from the East Asian experience, so much so that the ideas of the 'flying geese' model and the East Asian model of development are now closely intertwined (see, for example, Bernard and Ravenhill, 1995; Yamazawa, 1990). At its most basic level, the theory postulates that production and trade will follow a series of stages as a country moves from a developing to an industrial nation:

1 Initially, consumer goods are imported from more advanced countries.
2 Over time, techniques and capital goods are imported and what Akamatsu calls 'homogeneous industries' are established.
3 Less developed countries then acquire their own capital goods industries.
4 Local industries are able to compete in export markets, and trade disputes can arise.
5 As particular industries mature and become less competitive compared with the products of the more recently industrialized nations, the country will again import certain products, especially those at the lower end of the technology and value-added scale.

Many writers have argued that this is what happened, or is happening, in East Asia (see, for example, Shinohara and Lo, 1989). First Japan, then the ANICs, then the Little Dragons, now China and Vietnam achieve industrial take-off, and with the correct free market policies, India, Pakistan, the Philippines and Bangladesh will not be far behind. The achievement of assimilation and similarity is held out as a realistic goal. This is an extremely optimistic scenario and some question it. We now turn to their views.

The political economy-network view

Bernard and Ravenhill (1995) see the East Asian region not as a trading unit but a production unit, in which hierarchies of firms are linked across borders and where governments play important roles in the formation and defence of these production networks. They are strongly critical of the product cycle, 'flying geese' argument and, more generally, argue that orthodoxy does not tell us what is economically going on in the East Asian region. Rather than looking for the evidence for world blocs, they are more concerned with internal regional dynamics. Their argument is to a large extent concerned with demolishing the notion of product cycles and 'flying geese' and we will outline this criticism first.

They have three major criticisms. First, the 'flying geese'-product cycle version of the orthodox school assumes that as products and the technology producing them mature, they will migrate to, or be taken up by, less developed countries in the region by a technology transfer process. But technology is fluid, not standardized or tied to products in a staged way. Technological change is both continuous and rapid, and while this can provide opportunities for some firms in the less developed countries of the region to advance their products, it also allows established firms to engage in product innovation and product defence. Greater technological complexity can raise barriers to entry (e.g. higher start-up costs), make learning harder, increase specialization and decrease technology transfer. 'These trends,' argue Bernard and Ravenhill, 'make the establishment of backward linkages and indigenous industries far more difficult than was the case during the initial period of industrialization in Taiwan and Korea' (1995, p. 177).

In contrast to the 'flying geese' scenario and notions of assimilation and homo-genization (and to the findings of Frankel above concerning Japan):

> technological diffusion in East Asia has been partial, varies from country to country, and has remained linked throughout to a 'supply architecture' built around on-going Japanese innovation of components, machinery and materials ... [and] partial technological diffusion has brought about an intra-regional hierarchy of production (p. 177).

Secondly, there has been no significant development of an indigenous capital goods industries in the Southeast Asian latecomers, based on, as the theory implies, an experience of import-substitution (as in Korea and Taiwan). ASEAN export manufacturing depends on imported technology and components, from Japan and the ANICs. Thirdly, the regionalization process has yet to produce substantial reverse exports to the older industrialized countries, at least to Japan.

The East Asian region of Bernard and Ravenhill is not made up of national units increasingly trading with each other but is a production region in which networks of firms across borders are linked in chains of production in a number of industries. Exports beyond the region flow from the end of the chain, and components through the chain within the region. It is because of the spatial expansion of these networks since the Plaza Agreement in 1985, processed through outflows of FDI from Northeast Asia to ASEAN, and then Vietnam and China, that we can speak of *regionalization* (Bernard and Ravenhill 1995, p. 183). While the interaction between firms, the networks themselves, become the units of analysis, it is also true that states play important roles in attracting and rationalizing FDI inflow (as hosts) and (as exporters of FDI) in supporting firms in their defence of technological property rights. This is a hierarchical system, where power, and essentially technological power, resides in firms at the top of the chain and in states which have the bulk of such firms. A number of implications follow.

Japan is crucial in the system. It is the main investor and financial supplier, it is the source of most technically advanced components in the networks. But it is a poor absorber of exports. In 1991, for example, Japan traded more with the ANICs (US$94 billion) than with the European Community (US$91 billion), but the trade with the ANICs was biased. In 1992 Taiwan's trade deficit with Japan was three times the United States trade deficit with Japan on a per capita basis (Gipouloux, 1994, p. 26). Despite the rise in export production and intense efforts at indigenous R&D in Korea, that country still depends heavily on imports from Japan: in 1987 the Korean electronics industry imported 36 percent of its components from Japan; in 1993, one study found that only 38 percent of the value of semiconductors was added locally (Bernard and Ravenhill 1995, p. 191). ASEAN too is heavily and increasingly dependent on Japan: 45 percent of its machinery imports, for example, comes from Japan (Gipouloux, 1994, p. 27), and this is reflected in a blow-out in ASEAN's trade deficit; this imbalance is far less apparent in ASEAN's trade with the ANICs, on which ASEAN also depends heavily for machinery and components and for its FDI (see tables 2.la, 2.lb and 2.lc).

The strength of Japan in the region is also reflected in patterns of Japanese affiliates. A rising number in the region procure from local joint ventures (including local Japanese firms); and when exports go back to Japan for the less industrialized countries in the region it is, it seems, from these affiliates. In their operations in other countries in the region, Japanese firms sending capital goods down the network are not concerned to own the local affiliates or subcontractors; but when Japanese technology or part of the production process is involved in transfers overseas, Japanese firms 'aggressively pursue the acquisition of majority ownership of local production facilities' (Gipouloux, 1994, pp. 34-5). This supports the point of the importance of technology made above.

Table 2.l(a)
Japan's trade with

	ANICs	ASEAN-6	China	North America	EC 12
X/M					
1986	2.22	0.81	1.75	3.20	2.76
1990	1.82	1.19	0.66	1.74	1.88
1993	2.27	1.60	1.10	2.11	2.13
Trade Balance (US$ billion)					
1986	14.19	-2.92	4.22	60.37	19.68
1990	20.94	5.07	-3.18	42.52	25.33
1993	35.80	18.73	1.57	61.86	30.26
X growth					
1980-1986	1.67	0.92	1.94	2.49	1.71
1985-1990	1.80	2.65	0.62	1.14	1.75
1990-1993	1.38	1.55	2.82	1.17	1.05
M growth					
1980-1986	1.90	0.71	1.30	1.10	1.69
1986-1990	2.20	1.80	1.85	2.10	2.57
1990-1993	1.10	1.15	1.69	0.96	0.93

Table 2.1(b)
ANIC's trade with

	ASEAN-6	China	North America	EC 12	ANICs
X/M					
1986	0.94	0.72	3.06	1.40	
1990	1.16	0.77	1.67	1.33	
1993	1.09	2.34	1.90	1.31	
Trade Balance (US$ billion)					
1986	-0.35	-2.91	32.02	4.00	
1990	2.27	-5.91	25.97	7.46	
1993	2.37	35.38	39.56	9.76	
X growth					
1980-1986	1.18	6.03	2.65	1.39	ANICs
1985-1990	2.91	2.69	1.36	2.13	Intra-trade
1990-1993	1.65	3.04	1.29	1.36	growth
M growth					
1980-1986	1.23	2.38	1.24	1.69	1.95
1986-1990	2.37	2.51	2.36	2.23	2.74
1990-1993	1.74	1.01	1.13	1.37	1.59

Table 2.1(c)
ASEAN-6 trade with

	China	North America	EC12	ASEAN-6
X/M				
1986	0.51	1.66	1.06	
1990	0.65	1.45	1.07	
1993	1.07	1.51	1.16	
Trade Balance (US$ billion)				
1986	-1.19	5.75	0.01	
1990	-1.23	9.01	1.41	
1993	0.33	15.24	4.37	
X growth				
1980-1986	1.81	1.20	0.98	ASEAN
1985-1990	1.81	2.02	2.41	Intra-trade
1990-1993	2.21	1.53	1.48	growth
M growth				
1980-1986	1.42	0.92	1.11	0.94
1986-1990	1.43	2.33	2.38	2.26
1990-1993	1.34	1.46	1.36	1.52

Sources: see Appendix A

The working of the region as a production unit, as far as Japan is concerned at least, rests on what can be seen as a colonial division of labour. Japanese firms act vertically in Asia. Increasing their FDI in the region, and in manufacturing rather than services (services FDI goes elsewhere), and using other countries as export platforms. Table 2.1 reveals that the rate of growth of exports to, for example, the European Community, is greatest for the ASEAN countries, followed by the ANICs, and then Japan. In absolute terms, Japan's exports of US$56 billion to the European Community in 1993 were not all that greater than the exports from the ANICs (US$40 billion) to the European Community in 1993, and from ASEAN (US$31 billion). The differences would be much less in terms of manufacturing. The ANICs and ASEAN have trade deficits with Japan in this arrangement, but positive trade balances with the main markets in Europe and America (table 2.1). A similar pattern is emerging with some countries (Korea and Taiwan) in relation to Japan on the one hand to the growing Chinese market on the other.

It seems to us that this picture of a region of production networks, of hierarchies of forms and groups of competing states at different levels, of capital goods, components and investment flowing down the system and exports flowing out of the region, provides a better means of assessing the rhetoric surrounding the APEC and EAEC forums than the orthodox scenario described earlier. It is a more uncomfortable view, containing contradictions and competition (the contradiction between Japan's dominance and the benefits which flow from its investments and the competition between the ANICs at one level and the ASEAN countries at another), the uncertainty of China which has become part of this production region, and the unpredictability of international relations in a system where (networked) firms are major international actors and where government to government relations are subjected to firm-firm and firm-government decisions. The uncertainties help to explain the interest in the forums. In particular, in this view of the region, the EAEC is in some ways more promising than APEC, having the potential for the uncertainties within the hierarchy to be reduced, a potential that APEC does not have. That this is especially important for the smaller and dependent countries such as Malaysia may help explain Dr. Mahathir's continued promotion of the Caucus idea.

This view of the region, finally, provides a context for one of the conclusions drawn from a set of recent French-Japanese studies on regional economic strategies in East Asia:

... despite the long-repeated assumption about the irreducible diversity of the region, the traditional concept of the United States as a counterweight for allaying the fears of many Asian countries toward Japan is changing and something new is happening in East Asia which is challenging conventional wisdom ... the explosion of intra-Asiatic trade and quest for an identity ... cannot be reduced to the mere recognition of Western values (Gipouloux, 1994, p. 38).

Conclusion

What we have tried to argue in this chapter is that reality of change is far less simple, predictable and universally optimistic than is portrayed in much of the neo-liberal literature, and that this has fundamental implications for the social processes of economic integration now attracting so much attention in the region. We have made these arguments at both the political and economic levels.

Processes are less simple than they appear in the orthodox view, in that the issues of trade and trade liberalization that dominate the solemn declarations made at the APEC summit meetings are not the only factors driving the agenda. Indeed, these issues may not even be most important considerations. As we have tried to demonstrate, issues of defence, national pride, cultural identity and social goals are to varying degrees extremely important to the various countries of the region, and help to shape attitudes to the whole APEC process.

They are less predictable than is portrayed in the frameworks of the 'flying geese' model, because within Asia questions of power and power sharing are paramount in a far from stable post-Cold War era. The hegemony of the United States in the region is weakening, at a time when its trading interest is becoming greater, and the future role of the potential superpowers, Japan and especially China, is far from clear. Crone has argued that the political economy of the Asia-Pacific region is at a particularly difficult stage, and that this is having a major impact on all of the countries of the region:

> The erosion of extreme hegemony changes the incentives of all states. Subordinate actors may desire to provide a multilateral framework that keeps a larger actor in the system but also constrains its exercise of unilateral power; the subordinate actor may wish to use its size to preserve bargaining power that is perceived to be eroding. This line of argument suggests that regimes may form as hegemonic deflation opens political space that was previously closed to dependent actors and preserves some advantages for superordinate ones, but that engagement will be wary and cautions. Such an extended, more dynamic conception of the role of power structures in regime formation, then, might account for the pattern observed in the Pacific. Strategic incentives did not favour institutional formation under conditions of extreme hegemony, but with exogenous power changes those incentives changed too, creating a greater convergence of interest in mutual management (Crone, 1993, p. 505).

They are also less predictable than orthodoxy allows, because of the complexity of networks and the technological positioning of companies and states that we have outlined in Section 4. The emergence of growth triangles and other cross-border arrangements is a reflection of this complexity, which some would argue is seeing the emergence of natural economic regions which in some cases are relatively independent of the nation state.

Initiates such as the ASEAN are, in part, a symptom of this new multipolar and

36

multilateral reality. The growth of Japan and the ANICs has added new and important players in the region, and the success of Malaysia has increased Dr. Mahathir's credentials as a spokesman for the emerging nations of Southeast Asia and beyond. Yet the emergence of Japanese economic power and the growing presence of China are complicating a situation in which the United States, while in relative decline, is still a major force. The possibilities for trade wars and other kinds of conflicts are much greater in a multipolar world and in the absence of a dominant hegemony.

Fears of instability in the region are also intensified by the possibilities that in spite of GATT and the WTO, the world may split into competing trading blocs. Many Asians believe that in spite of its recent dramatic growth performance, the Asian bloc would be the least able to compete in the three bloc scenario — North America, Europe, Asia. This is in part because of the three leaders, Japan seems the least inclined to take on a true leadership role. A coming battle between China and Japan for regional dominance is widely predicted and many nations in the region, notably Korea and Taiwan, fear being caught in the middle of such a battle of giants.

The question of the emergence of regional production hierarchy in the region is a further complication. In spite of the predictions of the 'flying-geese' model, and of those who suggest that within Asia the dominant powers now have less influence, there is real evidence of such a hierarchy. This can only undermine relations in the region, when it is clear that the promised 'assimilation' is not taking place, and undermining the basic principles on which regional integration is supposed to take place. Finally we would raise the question of whether production hierarchies of the kind we have described exist or are being formed in all three of the emerging blocs. If the answer to this question is yes, what does this say about the form of globalization that is taking place in the region in the 1990s and what kinds of relationships will be created both between and within these groupings?

References

Anderson, K. and Nordheim, H. (1994), 'Is World Trade Becoming More Regionalised?', in Garnaut, R. and Drysdale, P. (eds), *Asia-Pacific Regionalism: Readings in International Economic Relations,* Harper Educational: Sydney, pp. 125-42.

Bernard, M. and Ravenhill, J. (1995), 'Beyond Product Cycles and Flying Geese: Regionalization, Hierarchy, and the Industrialization of East Asia', *World Politics,* 47, pp. 171-209.

Betts, R.K. (1993), 'Wealth, Power and Instability. East Asia and the United States after the Cold War', *International Security,* Vol. 18, No. 3, pp. 34-77.

Bonnor, J. (1995), 'APEC and Security', Australian Defence Studies Centre, Australian Defence Force Academy, Working Paper No. 31.

Byrnes, M. (1994), *Australia and the Asia Game,* Allen and Unwin: Sydney.

Crone, D. (1993), 'Does Hegemony Matter? The Reorganisation of the Pacific Political Economy', *World Politics*, Vol. 45, pp. 501-25.

Evans, G. (1995), 'Australia in East Asia and the Asia Pacific: Beyond the Looking Glass', Asia-Australia Institute, University of New South Wales, 14th Asia Lecture, Museum of Contemporary Art, Sydney.

Frankel, J.A. (1994), 'Is Japan Creating a Yen Bloc in East Asia and the Pacific?', in Garnaut, R. and Drysdale, P. (eds), *Asia-Pacific Regionalism: Readings in International Economic Relations*, Harper Educational: Sydney, pp. 227-49.

Gipouloux, F. (1994), 'Introduction: Globalization and Regionalization in East Asia: Stakes and Strategies', in Gipouloux, F. (ed.), *Regional Economic Strategies in East Asia: A Comparative Perspective,* La Maison Franco-Japonaise: Tokyo.

Grant, R.J., Papadakis, M.C. and Richardson, J.D. (1993), 'Global Trade Flows: Old Structures, New Issues, Empirical Evidence', in Bergsten, C.F. and Noland, M. (eds), *Pacific Dynamism and the International Economic System*, Institute for International Economics: Washington D.C., pp. 17-64.

Harris, S. (1993), 'Economic Cooperation and Institution Building in the Asia-Pacific Region', in Higgott, R., Leaver, R. and Ravenhill, J. (eds), *Pacific Economic Relations in the 1990s. Cooperation or Conflict?*, Allen and Unwin: Sydney, pp. 271-89.

Higgott, R. (1993), 'Competing Theoretical Approaches to International Cooperation: Implications for the Asia-Pacific', in Higgott, R., Leaver, R. and Ravenhill, J. (eds), *Pacific Economic Relations in the 1990s. Cooperation or Conflict?*, Allen and Unwin: Sydney, pp. 290-311.

Higgott, R., Leaver, R. and Ravenhill, J. (1993), 'The Pacific Economic Future: Towards Convention or Modernization?', in Higgott, R., Leaver, R. and Ravenhill, J. (eds), *Pacific Economic Relations in the 1990s: Cooperation or Conflict?* , Allen and Unwin: Sydney, pp. 312-24.

Huntington, S. (1993), 'The Clash of Civilisations', *Foreign Affairs*, Vol. 72, No. 3, pp. 22-49.

Jomo, K.S. (1994), *Japan and Malaysian Development: In the Shadow of the Rising Sun*, Routledge: London.

Lawrence, R.Z. (1993), 'Comment', in Frankel, J.A. and Kahler, M. (eds), *Regionalism and Rivalry: Japan and the United States in Pacific Asia*, University of Chicago Press: Chicago.

Mahathir, M. (1995), 'EAEC Could Be of Benefit to the World', *Yomiuri Shimbun*, 7, April 1995, p. 13.

Mahbubani, K. (1995), 'The Pacific Impulse', *Survival*, Vol. 37, pp. 105-20.

Manning, R.A. and Stern, P. (1994), 'The Myth of the Pacific Community', *Foreign Affairs*, Vol. 73, No. 6, pp. 79-93.

Mount, F. (1994), 'The Genesis of APEC: An Australian Viewpoint', United States Global Strategy Council, Occasional Paper Series.

Petri. P. (1994), 'The East Asian Trading Block: An Analytical History', in Garnaut, R. and Drysdale, P. (eds), *Asia-Pacific Regionalism: Readings in*

International Economic Relations, Harper Educational: Sydney, pp. 107-24.

Preston, P.W. (1995), 'Domestic Inhibitions to a Leadership Role for Japan in Pacific Asia', *Contemporary Southeast Asia*, Vol. 16, pp. 355-74.

Rix, A. (1994), 'Japan and the Region: Leading from Behind', in Higgott, R., Leaver, R. and Ravenhill, J. (eds), *Pacific Economic Relations in the 1990s: Cooperation or Conflict?*, Allen and Unwin: Sydney, pp. 62-82.

Ruggie, R. (1993), 'Unravelling Trade: Global Institutional Change and the Pacific Economy', in Higgott, R., Leaver, R. and Ravenhill, J. (eds), *Pacific Economic Relations in the 1990s: Cooperation or Conflict?*, Allen and Unwin: Sydney, pp. 15-38.

Shinohara, M. and Lo, F.C. (eds) (1989), *Global Adjustment and the Future of Asian-Pacific Economy*, Asian and Pacific Development Centre; Kuala Lumpur.

Soesastro, H. (1994), 'Pacific Economic Cooperation: The History of an Idea', in Garnaut, R. and Drysdale, P. (eds), *Asia-Pacific Regionalism: Readings in International Economic Relations*, Harper Educational: Sydney, pp. 77-88.

Yamazawa, I. (1990), *International TraEconomic Development: A Japanese Model*, University of Hawaii Press: Honolulu.

Yamazawa, I. (1994), 'On Pacific Economic Integration', in Garnaut, R. and Drysdale, P. (eds), *Asia-Pacific Regionalism: Readings in International Economic Relations*, Harper Educational: Sydney, pp. 201-11.

Young, S. (1994), 'Globalization and Regionalism: Complements or Competitors?', in Garnaut, R. and Drysdale, P. (eds), *Asia-Pacific Regionalism: Readings in International Economic Relations*, Harper Educational: Sydney, pp. 179-93.

APPENDIX A
Consolidated matrix of Asia Pacific trade — 1980, 1986, 1990 and 1993 (US$ million)

	Japan	ANICs	ASEAN-6	China	East Asia	N. America	ANZ	EC12	World
Japan									
1980	-	15,434	19,069	5,078	39,581	34,309	4,069	18,025	129,542
1986	-	25,812	12,081	9,856	47,749	87,811	6,331	30,871	209,081
1990	-	46,487	32,066	6,145	84,698	100,132	8,134	54,045	287,678
1993	-	64,024	49,691	17,353	131,066	117,206	9,013	56,917	362,583
1986/80		1.67	0.92	1.94	1.20	2.49	1.56	1.71	1.61
1990/86		1.80	2.65	0.62	1.77	1.14	1.28	1.75	1.38
1993/90		1.38	1.55	2.82	1.55	1.17	1.11	1.05	1.26
ANICs									
1980	6,114	3,312	4,901	1,253	15,579	17,910	1,369	10,175	56,969
1986	11,619	6,469	5,774	7,552	31,414	47,543	2,535	13,996	109,838
1990	25,548	17,740	16,800	20,335	80,432	64,664	2,526	29,796	208,996
1993	28,220	28,186	27,662	61,769	145,837	83,445	5,317	40,435	303,493
1986/80	1.90	1.95	1.18	6.03	2.02	2.65	1.72	1.38	1.93
1990/86	2.20	2.74	2.91	2.69	2.56	1.36	1.07	2.13	1.09
1993/90	1.10	1.59	1.65	3.04	1.81	1.29	2.10	1.36	1.45
ASEAN-6									
1980	21,032	4,975	12,934	693	39,634	12,080	2,042	8,897	71,036
1986	15,004	6,122	12,165	1,253	34,544	14,451	1,667	8,721	66,613
1990	27,000	14,532	27,500	2,268	71,300	29,260	3,113	21,039	137,965
1993	30,966	25,289	41,760	5,010	103,025	44,840	4,292	31,138	208,996
1986/80	0.71	1.23	0.94	1.81	0.87	1.20	0.82	0.98	0.94
1990/86	1.80	2.37	2.26	1.81	2.06	2.02	1.87	2.41	2.07
1993/90	1.15	1.74	1.52	2.21	1.44	1.53	1.38	1.48	1.51

	Japan	ANICs	ASEAN-6	China	East Asia	N. America	ANZ	EC12	World
China									
1980	4,323	4,401	1,722		10,447	1,362	283	2,748	18,120
1986	5,638	10,462	2,443		18,543	5,682	371	4,096	31,367
1990	9,327	26,243	3,493		39,063	8,132	644	6,720	66,518
1993	15,782	26,388	4,684		46,854	18,328	1,201	11,715	91,611
1986/80	1.30	2.38	1.42		1.78	4.17	1.31	1.49	1.73
1990/86	1.85	2.51	1.43		2.11	1.43	1.73	1.64	2.12
1993/90	1.69	1.01	1.34		1.20	2.25	2.25	1.74	1.38
East Asia									
1980	31,489	28,122	32,626	7,024	105,241	66,660	7,763	39,845	275,668
1986	32,281	48,865	32,463	18,661	132,250	155,487	10,722	57,686	416,899
1990	61,874	105,001	79,858	28,748	275,483	202,188	14,417	111,600	701,157
1993	74,968	143,887	123,797	84,132	426,784	263,819	19,823	140,205	966,444
1986/80	1.03	1.74	1.00	2.66	1.26	2.33	1.38	1.45	1.51
1990/86	1.92	2.15	2.46	1.54	2.08	1.30	1.34	1.93	1.68
1993/90	1.21	1.37	1.55	2.93	1.55	1.30	1.37	1.26	1.38
North America									
1980	24,919	12,486	9,413	4,587	51,406	97,641	5,317	66,148	291,431
1986	27,440	15,523	8,700	3,963	55,626	127,440	6,598	57,483	301,630
1990	57,609	38,694	20,246	6,230	122,779	228,611	10,674	112,132	554,520
1993	55,349	43,884	29,605	10,180	139,018	296,566	10,264	107,491	652,807
1986/80	1.10	1.24	0.92	0.86	1.08	1.31	1.24	0.87	1.03
1990/86	2.10	2.36	2.33	1.57	2.21	1.79	1.62	1.95	1.84
1993/90	0.96	1.13	1.46	1.63	1.13	1.30	0.96	0.96	1.18

	Japan	ANICs	ASEAN-6	China	East Asia	N. America	ANZ	EC12	World
ANZ									
1980	6,109	1,500	2,082	938	10,629	3,154	1,791	4,139	27,439
1986	6,095	2,419	1,484	1,163	11,161	3,208	1,845	4,238	27,775
1990	11,699	5,573	4,910	1,046	23,228	6,526	3,681	6,597	48,341
1993	11,997	7,637	6,513	1,751	27,898	5,909	4,561	6,272	52,977
1986/80	1.00	1.61	0.71	1.24	1.05	0.91	1.03	1.02	1.01
1990/86	1.92	2.30	3.31	0.90	2.08	2.03	2.00	1.56	1.74
1993/90	1.03	1.37	1.33	1.67	1.20	0.91	1.24	0.95	1.10
EC 12									
1980	6,617	5,894	7,416	2,444	22,371	45,773	5,156	381,562	688,113
1986	11,188	9,988	8,261	6,398	35,835	84,110	6,785	449,592	788,431
1990	28,713	22,333	19,627	6,728	77,301	112,933	10,285	889,742	1,364,346
1993	26,662	30,674	26,771	13,452	97,559	115,408	9,552	727,123	1,300,000
1986/80	1.69	1.69	111	2.62	1.60	1.84	1.32	1.10	1.15
1990/86	2.57	2.23	2.38	1.05	2.16	1.34	1.52	1.98	1.73
1993/90	0.93	1.37	1.36	2.00	1.26	1.02	0.93	0.82	0.95
World									
1980	139,892	63,918	63,882	20,020	287,712	327,578	25,384	768,328	1,993,312
1986	119,424	91,009	62,232	43,247	315,912	470,533	30,471	776,627	1,973,600
1990	235,307	205,055	159,441	55,378	655,181	668,864	48,700	1,419,062	3,322,100
1993	215,802	261,446	208,695	110,442	796,405	777,746	50,148	1,265,014	3,686,700
1986/80	0.85	1.42	0.97	2.16	1.10	1.44	1.20	1.01	0.99
1990/86	1.97	2.25	2.58	1.28	2.07	1.42	1.60	1.83	1.69
1993/90	0.92	1.28	1.31	1.99	1.22	1.16	1.03	0.89	1.11

Sources: 1980-90 Yamazawa (1994), 1990-93 IMF *Direction of Trade Statistics*

3 Economic Integration of the ASEAN Countries

Erja Kettunen

Introduction

This chapter discusses the economic integration of the Association of Southeast Asian Nations (ASEAN) countries, particularly the establishment of the ASEAN Free Trade Area (AFTA) in the 1990s. Originally, ASEAN was formed in the 1960s to promote regional economic cooperation and was fostered by regional security concerns. Until 1995, it comprised Indonesia, Malaysia, the Philippines, Singapore, Thailand, and Brunei. Vietnam became a member in 1995, while Laos and Myanmar were admitted in mid-1997 (figure 3.1). Despite the modest performance in intra-regional trade, the — original — ASEAN countries in 1993 agreed to establish a free trade area.

However, trade among the ASEAN has remained minor, and the countries seem not to aim at increasing intra-ASEAN trade, hence contradicting the basic explanations for a free trade area. Thus, the case of AFTA challenges the mainstream theorizing of economic integration. This chapter looks at the reasons for the formation of AFTA and discusses the relevance of the integration theorizing, considering the case at hand. Firstly, ASEAN's formation and institutionalization will be examined. Secondly, the aims of the ASEAN Free Trade Area will be presented against the backdrop of the international politico-economic developments of the 1990s. Finally, prospects for ASEAN and AFTA will be discussed, searching for the particular integrative and disintegrative factors prevailing within ASEAN. As a conclusion, some suggestions will be presented concerning the basic theorizing on economic integration.

Integration theory and ASEAN[1]

Basically, the formation of a free trade area falls into the category of international economic integration. The basic definition for integration, 'combining parts into a whole', is here understood as the process of sovereign countries forming a regional grouping in order to institutionalize economic and political cooperation. Indeed, international integration is manifested perhaps most clearly in regional organizations:

> The fundamental actors in the international system are sovereign states, and the main motive force directing their behaviour is the pursuit of the 'national interest' [... that] leads states variously towards conflict, competition and cooperation. Cooperation may become institutionalized in an international organization of states, [... and eventually,] the organization itself may develop a dynamic and vested interests of its own (Muir, 1987, p. 152).

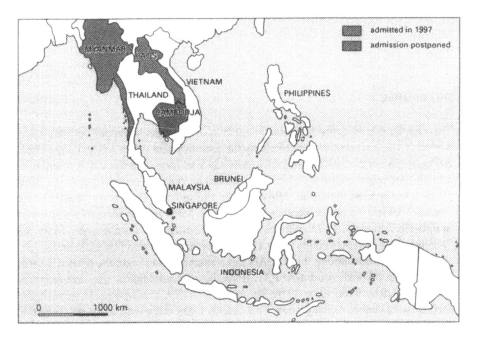

Figure 3.1   The ASEAN countries

The ASEAN organization was formed in 1967 by five countries: Indonesia, Malaysia, the Philippines, Singapore, and Thailand. According to the original agreement, the Bangkok Declaration, the formal objective of the Association was to promote cooperation in economic, social and cultural fields. It has been widely noted[2], however, that the strive to form a regional grouping arose from both internal and external political concerns during the Cold War. The aim was to enhance national integration in single countries, and to create peaceful relations among neighbouring nations. Despite the original objective of ASEAN, there have been few accomplishments in the field of economic cooperation. In the 1970s and 1980s, there were attempts at industrial and trade cooperation, for example the ASEAN Industrial

Projects (AIPs), the ASEAN Industrial Complementation (AIC), the ASEAN Industrial Joint Ventures (AIJVs), and the Preferential Trading Arrangements (PTAs), but the schemes were not realized in the way planned. The aims and outcomes of these plans have been discussed in detail earlier[3] and will not be taken into further consideration here. However, the formation of the ASEAN Free Trade Area is a more extensive attempt at economic integration, and also of great interest in regard to mainstream explanations for integration, and will be thus discussed in the following.

Mainstream theorizing

Integration studies have long traditions within two major disciplines, international economics and political science. In international economics, integration is explained by the aim of countries at increasing welfare through trade creation. Integration is basically understood as the integration of markets (Molle, 1990, p. 10) among the partner countries. It can only apply to product markets, or if deepened, also to markets of production factors. Eventually also economic policies can be integrated. The stages of integration that were distinguished by Bela Balassa in *The Theory of Economic Integration* (1966) have since been adopted as the main categorization of integration forms. The first stage of economic integration is a free trade area, in which all trade barriers are removed among the partners — as is the aim of the present AFTA agreement. The second stage is a customs union where, in addition to free trade area, one common external tariff is agreed upon. The third stage is a common market in which also the production factors, labour and capital, can move freely. The fourth stage is an economic union that also implies a unification of economic policy, market regulation, macro-economic and monetary policies and income redistribution policies. The final stage is a monetary union where one common currency is created for all the member states.

The other tradition of integration studies has evolved in political science and comprises two main bodies of international relations theories, the Realist and the Liberal.[4] The theories were largely built on the bipolarity of the Cold War. As to the Asia-Pacific region, this meant an explanation of the political relations by the hegemonic United States leadership. Since the passing of the Cold War, the changes in the region have been noteworthy and, as Higgott (1993, p. 109) notes, neither of the main traditions have articulated an adequate post-Cold War theory of leadership. The theories are now faced with the challenge of reconceptualizing the bases of international relations.

Summarizing the above, the general concept of integration comprises the following basic elements: (1) sovereign states are the major actors of international integration, (2) the countries are motivated by increasing national welfare through intra-regional trade, (3) integration proceeds in subsequent stages of a free trade area, customs union, common market, and economic and monetary union. It must be noted, however, that economic integration theorizing has largely originated from the European case, and thus it includes basic assumptions about the stage of economic development and similarity of the countries. The ASEAN countries are, in economic terms, still significantly behind Europe and also constitute a economically heterogeneous group of countries.

Furthermore, the analysis of trade and national welfare effects of economic integration are basically studied employing econometric models of a customs union. A problem concerning the customs union analyses of the Third world groupings arises from the point that intra-regional trade among developing countries is usually minor, and trading links to outside the region remain stronger. This renders modest customs union effects and implies that there are other motives for developing countries to integrate.

The establishment of ASEAN and AFTA have indicated progress in formal economic integration, although the performance of the Association has been more in the political sphere. All in all, it is not a simple task to evaluate the accomplishments of a regional grouping. The given 'ranking' depends heavily on the perspective, and as Thambillai (1991, p. 301) comments, from an economic viewpoint the modest success of ASEAN in economic integration has been criticized on the basis of the lack of trade, industrial cooperation, and harmonization of trade and investment regulations. Political analysts have been more generous in their evaluation of ASEAN's attempts at promoting friendly relations intra-regionally and in pursuing common policies on extra-regional issues.

The institutionalization of ASEAN

The notion of the stages of integration is important as it implies a process of institution-building. The various forms of integration require policy integration, for which common institutions, international organizations, are created (Molle 1990, p. 14). Institutionalization is thus inherent to international economic integration. Although the concept of institution and the term institutionalization have various interpretations, they are here employed for analyzing integration in accordance with the political relations studies regarding international cooperation. Higgott (1993, p. 105) has discussed the Asia-Pacific Economic Cooperation (APEC) and listed the characteristics and functions of institutions, including: (1) a shared recognition of the utility of cooperation, (2) retaining and transmitting of information, and (3) policy coordination.

The establishment of ASEAN by five developing countries was the first concrete step in the institutionalization process of the Association. The political will for integration emanated from a shared recognition of the utility of cooperation in the unstable environment. Since its formation, ASEAN has been a forum for mutual consultation among the member states. This denotes the function of the Association as retaining and transmitting information. Policy coordination has been achieved in mutual diplomacy, and the members perceive ASEAN as the cornerstone of their foreign policies. Kurus (1993, p. 824) has pointed out that ASEAN is the only Third world grouping that has managed to institutionalize annual discussion with Western industrialized countries within the so-called ASEAN Dialogue Partners system. Also, while the earlier record in industrial and trade cooperation might have been poor, ASEAN has created a solid image for itself and done much in creating an ASEAN 'consciousness' and providing at least the Southeast Asian elites with a sense of regional identity (Rigg, 1991, pp. 201, 224). ASEAN has thus developed a dynamic of its own (cf. Muir, 1987, p. 152), extended from the diverse interests of individual member nations. Evidently, the signing of AFTA has been another hallmark in the institutionalization of ASEAN. It has also expanded geographically as four countries have later joined the Association. In 1984, after having gained full independence, Brunei became the sixth member, and, arguably as a historical event, in 1995 Vietnam joined ASEAN as its seventh member. After having had a 'observer' status for a number of years, Laos and Myanmar were admitted to the Association in 1997. In line with the so-called Seven Plus Three Formula, ASEAN will encompass all ten countries of Southeast Asia by the year 2000.

The ASEAN countries

Contrary to the integration theory, ASEAN is composed of very different countries in terms of land area, population and macro-economic characteristics, as table 3.1 shows. The smallest states in terms of population, Brunei and Singapore, have the highest per capita gross national product (GNP). At the same time, the economies of Thailand and Malaysia have shown the most rapid growth. In aggregate terms, Indonesia is the group's giant, with a huge land area and a population of 190 million — a figure that gives the country a ranking as the fourth in the world.

Table 3.1
Macro-economic indicators of the ASEAN countries

	Area (km^2)	Pop. 1994 (million)	GNP 1993 (US$ bil.)	GNP PC 1993 (US$)	80-85	86-92	92	93	94
					GDP Annual Growth (%)				
Indonesia	1906.6	190.7	137.0	730	5.6	6.2	7.2	7.3	7.3
Malaysia	329.7	19.5	60.1	3160	5.5	7.4	7.8	8.3	8.5
Philippines	300.0	68.6	54.6	830	-0.1	3.2	0.3	2.1	4.3
Singapore	0.6	2.9	55.4	19310	6.8	7.5	6.0	10.1	10.1
Thailand	513.1	59.4	120.2	2040	5.3	10.0	7.9	8.2	n.a.
Vietnam	331.7	72.5	12.0	170	4.2	4.5	8.6	8.1	8.8

Source: Asian Development Bank (1995); n.a. = not available

As was mentioned earlier, trade among the ASEAN countries is relatively small; at the time of the signing of AFTA, intra-ASEAN trade was only about 15-20 percent of the total trade of the member countries. Furthermore, most of this intra-regional trade is conducted with Singapore. Also, the bulk of the trade, 63 percent, is constituted of minerals and fuels (Hussey, 1991, p. 91). For historical reasons, stronger trading links have developed with Japan, the United States, and Europe that also provide the developed infrastructure and technology for transportation and communication. In intra-ASEAN trade, an impediment to growth has traditionally been the lack of complementarity (Rigg, 1991, p. 219; Hussey 1991, p. 92) among the countries due to similar production structures. Regarding the basic theory of economic integration, the lack of intra-trade in the context of establishing a free trade area, implies that basically there are other reasons than trade for the establishment of AFTA.

The ASEAN Free Trade Agreement

The preparations for AFTA began in 1990. In October 29-30 in Denpasar, Bali, the 22nd ASEAN Economic Ministers Meeting (AEM) agreed to adopt a common effective preferential tariff on selected industrial products. The products initially included were cement, fertilizer, and pulp. The following year, the ASEAN Senior Officials Meeting (SEOM) in Kuala Lumpur agreed on amendments to the earlier Thai proposal to establish AFTA. Soon after, the 23rd AEM in Kuala Lumpur agreed to form a regional free trade area within 15 years. In December 1991, the first meeting of the Interim Technical Working Group on AFTA was held in Jakarta. The agreement reached completion at the highest level in the 4th ASEAN Summit in Singapore in 1992, where the ASEAN heads of government formally agreed to establish AFTA, and signed the Singapore Declaration and the Framework Agreement on Enhancing ASEAN Economic Cooperation. AEM signed the Agreement on the CEPT for AFTA (AFTA Reader, 1993, pp. 72-3).

The main institutional arrangement for the free trade area is the AFTA Council that was established by the ASEAN Economic Ministers (AFTA Reader, 1993, p. 8). The Council is composed of Ministers from the ASEAN member states, and the Secretary-General of ASEAN. The AFTA Council is responsible for supervising, coordinating and reviewing the implementation of the CEPT Agreement. The ASEAN Secretariat is primarily responsible for coordinating and monitoring the implementation of AFTA. According to the agreement, the ASEAN Free Trade Area will be established in ten years (1993-2003). Originally, 15 years was envisaged, but the schedule was tightened later. AFTA will be formed by gradually reducing tariffs on locally produced manufactured goods and processed agricultural goods to 0-5 percent in intra-ASEAN trade. The actual tariff reductions were started in January 1994. The main mechanism for the AFTA is the so-called Common Effective Preferential Tariff (CEPT) Scheme, under which there are two time schedules for tariff cuts, the Fast Track Program and the Normal Track Program. The fast track reductions will be completed by the year 2000 for fifteen product groups, e.g. textiles, pharmaceuticals, electronics, cement and plastics. The normal track tariff cuts for other products will take place by the year 2003. The CEPT is consistent with the General Agreement on Tariffs and Trade (GATT) and WTO.

AFTA covers all manufactured products, including capital goods and processed agricultural products. The local content requirement is 40 percent, referring to both single country and cumulative ASEAN content. The CEPT Scheme also covers quantitative restrictions (quotas, licences, etc.) and non-tariff barriers. Non-tariff barriers will be eliminated on a gradual basis within a period of five years after the enjoyment of concessions applicable to the CEPT products (AFTA Reader, 1993, p. 6).

The rationale for AFTA

From conventional economics point of view, the reason for AFTA seems obscure as trade among the member countries is not substantial, and, at least explicitly, the countries do not intend to increase intra-ASEAN trade as such. Indeed, the rationale behind the ASEAN Free Trade Area is distinct from the mainstream explanation. In the early 1990s, after the Cold War, the emphasis in international relations shifted from political towards economic matters, and ASEAN faced new challenges related to its existence. Increased integration of the European Union (EU) and progress in the North American Free Trade Agreement (NAFTA), as well as the opening of the Eastern European markets to foreign investments, created the need for ASEAN to intensify its economic integration. Within ASEAN a concern was shared about maintaining industrial competitiveness of the countries *vis-à-vis* outside the region (Ariff, 1992, p. 9). More exactly, single ASEAN countries aiming to maintain the competitive position of their industries perceived AFTA as a means to compete for foreign direct investments in the world market. In effect, this has also been noted by the ASEAN Secretariat itself: 'The ultimate objective of AFTA is to increase ASEAN's competitive edge as a production base geared to the world market' (AFTA Reader, 1993, p. 1).

Thus, AFTA was established along the 'global regionalization process', as integration in the other continents intensified with EU and NAFTA. Regionalization is here understood as the formation of so-called trading blocs that are based on industrial competition. In the 1990s, regional blocs are formed on economic and industrial grounds, and regionalization is thus an economically oriented phenomenon, in contrast to the blocs of the Cold War that were based on security and defence concerns.

Prospects for ASEAN?

AFTA is consistent with the economic and industrial policies of the ASEAN member countries which perceive the free trade area scheme as a means to attract foreign investments, thus maintaining economic growth. As to the integration theory, the ASEAN countries aim to increase national welfare, not through increased intra-ASEAN trade, but instead through expansion of their industries by means of foreign capital. For example, Malaysia seems committed to AFTA, having set high aims in industrialization and economic development — as expounded in 'Vision 2020', which expresses Prime Minister Mahathir's goal of a fully industrialized Malaysia by the year 2020. The future of ASEAN and AFTA will rest on developments both within the member countries and in the international arena. In general, arguments for regional cooperation that are and will be invoked in the ASEAN case include: (1) regional peace and stability, (2) trade creation, conferring substantial economic advantages, (3) regional liberalization being politically easier than global liberalization, (4) regional association being more effective in international negotiations (Hill, 1987, p. 82).

These can be regarded as integrative factors for a regional grouping. The first and fourth arguments — regional stability and the effectiveness of an association in the international arena — seem by far the most important aspects of ASEAN integration. However, the second notion, trade creation, is as yet an overstatement in the case of ASEAN, as has been argued earlier.

However, besides integrative factors, also disintegrative factors can be identified among ASEAN. These include, for example, the competitive rather than complementary nature of the ASEAN economies (Rigg, 1991, p. 219) and the strong economic links of the ASEAN countries outside the region, related to the importance of the western export markets. In addition, ASEAN's institutional structure and '*modus operandi*', implying that national interests prevail over regional interests, have caused regional economic cooperation to progress slowly (Rigg 1991). For example, as to AFTA some countries decided to stagger the timing of their tariff cuts soon after the establishment of the free trade area (Vatikiotis, 1993, p. 61). ASEAN integration is also hampered by the geographical scatteredness of the countries, colonial history, political heterogeneity and cultural pluralism. Many of the ASEAN nations have a ethnically heterogeneous population, comprising Malay, Indian, Chinese, and indigenous groups, affecting the coherence of both a state and a regional grouping. In general, cultural and political factors always underly economic relations (for example, foreign trade or economic cooperation). As Muir (1987, p. 158) points out, the pattern of world trade is conditioned by political factors of affinity and animosity to a very considerable degree. Furthermore,

.. such factors as geographic proximity; ethnic, cultural or linguistic similarity; traditional affinities; and formal political linkage and commitment also help to determine trade flows (Alker and Puchala, 1968, p. 290; quoted by Muir, 1987, p. 158).

Discussion

In this chapter, the concept of economic integration has been discussed in the light of the case at hand, ASEAN and its free trade area. Usually, free trade areas are treated applying the standard economics textbook presentation of the concept of integration. Regarding the three basic elements of integration presented earlier, and the case of ASEAN and AFTA, some remarks and suggestions are raised:

1 The concept only applies to the integration of sovereign states where whole countries form an integrated economic area. Other actors of integration, or other scales of integration, are neglected.
2 Considering the standard assumption of national interest in international relations, there is an opposite view as well. In political relations studies, the Liberal tradition stresses interactions among states and altruism over the self-help assumption (Nye, 1987, pp. vi-vii). However, in this study the former assumption is applied in the ASEAN case: of national interests prevailing over collective interests.
3 As to the stages of integration, it must be noted that the popular usage of the terms may be misleading. For example, the 'common market' is more often applied as a label than practiced in reality, as in the so-called Arab Common Market (Nye, 1987, p. 29). Although ASEAN strives to proceed moderately beginning from the first stage, it is virtually impossible to figure out the future development and potential deepening of its integration. It may be more probable that the removal of economic obstacles among ASEAN continues only along multilateral economic cooperation, for example, the Asia-Pacific Economic Cooperation (APEC) scheme.
4 In integration theory, spatial features have not played a prominent role. Both the mainstream neoclassical economics and the international relations studies have basically neglected the spatial dimension, for example distance. But as is evident from the case of the European integration, physical proximity and the compactness of the region have but advanced the region's economic integration. Also, the performance of ASEAN reveals the importance of distance, be it physical, cultural, political or economic, in the accomplishments of political cooperation or the activity of economic interchange.

Indeed, there is a need for a spatial theory of integration. Hartshorne's (1950) classical work on the 'functional approach to political geography' has been later presented by Taylor (1985, p. 113) as the theory of territorial integration. It is based on the idea of two opposing forces binding and pulling apart a state: the centripetal (integrative) and centrifugal (disintegrative) forces. The basic and most important integrative force is the '*raison d'être*', the reason for existence of a state. The concept should be further modified and adapted, to be applied to a regional grouping. Arguably, ASEAN's '*raison d'être*' was originally to strengthen the political stability in the region (Rolls, 1991, p. 323).

Summing up, it has been found that on a regional level, ASEAN as an entity is crucial for political stability and international diplomacy of the member countries. As such, ASEAN shows a steady process of institution-building. ASEAN's Free Trade Area, on the other hand, aims at enhancing the industrial competitiveness of the countries. The pursuance of the new objectives, as well as the expansion of ASEAN, occur alongside the regional and global politico-economic developments of the 1990s.

Notes

1. Although the operative expression for ASEAN has throughout been 'cooperation' rather than 'integration', as Punyaratabandhu-Bhakdi (1991) points out, the latter concept will be employed here. Along with the development of the free trade area, ASEAN will also operationally go under the heading of economic integration.
2. For example, Hussey (1991, p. 87); Rigg (1991, p. 209); Rolls (1991, pp. 324-5); Rigg & Stott (1992, pp. 107-108).
3. See, for example, Balasubramanyam (1989, pp. 172-4); Hussey (1991, pp. 89-90); Rigg (1991, pp. 213-19); Kurus (1993, pp. 32-5).
4. The main schools within international relations studies are further discussed in, for example, Nye (1987).

References

AFTA Reader (1993), *Questions and Answers on the CEPT for AFTA*, Volume I, ASEAN Secretariat: Jakarta.

Ariff, M. (1992), ASEAN Free Trade Area (Afta): Problems and Prospects. Paper presented at the Malaysian Institute of Economic Research (MIER), National Outlook Conference, 8-9 December, Kuala Lumpur, Malaysia.

Asian Development Bank, Economics and Development Resource Center (1995), *Key Indicators of Developing Asian and Pacific Countries*, Vol. XXVI, Oxford University Press: Manila.

Balasubramanyam, V.N. (1989), 'ASEAN and Regional Trade Cooperation in Southeast Asia', in Greenaway, D., Hyclak, T. and Thornton, R.J. (eds), *Economic Aspects of Regional Trading Arrangements*, Wheatsheaf: Exeter/ Harvester.

Hartshorne, R. (1950), 'The Functional Approach in Political Geography', *Annals of the Association of American Geographers*, Vol. 40, No. 2, pp. 95-130.

Higgott, R. (1993), 'Economic Cooperation: Theoretical Opportunities and Practical Constraints', *The Pacific Review*, Vol. 6, No. 2, pp. 103-17.

Hill, H. (1987), 'Challenges in ASEAN Economic Co-operation: An Outsider's Perspective', in Sopiee, N., Chew, L.S. and Lim, S.J. (eds), *ASEAN at the Crossroads: Obstacles, Options and Opportunities in Economic Cooperation*, Institute of Strategic and International Studies (ISIS): Kuala Lumpur, pp. 81-9.

Hussey, A. (1991), 'Regional Development and Cooperation Through ASEAN', *The*

Geographical Review, Vol. 81 , No. 1, pp. 87-98.

Kurus, B. (1993), 'Understanding ASEAN: Benefits and Raison d'Être', *Asian Survey*, Vol. 33, No. 8, pp. 819-31.

Molle, W. (1990), *The Economics of European Integration. Theory, Practice, Policy*, Dartmouth Publishing Company Ltd: Worcester.

Muir, R. (1987), *Modern Political Geography*, The MacMillan Press Ltd: Trowbridge and Esher.

Nye, J. Jr. (1987), *Peace in Parts. Integration and Conflict in Regional Organization*, University Press of America, Inc.

Punyaratabandhu-Bhakdi, S. (1991), 'Administrative Aspects of Regional Economic Co-operation: The Case of ASEAN', *International Review of Administrative Sciences*, Vol. 57, No. 4, pp. 577-90.

Rigg, J. (1991), *Southeast Asia: A Region in Transition. A Thematic Human Geography of the ASEAN Region*, Cambridge University Press/Unwin Hyman: Cambridge.

Rigg, J. and Stott, Ph. (1992), 'The Rise of the Naga: The Changing Geography of South-East Asia 1965-90', in Chapman, G. and Baker, K. (eds), *The Changing Geography of Asia*, Routledge/Guilford and King's Lynn: London, pp. 74-121.

Rolls, M.G. (1991), 'ASEAN: Where from and Where to?' *Contemporary Southeast Asia*, Vol. 13 , No. 3, pp. 315-32.

Taylor, P. (1985), *Political Geography: World-Economy, Nation-State and Locality*, Longman Group Limited: Singapore.

Thambillai, P. (1991), 'The ASEAN Growth Triangle: The Convergence of National and Sub-National Interests', *Contemporary Southeast Asia*, Vol. 13, No. 3, pp. 299-315.

Vatikiotis, M. (1993), 'Less Haste, Less Speed: ASEAN Scheme Starts with Tariff Cuts', *Far Eastern Economic Review*, Vol. 156, No. 1, p. 61.

4 Intra-Regional Division of Labour and Industrial Change in East Asia

Emerging High-Technology Interaction Between Korea and Taiwan

Claes G. Alvstam and Sang-Chul Park

Introduction

One of the most important new tendencies in East Asian industrial transformation in the 1990s is the rapid growth of intra-regional trade. Hitherto export flows from the newly industrializing economies have been mainly directed towards the United States and Japan, while intra-regional exports have amounted to marginal volumes. Particularly obvious is this imbalance within the high-technology industries, in which one can talk about an almost watertight bulkhead between the national markets, despite the fact that American, Japanese and, to some extent, European firms traditionally have served as the main sources of technology transfers and acted as major consignees of assembled goods in the cases of Korea and Taiwan, as well as in Hong Kong, Singapore and Malaysia. The emergence of strong domestic firms within high-technology industries in the NIEs since the 1970s for a long time strengthened the bilateral links to the Old Industrial Core, rather than of intra-regional contacts. High physical and technical barriers protecting infant industries, particularly in Korea and Taiwan, served as effective obstacles to the growth of the tendencies towards product differentiation in a regional market, which was a major feature of the deepening of economic interaction in Western Europe during the 1960s and 1970s.

The pattern we have seen up to now is about to change. Korean FDI, initially directed to the Middle East and Southeast Asia, entered the take-off phase in the late 1970s. A notable widening, in terms of actors, objectives and geographical spread can be observed after 15-20 years of Korean FDI experience. The dominance of a few big actors, to a large extent within the infrastructural sector, and with investment activities directed to relatively few countries, has gradually been replaced by a higher degree of company diversification within a wider range of manufacturing sectors, targeting a larger number of host countries. Taiwanese overseas investments have soared from almost non-existent volumes in 1985 to becoming one of the main sources of investments in Asia in the mid-1990s. The FDI was initially particularly directed to

54

Southeast Asia, but since the early 1990s overwhelmingly to mainland China. Regarding sectoral composition, Taiwan is following roughly the same tracks as Korea, but incorporating a larger number of individual investors. The delicate political relations with the People's Republic of China have implied a slower growth of FDI and trade with the Chinese mainland, although it has not been a definite obstacle. The PRC is now by far the largest trade and investment partner for Taiwan. Rather it is appropriate to see Korean and Taiwanese investment on the Chinese mainland as a time-lagged process.

Korea's and Taiwan's present industrial challenge is to keep ahead of the ASEAN-4 [1] and mainland China by maintaining and expanding the existing technological gap on the one hand and on the other to achieve higher levels of product sophistication, in order to compete with other members of the first generation of Asian tigers, as well as with Japan, the USA and Europe. Korean and Taiwanese investors have hitherto avoided competition in their respective domestic markets, instead putting priority on global competition. Now, when there are signs of a rapid increase of intra-regional trade connections in high-technology and knowledge-intensive goods and services, there are also far-reaching implications for a radical restructuring of Korean and Taiwanese industry, to meet the new challenges of intra-regional competition.

This chapter aims to assess the conditions for such a change, and to contribute to the theoretical debate on how to interpret and explain the present as well as the future development. Key issues to be raised here include the role of governments, the absence of a common industrial network between the two countries, and the potential implications for other countries in the region, mainly the ASEAN-4, mainland China and Vietnam. The methodology used is to inquire deeply into trade and investment statistics from the two countries, and to relate the growing bilateral flows of economic interaction to the contemporary theoretical debate on previous lessons of economic integration between Western European countries. The more detailed case-study will focus on the electronics industry within the commodity groups SITC 76-77, particularly in chapters 83-85 according to the Harmonized Commodity Coding and Description System (HS).

Emerging intra-regional division of labour

There are basically four main explanations behind the deepening intra-regional economic interdependence in the Asia-Pacific Region. The first is the continuously declining role of US economic power and the diminishing welfare gap between the industrial countries in North America and Western Europe on the one hand, and the NIEs in East and Southeast Asia on the other; second, the threats of increasing trade friction and protectionist measures in a scenario of rising regionalism in the post-Uruguay world trade order; third, a new phase in the internationalization process of Asian economies, resulting in a more diversified and technologically advanced trade pattern, and growing significance of foreign direct investment; and fourth, the successive removal of political barriers, enabling countries with a huge development potential, like China and Vietnam, to participate in the international economy (Chi, 1993). Those bilateral trade flows of significance, which have recorded the largest rates of growth in intra-regional trade in the Asia-Pacific during the first half of the 1990s have all been related to Greater China, i.e. the mainland, Hong Kong, Taiwan and Macau (Alvstam, 1995, p. 116). Taking the commodity composition into consideration, the largest growth has taken place within the intermediate sector, i.e. capital goods within the machinery and apparatus industries, as well as different kinds of parts and components in these industries, followed by semi-manufactured goods. An important trend is diversification. While previous intra-regional trade mainly occurred within raw material sectors, textiles and apparel, food, light consumer goods, and electronic components, there is in the 1990s an obvious shift in the direction of general machinery, capital goods, and equipment within a broad industrial range. The average manufacturing value added has soared in a remarkably short period of time.

However, regional cooperation in Asia is still weak compared to Western Europe. Its multilateral economic cooperation has mainly been based on the government level rather than on private sector initiatives. Even ASEAN, the most well-known symbol of regional economic cooperation, has yet to achieve lasting results regarding intra-trade development. The schedule to create an ASEAN free trade area (AFTA) within a 10-15 years' timeframe is still subject to doubt regarding pace and progress. On the other hand, the rapid progress of economic integration between the island of Taiwan and the Chinese mainland during the past ten years is an illustrative example of how regionally based trade and FDI can grow, despite, rather than because of governmental cooperation (Johansson and Alvstam, 1995).

Economic development in Korea and the role of the government

A major change in the direction of Korean economic development began with the military government that took power in 1961. Its economic policy aimed at rapid industrial development based on a 'growth-first', export-oriented industrialization strategy (*Sungjang Chaeil Jongchaeck*), active inducement of foreign capital and various institutional reforms (Sakong, 1993; Kim Kwang-Suk, 1994). To carry out this outward-looking strategy, the government devaluated its currency in May 1964 by almost 50 percent from 130 to 214 won per US dollar. This measure was accompanied by large-scale foreign borrowing in order to finance investments in export industries. Furthermore, substantial imports of raw materials, components and machinery were also necessary. It provided the most successful exporters a range of benefits, including preferential access to loans at subsidized interest rates, discounts on power and freight costs, and access to import licences for procuring machinery and components (Bloom, 1993; Kim Kwang-Suk, 1994, p. 534).

These measures enabled a few major actors to expand their exports and led to a concentration of economic power in the huge conglomerates, *chaebol*. A major factor behind the fast growth of the conglomerates was also the new industrial policy based on '*Jung Hwahak Kongyop*', the heavy and chemical industries in the 1970s. It resulted in the neglect of the light manufacturing industries, which were significant exporters as well as producers of daily necessities, and at the same time an over-investment in targeted industries based on supply-side considerations rather than realistic demand-side forecasts at the corporate level.

Consequently, the government announced a set of comprehensive stabilization measures (*Anjong Jongchaeck*) in 1979, particularly characterized by a much tighter monetary and fiscal stance than during the 'growth-first' period. This shift of policy caused severe problems in the non-targeted, labour-intensive sectors. The new strategy was negatively affected by the balance of payment crisis created by the second oil shock in the early 1980s, but generally it was well-timed, and enabled Korea to take advantage of the boom in manufactured exports, particularly to the USA, in the early and mid-1980s.

Moreover, selective industrial promotion laws oriented to sunrise industries, such as electronics and petrochemicals, were replaced by the Industrial Development Law in 1986, which mainly focused on restructuring. The new law also supported industrial technological upgrading, and enabled the government to establish a basic principle, namely to intervene actively in industry only in cases of obvious market failure. The close association between government and business in Korea's economic development had unquestionably contributed to the rapid industrialization, but at the same time the national economy had suffered from fundamental distortions of competitive market structures, misallocation of resources, severe inflationary pressure, and unbalanced industrial and regional development (Kim Yoon-Hyung, 1994, p. 50). Since the second half of the 1980s, trade liberalization has become essential in order to maintain the economic cooperation with other countries, particularly the USA, and a liberalization of the financial sector started at a limited scale (Sakong, 1993, p. 75; Leipziger and Petri, 1994, p. 593).

Furthermore, the domestic environment has changed rapidly since the end of the 1980s. The technology-intensive sectors have continuously expanded, and at the same time the manufacturing sector is becoming more sophisticated and diversified. The *chaebol* are gradually more and more integrated into the world economy through corporate alliances and foreign direct investments, that enable them to evade government directives. Under these circumstances, the government announced '*Upjong Junmun Hwa*', the Industrialization Specialization Plan, in October 1993. The objective of the plan was that the more specialized top 30 conglomerates should, on the basis of their core businesses, increase their competitiveness in the global market on the one hand, while the small and medium sized firms should gain economic vitality through a taking over of the non-strategic industries of the *chaebol* on the other hand (*The Maekyoung Business Week*, 9 Nov. 1993, pp. 18-21; McKay and Missen, 1995, p. 74). The role of the government is now to focus on supporting R&D activities, in order to upgrade technological standards, and on promoting industrial diversification (White Paper, 1994, pp. 250-54). McKay and Missen point out that the immediate future of the Korean economy will depend upon a few key industries. In the case of electronics, the development of an efficient and technologically innovative network of subcontractors is seen as a major priority.

While the *chaebol* will continue to dominate, the role of small and medium enterprises is likely to be more important, and therefore less attention should be paid to the issue of firm size in the future economic development (White Paper, 1994, p. 62).

The emerging high-technology sector

In the mid-1960s, a number of American electronics companies established a couple of mostly wholly-owned operations in Korea. These were mainly assembling components for exports, using imported parts and components. The advantages of these investments to the Korean economy were limited. Far more visible was the result of the Japanese investment projects that began in 1969 and grew rapidly in the beginning of the 1970s. At that time Japanese production, moving overseas, based on a strategy of globalization, provided the embryonic Korean producers of consumer electronics products an opportunity to establish joint ventures with Japanese counterparts. Examples of Korean companies that particularly took advantage of the mutual benefit by combining the Japanese strategy for globalization and the Korean strategy to encourage industrial development were Samsung, establishing joint ventures with NEC and Sanyo Electric, and Lucky Goldstar Group, which was linked to NEC and Alps Electric (Bloom, 1993).

Needless to say, there was little technology available to Korean companies in the 1960s because of inadequate research infrastructure and lack of skilled manpower, as well as the limited technology transfers provided by the wholly-owned American companies. These experiences resulted in a restrictive development strategy to obtain foreign production technology in the form of machinery and equipment for electronics assembly. In order to handle the procured equipment, the domestic companies developed gradually the required managerial skills and hired low-cost female labour to assemble the basic components. Furthermore, the finished products were mainly exported, usually on an OEM basis, and own brand sales were restricted to the domestic market.

The next step in the cooperation with Japanese electronics companies, when the R&D activities within the Korean industry expanded, and licensing and OEM agreements became more significant, was to take over step-by-step the majority role in the joint ventures. The Japanese counterparts started a slow withdrawal in the late 1970s and the early 1980s. In order to conduct R&D activities in the high-technology sector, the Korean government established in the 1970s special material research institutes, which had considerable impacts in increasing the R&D efforts in the private sector. Finally in the 1980s, the leading companies, mainly Samsung, Daewoo and Goldstar, later also Hyundai, began to grow rapidly abroad within the consumer electronics sector. This success could be seen as a direct result of the government's technology policy, encouraging a concerted effort in the electronics industry as part of its export promotion policy on the one hand, and the recruitment of production management from the foreign joint ventures established in Korea and the recruitment of Korean engineers educated in and working in the electronics industry in the United States on the other hand (Wakabayashi and Sumita, 1993, p. 45).

Table 4.1
Export of semiconductor products from Korea, 1991-1993
(US$ million)

	1991	1992	1993
Manufactured	2,140	2,841	5,092
Memory	1,673	2,417	4,185
DRAM	1,401	2,015	3,516
1M	799	490	401
4M	451	1,392	2,586
16M	-	38	499
Non-memory	467	424	907
Assembled	3,520	3,963	2,936

Source: Ministry of Trade Industry and Energy (1994), The White Paper, p. 416; revised by the authors

Table 4.2
Production and exports within the Korean semiconductor industry, 1990-1993 (US$ million and %)

	1990	1991	1992	1993
World market (A)	58,200	59,694	65,587	85,641
Domestic production (B)	5,200	6,500	7,800	8,800
Market share (B/A)	8.9	10.9	11.9	10.3
Exports (C)	4,541	5,660	6,804	8,028
Export dependence (C/B)	87.3	87.1	87.2	91.2
Imports (D)	4,093	4,830	5,426	5,042
Import dependence (D/(B-C+D)	86.1	85.2	84.5	86.7
Trade balance (C-D)	448	830	1,373	2,986

Sources: Ministry of Trade Industry and Energy (1994), The White Paper, and Dataquest; revisions and adaptations by the authors

In the semiconductor industry there has been a clear shift during the 1990s toward the more advanced memory chips, phasing out the 1M DRAMs, and recently introducing the 16Ms (table 4.1). Samsung Electronics produced 8.0 million 4M

DRAM-chips per month in 1993. Hyundai Electronics and Goldstar Electron had a monthly output of 4.5 million and 3.5 million respectively in the same year (Wakabayashi and Sumita, 1993, p. 40; *Korea Economic Weekly*, 1 May 1995). The exports of semiconductor products have been growing continuously. The world market share of Korean semiconductor products increased to 10.3 percent in 1993, and the export share of production amounted to 91 percent (see table 4.2). The increasing level of export-dependence and the continuously high import-dependence, signify a high level of intra-industry trade within the semiconductor sector.

Although the Korean semiconductor industry has expanded to become the second largest producer in the world, it has still weaknesses in the non-memory production, incorporating basic technology and design technology.[2] The demand for non-memory chips, Application-Specific Integrated Circuits (ASICs), is increasing rapidly, since electronics products have gradually become more complex and the life cycle of products has decreased (Hobday, 1991). The Korean semiconductor industry is still heavily dependent on foreign suppliers, mainly in the USA and Japan for more than 80 percent of its domestic non-memory consumption, as well as equipment for semiconductor production (The White Paper, 1994, p. 174; Wakabayashi and Sumita, 1993, pp. 42-3). In order to solve these problems, Samsung is keen to move into more lucrative chips, such as ASICs, and has invested in a 40 percent stake in the PC maker AST Research in the USA (*Business Week International*, 31 July 1995, pp. 34-6).

The transformation of the Taiwanese economy

The extraordinary evolution of the Taiwanese economy has been well documented and analyzed in numerous monographs and articles (see e.g. Fei, Ranis and Kuo, 1979; Galenson et al., 1979; Kuo, 1983). The most generally accepted explanations have stressed the export expansion, the initial successes in bringing down the high inflation rates of the late 1940s, and then keeping the level low since then, the high savings and investment rates, the massive allocation of financial resources from the United States in the 1950s, as well as a unique political context, being initially governed by a leadership aiming at returning to the mainland as quick as possible, and later finding itself internationally isolated and unrecognized. There is indeed no single theoretical framework within which such an evolution could take place in reality. Chan and Clark (1992) have pointed out how the economic success of Taiwan is contradictory to all different mainstream paradigms that dominate current development theory:

> Dependency theorists would have expected catastrophe in view of its extreme economic and political dependence upon the core of capitalism (the United States), its backward agrarian economy, and its authoritarian capitalist ruling class divorced from the sullen masses. Developmentalists would have been quite dismayed by the island's economic chaos, hyperinflation, and the heavy hand of the state which controlled over half of industry, as well as by the alleged anti-

market biases in a Confucian culture. The statists, for their part, would have pointed to the economic failure of the KMT on the mainland and the existence of a garrison state dominated by the military as reasons for being extremely pessimistic about the emergence of a developmental state. From the tradeoff perspective, the heavy commitment to defence by an authoritarian regime would have been seen as almost inevitably precluding progress in terms of growth, welfare, and democratization which, in turn, could well sow the seeds of future instability (Chan and Clark, 1992, pp. 32-3).

A key factor in the general economic growth of the island has been the ability to transform successfully the traditional agrarian structure into a modern industrial economy, continuously upgraded to more and more advanced segments of manufacturing. The current challenge in the mid-1990s is how to manage the transformation into a service economy, where the future welfare growth of its population will be dependent on sustaining its competitive edge in creating own technological and industrial innovations rather than imitating and copying breakthroughs reached in other countries. Taiwanese companies and Taiwanese scientists have during an astonishingly short period of time diminished the original gap with the worldwide technological front in a great number of industrial sectors, and have reached the position of being recognized as equals by their American, Japanese, German and Korean competitors. Another great challenge will be the transformation from export dependence in becoming a source country for extensive foreign direct investment in the entire Asia-Pacific region as well as in the old industrial core. Starting in the 1950s at the stage of 'young debtor', capital poor and lacking foreign trade, the country passed between 1975 and 1985 through the stage of being a 'mature debtor', displaying considerable success in economic development and trade and possessing the ability to obtain private loans and inward foreign direct investment. In the late 1980s Taiwan entered the stage of becoming a 'young creditor', where the trade surplus increased rapidly, the net possession of foreign currency soared and outward foreign direct investment began to rise. The final stage, which Taiwan is about to reach in the middle of the 1990s, is one of being a 'mature creditor' living off the interests and dividends on its overseas claims. At this stage the Taiwanese economy has become even more closely integrated with the world economic system, whereas the outflows as well as inflows of foreign capital have increased significantly.

The Taiwanese electronics production

Also in Taiwan the electronics industry is a good example of how industrial change takes place in a newly industrializing economy. Furthermore, electronics technologies are important in Taiwan's general strategy to design and manufacture innovative products. Taiwan is now the world's seventh largest producer of electronic goods, far exceeding several European countries like Italy and the Netherlands. Since 1984, electronics is furthermore the largest export sector when it overtook textiles. Around

85 percent of the total output is exported (McDermott, 1991, p. 78). Within the sector all different types of production can be found, from extremely labour-intensive production processes, to large-scale capital-intensive production and small-scale research and technology-based sequences. The origin of the electronics sector in Taiwan derives from the inward foreign direct investment in offshore production, mainly from USA and Japan. The first leading electronics company to establish in Taiwan was the American multinational General Instrument, who started to manufacture radios in 1964 (McDermott, 1991, p. 82). Apart from the simple assembly of consumer products, lay-off production of components started in the 1960s in a large number of domestic small-scale firms. At that time Taiwan concentrated on components production and consumer electronics assembly rather than on industrial electronics. Labour-intensity in the components production and assembly are generally higher, while the industrial products segment is on average far more knowledge-intensive and capital-intensive. In the next phase, when Taiwan started to build up an electronics industry on their own in tandem with the foreign companies, consumer electronics was given priority while industrial electronics was still very small in size. Within the consumer segment Taiwan emphasized low-technology products, such as radios and sound recorders, and within the industrial sector particularly low-technology capacitors and resistors. Later there was a quick transformation in the direction of industrial electronics which now accounts for more than 40 percent of the total output. Compared with its main competitors, however, Taiwan still has a low share of industrial electronics. Corresponding shares for USA, Western Europe and Japan in 1988 were 73 percent, 67 percent and 58 percent respectively (McDermott, 1991, p. 79).

These changes do reflect not only the production life cycles and the time of introduction of various new products, but also the strategies adopted by domestic as well as foreign companies operating within the electronics sector in Taiwan. The domestic actors are originally companies emanating from electric machinery and home appliances and relatively large in size, while the foreign actors started to use small and medium-sized Taiwanese companies as subcontractors, which later often were transformed into foreign-owned production plants. Many of these new firms have located in the three Export Processing Zones.

The centre of the Taiwanese semiconductor industry has been the Electronics Research and Service Organization (ERSO) established in 1975. It is an example of an organization that was part of the general industrial development strategy of the government at that time and substantial grants were its main source of finance for the first ten years. Its purpose is mainly to assist new entrants by giving them service regarding production and design of Integrated Circuits through an own production facility, and thus to become a source of spin-off for new firms. One example is the largest Taiwanese manufacturer of semiconductors, the United Microelectronics Corporation (UMC), that was spun off from ERSO in 1979. UMC was the only Taiwanese firm with wafer production facilities until 1987 when the Taiwan Semiconductor Manufacturing Corporation (TSMC) started an own plant. The larger Taiwanese electronics firms, Tatung and Sampo, opted early not to enter the semiconductor market. UMC is also to some extent backed by the government, that placed capital in ASICs, opting for a niche-market strategy, since unlike mass-produced semiconductors, ASICs are tailored to specific needs and produced in smaller volumes. Its vision is that small design houses will provide designs customized to end-user requirements, and TSMC will manufacture them. TSMCs prospects depend heavily on whether their assumptions about ASIC production and design are correct. As ASIC production is maturing, economies of scope are emerging, manifested in the increasing share of large established firms in ASIC production. Large firms are coordinating production lines to facilitate the move from standardized products to ASICs. Design sophistication depends upon access to 'libraries' consisting of a variety of circuit elements. Small firms cannot support large libraries. If such economies of scope eventually predominate, Taiwan may have to rely heavily on low value-added ASICs (Mody, 1991, p. 46f).

The disadvantage of being a relatively small country by international standards with little or no access to the common resources of a larger corporate group in the case of high-technology products with subsequently high entry barriers, may be an advantage within segments where entry barriers are low, the technology is widely known, the labour intensity is higher, and where the flexibility and ability swiftly to respond to new market opportunities are most important. The assembly of telephone sets is such an example. In the beginning of the 1980s, the US telecommunications market went through a deregulation process. Suddenly there was an opportunity to compete in a formerly protected domestic market and Taiwanese firms responded quickly to the surge in US demand for cheaper imported telephones. Between 1982 and 1983 the output rose from 3.5 million to 26 million sets. Because of different technical and quality problems, the production fell dramatically in 1984, but climbed again to 22 million units in 1986. After a peak in 1986-87, the output has fallen due to a phasing out of Taiwanese production and replacement by even cheaper telephones from Southeast Asia in the US market. In 1994 the production of telephone sets by Taiwanese companies in Taiwan had declined to 6.7 million sets, predicting a further decrease to 5 million sets in 1995. In the continuous process of technological upgrading within single products, it is still possible to trace growing, stagnating and declining product groups in Taiwanese manufacturing (see table 4.3). In the declining product groups the peak was often reached around 1990. A large number of products are underway of being phased out and moved elsewhere.

Comparisons between Taiwan and Korea

Both are latecomers in the electronics sector compared to the old industrial core countries. Initially in the 1970s, Taiwan's production was higher than Korea's and grew more rapidly, but in 1985 Korea's production exceeded Taiwan's and has since then increased at a higher rate, even though Taiwan's growth of electronic production has indeed been impressive as well. Furthermore, Korea has been much more successful in upgrading its technological level and capital intensity.

Table 4.3
Growing, stagnating and declining product ranges in Taiwanese electronics industry, 1986-1994 ('000 units)

Product	1986	1988	1990	1992	1994
Growing					
Portable computers	-	45	217	862	1302
Monitors	4449	7168	8569	11480	14070
Color-image scanners	104	169	441	694	1652
Mother boards	2225	3620	4983	5947	10761
Interface cards	2462	4367	9194	14586	19258
Telephone exchanges	849	973	1698	1670	3929
Facsimiles	-	38	108	280	671
Modems	340	693	1100	2102	6040
Integrated Circuits (mill)	1801	2273	3738	5850	7294
Diodes (million)	6461	9241	9880	11199	17685
Transistors (million)	797	1087	1156	1770	2345
Electr. condensers (mill)	16075	22835	23625	26577	36974
Power supplies	5280	5156	11175	15056	17815
Stagnating					
Desktop computers	1218	2271	2498	2941	3584
Computer terminals	1572	2262	1861	1417	1117
Floppy disks (million)	-	-	274	475	664
TV games	1924	2700	1897	3463	3395
Picture tubes (million)	15	18	19	16	13
Declining					
Electronic calculators	44925	68264	50014	18208	10631
Printers	85	84	66	66	17
Key boards	1008	2177	5277	5655	4480
Color TV sets	3988	3743	2403	1745	1482
Video tape Recorders	414	1784	571	760	474
Telephone sets	22288	18324	13992	10975	6715
Citizen band radios	2470	1005	247	317	116
Diode displays (million)	68	80	71	90	32

Source: Industry of Free China, LXXXIII, No. 6, June 1995, pp. 92-3

Mody (1989) suggests a couple of factors that put together explains why Korea has overtaken Taiwan in several sectors, despite Taiwan in many respects being a more industrially advanced country than Korea with a higher educational attainment (Balassa, 1981), a roughly eight-year lead in income level (Kim and Roemer, 1979), and a greater revealed comparative advantage in some skill-intensive and heavy manufacturing industry products (Lee, 1986). One factor is that the Korean government has actively promoted conglomerates. In the early 1960s electronics products were produced by relatively small firms in both Korea and Taiwan, and the number of involved companies was roughly the same in the two countries. During the 1960s the new political leaders of Korea initiated a policy in favouring large business groups with production becoming concentrated in a small number of conglomerates each of which spanned a wide range of products, while Taiwan at the same time maintained its smaller-scale approach (Myers, 1984; Scitovsky, 1986). In the early 1990s, Taiwan had more than 3,300 firms producing electronics, three to four times as many as in Korea, although Korea's production value in electronics was higher. The average number of employees per company was as low as 100, despite the presence of a couple of big foreign multinationals with 3,000-5,000 employees. The conglomerate organizational mode permits major investment in high technology markets, where late entrants face high entry barriers because product cycles are short. A conglomerate can better than a smaller-scale firm surmount the entry barriers through their ability to raise large amounts of capital efficiently (Mody 1991, p. 33f). In addition, conglomerates can also gain from economies of scale in manufacturing and in R&D, and are able to shift production from one production line to another to ride out temporary fluctuations in demand. Though both countries have been export-oriented, the domestic market has been more important in Korea, being a country with twice the Taiwanese population size. Korea's domestic market has been a more important home-base for export growth. Mody takes the example of television production in the two countries. Initially four firms shared television production in Korea. As parts of conglomerates, they were able to invest rapidly in large plants. Television imports were virtually banned until the early 1980s. In contrast, Taiwanese firms, when they were initially producing mainly for the domestic market, faced stiff competition from foreign firms, and of the dozen firms producing television sets in Taiwan at that stage, domestic firms accounted for a minority share of total output. When export possibilities emerged in the early 1980s, domestic Taiwanese firms lacked the financial capability to expand capacity rapidly to achieve substantial scale economics (Mody, 1991, p. 40). Another example is the development of PC production where both countries have had substantial success. When Korean producers entered this market, severe quantitative restrictions were placed on PC imports. Direct foreign investment by foreign firms in these products was almost completely restricted. Taiwanese firms were exposed to greater international competition, relying on high tariffs to protect domestic production of key electronic items, and Taiwan permitted considerable FDI in industry (Mody, 1991, p. 40; Schive and Yeh, 1980).

Another important difference is the monetary policy carried through by the two countries as expressed by the exchange rate of the domestic currencies to US dollars. When the US dollar started to tumble heavily relative to the Japanese yen in Autumn 1985, actually forcing the yen to appreciate by 100 percent between 1985 and 1987, and thus doubling the price of Japanese consumer goods on the US market between these two years, the Korean won fell at around the same rate as the US dollar, while the Taiwanese NT dollar was forced to appreciate at about the same pace as the yen. Consequently the US market was suddenly opened widely for low-priced Korean products gaining from plummeting Japanese market shares, while Taiwan never was faced with such a golden opportunity. Taking Samsung Semiconductor and Telecommunications (SST) as an example for comparison with UMC, it is much larger and is a member of a larger group of companies, where loans are guaranteed within the family. Consequently SST has been able to maintain a considerably higher debt-equity ratio than its Taiwanese competitor, and thus has had the opportunity to expand at a higher pace (Mody, 1991). Even though the initial investors in UMC included the Bank of Communications, China Development Corporation, China Development Corporation, Kuang Hua Investment Co. and a number of electronics manufacturers, it has no big brother and in 1985 had to go public in order to finance part of its projected capital expenditure over the next years.

Moreover, SST is much more dependent on foreign technology and has been able to keep pace with the research frontier through its direct or indirect links with a number of leading Japanese and American firms, has a large design facility of its own, and has through its parent company, Samsung Electronics, accessibility to a generous budget for research in several interrelated fields of electronics (Mody, 1991, p. 44). UMC has, in contrast to SST, a much more home-grown technology and has relied to a large extent on its own engineers. UMC has an indirect link with foreign companies through ERSO, which had an early collaboration with the American RCA. In addition UMC has cooperated with the American firms Mosel and Quase, which in fact are competitors. Similar cooperation arrangements between Korean and American competitors cannot be found. Finally UMC has established a company in Silicon Valley, Unicorn, which is much smaller in capital and strength than its Korean counterparts. Unicorn is expected to design custom chips for UMC and eventually for outside buyers as well (Mody, 1991, p. 46).

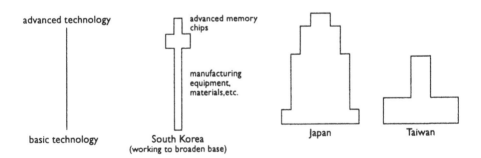

Figure 4.1   Technology structure of Korean, Japanese and Taiwanese semi-conductor companies in the early 1990s

Source: Nomura Research Institute, *NRI Quarterly*, 1993, 2, p. 43

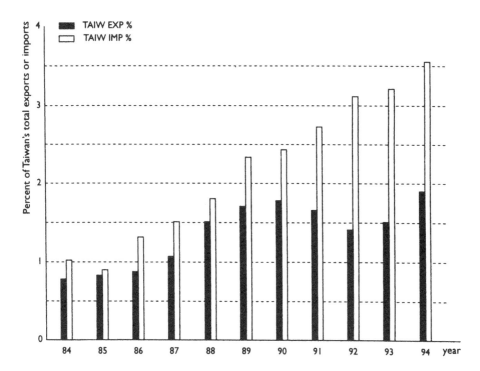

Figure 4.2   **Korea's share of Taiwan's foreign trade, 1984-1994**

Source: Industry of Free China

When the deregulation process started in the USA, the strategic difference between Taiwan and Korea was Taiwan's higher flexibility and more rapid response to the market signals. Thus Taiwan had a market share in the US three times as high as Korea in 1984 despite a similar price. The Japanese competitors had a unit price almost three times as high as the Taiwanese and the Koreans. During the following years, price became the single most important competition factor. In 1987, Korean phones were twice as expensive as the Taiwanese ones. In the third stage there was a successive upgrading of the market. The Korean competitors were more successful in developing the market for more expensive multi-line phones when the Taiwanese exports consisted dominantly of singe-line units. (Mody, 1991, p. 47f). Recently a change has occurred in the direction of more complex telephone exchange manufacturing. The experiences have been the same in other sectors of electronic equipment. Both Korean and Taiwanese companies have mainly used price as their competitive edge, been keen on rapid response to changing market signals, and have in addition relied mainly on the US market.

The Korean semiconductor industry indicates a wide technological gap even with

Taiwanese competitors, especially in basic technologies, materials and manufacturing equipment. According to Nomura Research Institute, Japanese and Taiwanese producers are characterized by broad basic technologies, whereas Korean producers hold a much more unbalanced technology structure (figure 4.1). The *chaebol* dominance in the Korean semiconductor industry implies a lack of innovative capacity, despite rapid production growth of DRAM chips, while small and medium sized Taiwanese competitors succeeded in developing a superior technology and in negotiating with foreign companies. The *chaebol*-led economic system also lacks the capacity and willingness to cooperate with foreign firms. As a new trend, however, the multi-layered structure of the emergent computer industry needs to work more closely with many others in order to gain access to technological and manufacturing research frontiers. Therefore, any single firm, even a big conglomerate that is left out of alliances and linkages, will face difficulties in maintaining its viability in the future (Simon and Soh, 1994, pp. 89-104).

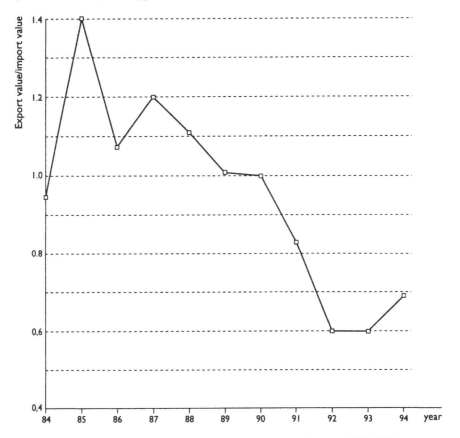

Figure 4.3   Taiwan's export/import ratio with Korea, 1984-1994

Source: Industry of Free China

The current level of Taiwanese-Korean division of labour within the electronics sector

The striking pattern of the development of Taiwanese-Korean economic interaction during the period of extraordinary growth, transformation and industrial upgrading has been its low speed of progress. Despite the obvious potential for change, the mutual trade and investment activities have been almost negligible. The hierarchical pattern that was created in the 1950s and 60s, putting the United States and Japan in a dominant position towards the emerging NIEs, still holds true, although the relative dominance of the economic superpowers has decreased since the peak in the mid-1980s. However, as seen from the Taiwanese viewpoint, the share of Korea in imports has grown at a considerable rate during the last ten years, although from a very low position (figure 4.2).

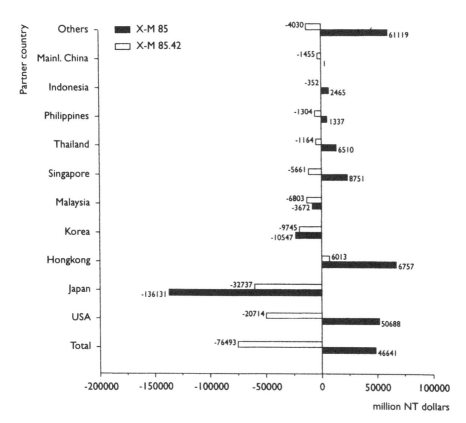

Figure 4.4   Taiwan's trade balance in electronics, 1993

Source: Industry of Free China

69

At the same time Korea's share of Taiwanese exports has shown a much slower progress. This imbalance between growth of import and export flows has created a situation where the Taiwanese export/import ratio towards Korea has deteriorated almost incessantly (figure 4.3).

A closer look at the commodity composition in the mutual trade relations shows that this imbalance to a large extent has occurred within the electronics sector, and that the single most important commodity group in Taiwanese imports from Korea is to be found in HS chapter 85[3] (29 percent of total imports in 1993), within which the sub-group 85.42 (integrated circuits) — 19 percent of total imports and 65 percent of the import value of the sub-group is by far most important. The data regarding HS 85.42 can then be disaggregated into thirteen items according to the Taiwanese customs schedule, among others 85.42.80901-DRAMs. Thus, it is possible to identify separate product groups where Taiwanese and Korean companies respectively have a competitive advantage towards each others. Some of the results from the detailed study are presented in figures 4.4-4.7.

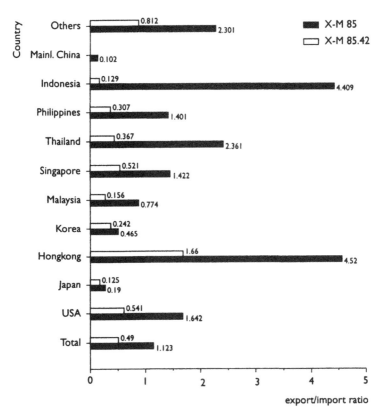

Figure 4.5   **Taiwan's export/import ratio in electronics, 1993**

Source: Industry of Free China

70

An important conclusion of the in-depth study is the negligible level of intra-Taiwanese-Korean trade within most electronics groups, with the exception of 85.42 and secondly 85.40[4], Taiwan has a trade surplus within chapter 85, explained by huge surpluses with the United States, Hong Kong and non-Asian countries (mainly in Western Europe). These surpluses can easily be traced to less advanced consumer electronics products. On the other hand, Taiwan has a significant deficit with Japan, which is explained by import surplus within more advanced products, mainly within the industrial electronics sector.

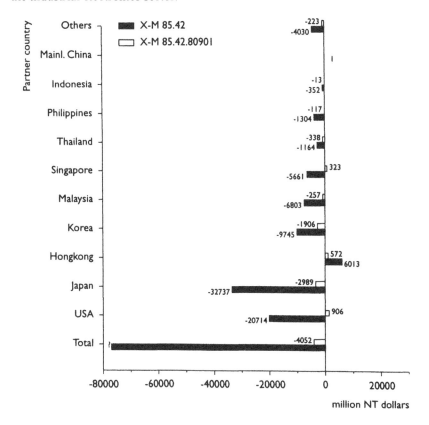

Figure 4.6   Taiwan's trade balance in integrated circuits, 1993

Source: Industry of Free China

Taiwan has also a deficit with Korea, that is mainly explained by the deficit within the IC-sector, where Korea has a clear lead. However, the major explanations behind the deficit in IC trade are to be found in the relations with Japan and the United States. A longitudinal study carried through from 1985 onwards shows a clear shift in the direction of upgrading in Taiwanese electronics trade with USA, Japan, Hong Kong

71

and Southeast Asia, but not in relation to Korea, where the interaction has remained at a low level. However, by disaggregating to an even lower level — e.g. DRAMs — it is evident that a process of specialization and increasing intra-trade has taken place between Korea and Taiwan. Korea has had a clear advantage in DRAMs, but Taiwanese companies have increased their exports to Korea as regards other, less advanced, integrated circuits. Within the DRAM group, a shift towards a phasing out of the 1M and DRAMs is obvious in Korea, which has given Taiwanese companies an export opportunity in that sub-sector. The only electronics sub-group with significant bilateral trade where Taiwan has a bilateral surplus with Korea is 85.40.

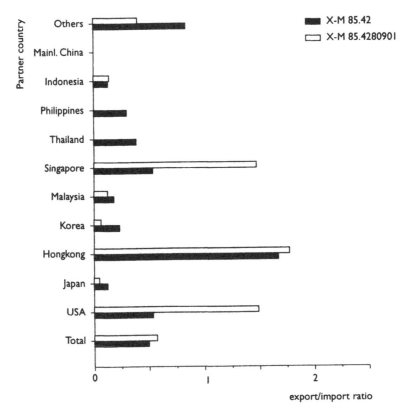

Figure 4.7   **Taiwan's export/import ratio in integrated circuits, 1993**

Source: Industry of Free China

In the process of the opening up of the Korean market, world PC giants have recently established local production. Among these a Taiwanese producer, Acer, launched an independent marketing company in March 1995, and established own production in order to supply Pentium level PCs for corporate users (*Korea Economic Weekly*, 1 May 1995, p. 3).

A generalized model of Korean-Taiwanese electronics interaction

Is there a general pattern to be found in the gradual restructuring of the electronics industry in Korea and Taiwan, and, in such a case, can it be used to explain the intra-trade pattern? A scrutiny of the transformation pattern since the 1960s reveals that although the time of introduction of technologically dependent electronics production has been almost the same, with a brief lead in Korea's favour, the sequential order of introduction of new processes and technologies has to some extent been different. These differences are summed up in figure 4.8, presenting a classification of 600-odd different electronic products, as identified in the customs nomenclatures, into fifteen broad categories.

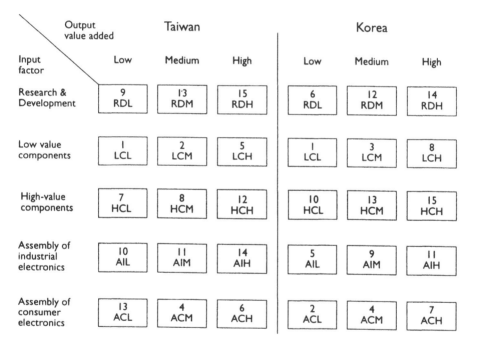

Output value added / Input factor	Taiwan			Korea		
	Low	Medium	High	Low	Medium	High
Research & Development	9 RDL	13 RDM	15 RDH	6 RDL	12 RDM	14 RDH
Low value components	1 LCL	2 LCM	5 LCH	1 LCL	3 LCM	8 LCH
High-value components	7 HCL	8 HCM	12 HCH	10 HCL	13 HCM	15 HCH
Assembly of industrial electronics	10 AIL	11 AIM	14 AIH	5 AIL	9 AIM	11 AIH
Assembly of consumer electronics	13 ACL	4 ACM	6 ACH	2 ACL	4 ACM	7 ACH

Figure 4.8 A generalized and simplified picture of the sequential transformation process in the Taiwanese and Korean electronics industry

Although very simplified and schematic, it represents roughly the real transformation pattern as it has developed hitherto, and the likely transformation process within the next 5-10 years according to existing plans and visions. While both countries started in the segments of low-value components, and proceeded in the field of assembly of consumer electronics, Korean companies seem to have been earlier in introducing the assembly of industrial electronics and setting up own research and development units. Taiwanese companies have on the other hand been earlier in upgrading the low-value components production into higher value-added segments, and they seem also to have a lead within small-scale, specialized high-value component production in narrow niches.

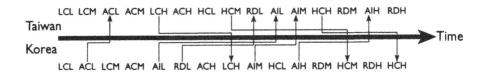

Figure 4.9 **Potential opportunities for specialization and division of labour between the Taiwanese and Korean electronics industry**

Given the fact that such a sequential differentiation represents differences in competitive advantages in the both countries, the potential for intra-trade growth could be largest in cases where time-lags are to be found in both directions (figure 4.9). The two countries have in the mid-1990s roughly proceeded half-way in the process, and have markly reduced the American and Japanese technological lead. The present trends show a transformation from similarities to diversification and specialization. Furthermore, there is an obvious shift from non-integrated via integrated to specialized production. The externally managed production and technology system that has dominated the electronics industry in both countries is slowly replaced by domestically controlled product development. The technologically dependent and subordinated production will change into a higher level of technological self-sufficiency and, in some cases, to technological leadership in limited segments.

Notes

1. ASEAN-4 includes Indonesia, Malaysia, the Philippines and Thailand.
2. According to government statistics, the capacity of Korean basic and design technology in the semi-conductor industry accounted for 20 percent of its Japanese and US counterparts (*The Maekyung Business Week*, 9 Feb. 1994, pp. 20-21).

74

3. Electrical machinery and equipment and parts thereof; sound recorders and reproducers, television image and sound recorders and reproducers and parts and accessories of such articles.
4. Thermionic, cold cathode or photo-cathode valves and tubes (for example, television camera and video monitor tubes).

References

Alvstam, C.G. (1995), 'Integration Through Trade and Direct Investment: Asian Pacific Patterns', in Le Heron, R. and Park, S.O. (eds),*The Asian Pacific Rim and Globalization*, Avebury: Aldershot, pp. 107-128.

Balassa, B. (1981), *The Newly Industrializing Countries in the World Economy*, Pergamon Press: New York.

Bloom, M.D.H. (1993), 'Globalization and the Korean Electronics Industry'. *Pacific Review*, Vol. 6, No. 2, pp. 119-26.

Business Week International Edition, July 31, 1995.

Chan, S. and Clark, C. (1992) *Flexibility, Foresight and Fortuna in Taiwan's Development*, Routledge: London.

Chi, H.K. (1993) 'Asia's Economies: Outlook to the Year 2000', *NRI Quarterly*, Vol. 2, No. 3, pp. 2-17, Nomura Research Institute: Tokyo.

Fei, C.H., Ranis, G. and Kuo, S.W.Y. (1979), *Growth with Equity: The Taiwan Case*, Oxford University Press: London.

Galenson, W. (ed.) (1979), *Economic Growth and Structural Change in Taiwan: The Postwar Experience of the Republic of China*, Cornell University Press: Ithaca.

Hobday, M. (1991), 'Semiconductor Technology and Newly Industrializing Countries: The Diffusion of ASICs', *World Development*, Vol. 19, No. 4, pp. 375-97.

Industry of Free China, Council for Economic Planning and Development, Executive Yuan, Republic of China, Taipei (monthly).

Johansson, B. and Alvstam, C.G. (1995), 'Taiwan's Investment in Mainland China', *Working Papers*, No. 2, Göteborg University, Centre for East and Southeast Asian Studies: Gothenburg.

Kim, K.S. (1994), 'Industrial Policy and Trade Regimes', in Cho, L.J. and Kim, Y.H. (eds), *Korea's Political Economy*, Westview Press: Boulder, CO, pp. 531-55.

Kim, K.S. and Roemer, M. (1979), *Growth and Structural Transformation. Studies in the Modernization of the Republic of Korea 1945-1975*, Harvard University Press: Cambridge, MA.

Kim, Y.H. (1994), 'An Introduction to the Korean Model of Political Economy', in Cho, L.J. and Kim, Y.H. (eds), *Korea's Political Economy*, Westview Press: Boulder, CO, pp. 45-62.

Korea Economic Weekly, May 1, 1995. Seoul.

Korean Customs Administration/Korea Customs Research Institute (1992), *Statistical Yearbook of Foreign Trade*, Seoul.

Kuo, S.W.Y. (1983), *The Taiwan Economy in Transition*, Westview Press: Boulder, CO.

Lee, Y.S. (1986), 'Changing Export Patterns in Korea, Taiwan and Japan'. *Weltwirtschaftliches Archiv*, Vol. 122, No. 1.

Leipziger, D.M. and Petri, P.A. (1994), 'Korean Industrial Policy: Legacies of the Past and Directions for the Future', in Cho, L.-J. and Kim, Y.H. (eds), *Korea's Political Economy*, Westview Press: Boulder, CO, pp. 581-619.

Maekyung Business Week, Feb 9 , 1994 (in Korean), Seoul.

McDermott, M.C. (1991), *Taiwan's Industry in World Markets*, The Economist Intelligence Unit: London.

McKay, J. and Missen, G. (1995), 'Keeping Their Miracles Going: Questioning Big Firms in Korea and Small Firms in Taiwan', in Le Heron, R. and Park, S.O. (eds), *The Asian Pacific Rim and Globalization*, Avebury: Aldershot, pp. 61-85.

Mody, A. (1989), 'Information Industries and the Newly Industrializing Countries', in Crandall, R.W. and Flamm, K. (eds), *Changing the Rules: Technological Change, International Competition and Regulation in Telecommunications*, Brookings Institute: Washington D.C.

Mody, A. (1991), 'Institutions and Dynamic Comparative Advantage: The Electronics Industry in South Korea and Taiwan', *Industry of Free China*, Vol. LXXVI, No. 2, pp. 33-62.

Myers, R.H. (1984), 'The Economic Transformation of the Republic of China on Taiwan', *China Quarterly*, No. 99, pp. 500-528.

Sakong, I. (1993), *Korea in the World Economy*, Institute for International Economics: Washington D.C.

Schive, C. and Yeh R.S. (1980), 'Direct Foreign Investment and Taiwan's T.V. Industry', *Economic Essays*. Vol. 9, No. 2.

Scitovsky, T. (1986), 'Economic Development in Taiwan and South Korea 1965-1981', in Lau, L.J. (ed.), *Models of Development: A Comparative Study of Economic Growth in South Korea and Taiwan*, Institute of Contemporary Studies: San Francisco.

Simon, D. F. and Soh, C. (1994), 'Korea's Technological Development', *The Pacific Review*, Vol. 7, No. 1, pp. 89-104.

Wakabayashi, H. and Sumita, M. (1993), 'South Korea's Semi-Conductor Industry', *NRI Quarterly*, Vol. 2, No. 2, pp. 40-49, Nomura Research Institute: Tokyo.

White Paper (1994), Ministry of Trade, Industry and Energy (MOTIE) (in Korean), Seoul.

5 Diaspora Investments and Their Regional Impacts in China

Chung-Tong Wu

Introduction

The location of investments has always attracted the attention of researchers in regional development. Classical location theory and its extensions focus on the locational decision of firms based on evaluations of costs of transportation (Alonso, 1968), the availability of infrastructure, the cost of labour and institutional context (Isard, 1975). Critiques of locational theory point to those factors which are not necessarily purely economic, such as the desire of managers to be near particular locations simply because of social and cultural ties (Alonso, 1975). More recently, studies such as that of Leung (1993) and Hsing (1995) point to the kinship ties that influence the location of foreign investments in China. Not only do these studies question the strictly economic evaluation of locational choices, they also point to a whole different literature on business networks and what is now recognized as diaspora capital.

Studies of business networks, family business enterprises and ethnic entrepreneurs detail the importance of family, ethnic identity, clan and kinship as the basis of establishing trust and business alliances. These studies tend to focus on the overseas Chinese, especially those located in Southeast Asia (Kunio, 1988) though there is now an emerging literature on the various diasporas, or global tribes (Kotkin, 1993). Southeast Asia-based Chinese enterprises have attracted plenty of interest among researchers. Most of the studies focus on the behaviour of entrepreneurs in their cultural settings (Hamilton, 1991), family business and national industrialization (Suehiro, 1989, 1993), changes in business groupings (Sieh, 1989), the relationship of ethnic business and the state (Sesudason, 1989) and the evolution and intricate networks established by large ethnic conglomerates (Sato, 1993). There are also studies that contrast the various types of business networks found in East Asia (Hamilton et al., 1990), that of the Chinese network extending into North America and other locations (Goldberg, 1989) and more recently, how this network has invested in southern China (Lever-Tracy et al., 1996). Most of these studies are chiefly concerned with the inner workings of Chinese businesses and enterprises, their business methods and the multiple linkages and networks that emerge around groups of families and the enterprises they control. Much of the interest is either political or sociological in that the researchers are mostly concerned with the political and social implications of these ethnic businesses in a political environment largely controlled by non-Chinese ethnic groups. Lever-Tracy et al., (1996) in particular examine the diaspora Chinese capital and the associated business networks' investments in various parts of southern China. They demonstrate that indeed a Chinese diaspora do exist and that the diaspora has made significant impacts on the development of China. However, none of the studies on Southeast Asian businesses deal explicitly with the spatial or regional impacts of their investments.

In a recent article on the development of the Pearl River Delta, Wu (1997) sketched the links of the developments in this region with investors based in Hong Kong and elsewhere. Leung (1993) studied in detail kinship ties and regional development in the same region and provided specific examples in the garment and textile industry. Hsing (1995) studied Taiwan-based investors and their investments in the province of Fujian. The latter two studies illustrate the importance of micro-studies and the insights gained through detailed understanding of specific groups or of the entrepreneurs in specific industrial sectors.

This chapter takes a broader view. Its focus is on the evidence of regional concentration of investments from particular sources, using China as an example. A brief section sketches the emerging concentration of South Korean investments in northeastern China. It then discusses the motivations and modes of operation of overseas Chinese investors. The final section identifies future research areas.

Diaspora capital

It is well known that in most Southeast and East Asian nations, ethnic Chinese-owned enterprises are prominent in number and the economic clout they represent. While this has sometimes created social and political tensions, the domination of Chinese capital in most of these countries continues. Though a few entrepreneurs from East Asia, notably those from Hong Kong and Taiwan, have made headlines with their huge investment forages in North America and in Australia, much of the diaspora capital is in small and medium sized firms and in a relatively few conglomerates. The great majority of these conglomerates does not compare in terms of capital base to the large Japanese, North American, European or even South Korean conglomerates. However their strength is not merely their own wealth and capital but the network of others in the region that would join with them in any number of ventures.

Careful scrutiny of foreign direct investment in China, for example, would indicate that its economic growth is largely reliant on Asian-based capital. By the late 1980s, within Southeast Asia, the Japanese and other Asian based investors have displaced North American and European investors as the most important drivers of economic growth. In fact, by the early 1990s, non-Japan-based Asian investors began to overtake Japanese investors in some countries in Southeast Asia. In part this is a reflection of the growing wealth of these other economies, notably Taiwan, Korea, Hong Kong and Singapore, but it is also partly the direct result of the economic restructuring process in these economies and the deliberate response of governments and private capital of these countries.

What are some of the Asian-based investors and does Asian capital tend to have specific regional development impacts? This chapter explores these questions within the context of regional development in China.

Regional impacts of diaspora capital

No where is the impact of diaspora capital so clearly defined as in China. This is partly because China presents a case where the nation was for all practical purposes closed to foreign investments and therefore it is comparatively easy to track direct foreign investment since policies changed. It is also a case where the diaspora Chinese have made significant investments.

Before a closely examining foreign direct investments (FDI) in China, it is necessary to first explain the data, the sources and data reliability. Although data published by China have expanded in scope, it is still difficult to track the sources of foreign investments, the sectors in which foreign capital is invested and the regional locations of these investments.[1] Much of the available data refer to 'agreements' or commitments that do not always come to fruition. Admittedly the 'agreements' do provide a hint of the intentions of foreign investors and could still give a sense of the opportunities that have been explored by the foreign investors. However, even the published 'agreements' do not give a complete coverage of the total foreign investments since many might be channeled through the central government and the ministries.[2] While these investments are sometimes separately identified, it is not possible to specify the spatial distribution of these investments nor exactly in which sectors these were made.[3]

It would be ideal to focus on 'actual' or realized foreign direct investments but these are usually published in aggregate terms only, with few details about the sectors or the origins of the investments. Identification of the origins of the investments is often difficult due to the indirect nature of some investments and the deliberate attempts of some foreign investors to disguise the origins either for commercial reasons or, very often, for political reasons. This chapter utilizes data on both '*agreements*' and actual or '*realized*' investments published in China, data on officially sanctioned investments published in the NIEs, as well as data derived from reports in newspapers published in the latter countries. Without a comprehensive set of data it is difficult to be absolutely definitive about the pattern of foreign investments in China, but the identifiable patterns do present important avenues for further investigation.

The next section presents an overview of foreign investments in China for the period since 1979 when the economic reforms were first announced. A comparison of the patterns of investments from the NIEs will follow.

Overview of foreign direct investment in China

The first economic reform programs announced in 1978/79 were timid in that the localities where foreign investments were allowed and the sectors in which they could invest were strictly limited. Four Special Economic Zones (SEZs) and subsequently fourteen coastal cities were designated as areas 'open' to foreign investments. Light industries and the tourism sector were the sectors open to foreign investors. It took several years before foreign investors warmed to the idea of investing in China and for the investments to filter through to various parts of China.

Up to the mid-1980s though, it is possible to discern a clear pattern of preferences for locations by foreign investors. Japanese and United States-based investors, chiefly multinational companies, tended to favour the large established industrial centers of Beijing, Tianjin and Shanghai. The investors from Hong Kong and Southeast Asia, however, overwhelmingly favoured Guangdong and Fujian.

The regional pattern of investments has, since 1985, continued to concentrate on the coastal provinces with Guangdong continuing to dominate as the province with close to half of all *realized* foreign investment. The top four provinces (Beijing, Shanghai, Fujian and Guangdong) attracted 56 percent of all cumulative FDI between 1985 and 1995. While the coastal provinces have increased their share of the total realized foreign direct investment (85 percent), the inland provinces, as a group, have lost in relative terms (table 5.1). Several other observations can be made. The dominance of Guangdong and the rise of Hainan Province as centers of FDI are due largely to their proximity to Hong Kong. Southern Guangdong in particular, is benefiting from the industrial decentralization from Hong Kong that has proceeded apace during the 1980s.[4] Fujian Province has maintained a strong inflow of FDI and in cumulative terms, stronger than Shanghai. The continuing inflow of FDI to Fujian is said to be largely due to the ties with Southeast Asia-based and Taiwan-based investors, many of whom have kinship ties with Fujian (Hsing, 1995). Shanghai, being the largest industrial center of China is an attraction on its own but probably also benefits from the inflow of investments from Hong Kong, Taiwan and elsewhere.

Fujian on the other hand seems to be enjoying a rising tide of FDI whereas Shanghai's attractions slipped during the early 1990s. The evidence from China is that the national and city officials recognize that Shanghai has slipped in recent years as a center for FDI and the development of Pudong (the eastern district of Shanghai) is a move aimed at redressing that imbalance. In this connection, the strong showing of Jiangsu Province is probably due to its proximity to Shanghai and the perception that the province is an area where foreign investors are welcomed with open arms.

Beijing, being the national capital, is the second most favoured location for FDI though it has attracted merely a tenth of what Guangdong Province has garnered. Its share of the total seems to be declining though, as other areas open up for investment and their infrastructures rival that of Beijing. Furthermore, many investors regard Beijing as the place to avoid due to the perceived intrusiveness of its officials.

Table 5.1
Realized foreign direct investment in China, by province
(percentage of total)

	1985	1986	1987	1988	1989	1990
Coastal						
Beijing	6.80	10.19	6.58	18.17	10.11	8.47
Tianjing	4.28	2.13	8.79	1.15	0.89	1.07
Shanghai	8.23	10.75	14.74	8.43	13.39	5.32
Hebei	0.63	0.50	0.51	0.60	0.85	1.20
Shandong	2.73	1.41	1.64	1.56	4.17	4.61
Jiangsu	2.56	1.32	3.21	3.72	2.97	3.80
Zhejiang	2.04	1.35	1.61	1.07	1.64	1.48
Anhui	0.23	0.58	0.10	0.42	0.15	0.29
Fujian	9.08	4.48	3.54	4.71	10.43	8.87
Guangdong	49.84	52.63	41.60	38.75	39.71	47.78
Guangxi	2.35	2.69	2.60	0.75	1.46	0.88
Hainan	0.00	0.00	0.00	4.13	3.01	3.15
Non-Coastal						
Shanxi	0.04	0.01	0.16	0.24	0.28	0.10
Inner	0.20	0.07	0.08	0.12	0.01	0.33
Liaoning	1.88	3.01	4.45	4.17	3.76	7.45
Jilin	0.37	0.04	0.01	0.22	0.11	0.54
Heilongjiang	0.30	1.27	0.78	1.45	0.71	0.75
Jiangxi	0.80	0.33	0.27	0.19	0.19	0.19
Henan	0.63	0.44	0.31	2.32	1.35	0.32
Hubei	0.61	0.90	0.82	0.81	0.73	0.89
Hunan	2.09	0.69	0.16	0.28	0.20	0.34
Sichuan	2.20	1.11	1.46	0.85	0.25	0.49
Guizhou	0.75	0.16	0.00	0.16	0.24	0.14
Yunnan	0.12	0.26	0.33	1.34	0.23	0.08
Tibet	0.00	0.00	0.00	0.00	0.00	0.00
Shaanxi	1.19	2.71	5.02	4.04	3.08	1.28
Gansu	0.04	0.03	0.01	0.07	0.04	0.03
Qinghai	0.00	0.00	0.00	0.10	0.00	0.00
Ningxia	0.00	0.00	0.00	0.01	0.00	0.01
Xinjiang	0.00	0.93	1.21	0.18	0.03	0.16
Total	100.00	100.00	100.00	100.00	100.00	100.00

Table 5.1
Realized foreign direct investment in China, by province
(continued)

	1991	1992	1993	1994	1995	1985-95
Coastal						
Beijing	5.68	3.18	2.44	3.13	2.79	3.70
Tianjing	3.07	0.98	2.24	2.64	4.00	2.80
Shanghai	3.37	4.49	11.58	5.86	7.57	7.65
Hebei	1.03	1.03	1.45	1.20	1.54	1.29
Shandong	4.17	9.12	6.85	5.91	6.96	6.32
Jiangsu	4.93	13.30	10.40	8.59	13.41	10.05
Zhejiang	2.13	2.18	3.77	2.63	3.25	2.87
Anhui	0.22	0.50	0.94	0.94	1.30	0.92
Fujian	10.82	12.94	10.51	8.45	10.45	9.74
Guangdong	46.48	33.63	27.63	43.19	26.86	34.93
Guangxi	0.59	1.65	3.24	1.93	1.78	2.04
Hainan	4.16	4.11	2.59	2.12	2.98	2.70
Non-Coastal						
Shanxi	0.09	0.49	0.32	0.56	0.24	0.36
Inner	0.03	0.05	0.31	0.11	0.22	0.18
Liaoning	8.10	4.69	4.68	3.44	3.95	4.18
Jilin	0.42	0.68	1.01	0.55	1.21	0.81
Heilongjiang	0.22	0.66	0.85	0.79	1.57	1.01
Jiangxi	0.45	0.91	0.76	0.67	0.87	0.72
Henan	0.88	0.48	1.12	1.05	1.63	1.18
Hubei	1.08	1.85	1.98	1.52	2.23	1.75
Hunan	0.53	1.21	1.60	0.77	1.41	1.12
Sichuan	0.57	1.02	2.09	2.17	1.56	1.72
Guizhou	0.17	0.18	0.16	0.14	0.23	0.18
Yunnan	0.07	0.26	0.35	0.16	0.30	0.27
Tibet	0.00	0.00	0.00	0.00	0.00	0.00
Shaanxi	0.73	0.41	0.86	0.79	0.99	1.02
Gansu	0.02	0.00	0.04	0.22	0.21	0.14
Qinghai	0.00	0.01	0.01	0.01	0.01	0.01
Ningxia	0.00	0.00	0.04	0.02	0.02	0.02
Xinjiang	0.01	0.00	0.19	0.45	0.48	0.34
Total	100.00	100.00	100.00	100.00	100.00	100.00

Source: China Statistical Yearbook (various issues)

Table 5.2
Realized foreign investment as a percentage of total fixed assets investments for selected provinces

	1985 RFI/FAI	1985 % FDI	1987 RFI/FAI	1987 % FDI	1990 RFI/FAI	1990 % FDI
Beijing	3.61	6.80	4.30	6.58	9.83	8.74
Tianjin	2.80	4.28	10.69	8.79	5.33	1.10
Hebei	0.27	0.63	0.22	0.51	2.57	1.24
Liaoning	0.52	1.88	2.97	4.45	13.66	7.69
Shandong	0.94	2.73	1.17	1.64	3.29	4.76
Shanghai	2.70	8.23	11.56	14.75	6.76	5.49
Jiangsu	1.00	2.56	1.68	3.21	3.28	3.92
Zhejiang	1.72	2.04	2.15	1.61	2.37	1.53
Fujian	9.14	9.08	6.79	3.54	18.81	9.15
Guangdong	11.04	49.84	15.67	41.60	22.88	49.33
Guangxi	2.15	2.35	2.60	2.60	4.37	0.90
Hainan	n.a.	n.a.	n.a.	n.a.	n.a.	3.25

Source: China Statistical Yearbook (various years) based on Zhou (1993)
Note: Fixed Assets Investments represent the total investment by the state, including foreign investments and international loans invested through government agencies.

The two other provinces with a significant share of the total FDI are Liaoning and Shandong that have probably benefited from the interest shown by Japan and Korea in expanding their investments in China. These provinces are geographically close to South Korea and Japan and have historical links that would attract the interest of investors based in these countries.

The increasing importance of foreign investments in the development of the coastal provinces can be ascertained through the data in table 5.2 which lists utilized foreign investment as a percentage of total fixed assets investments for the twelve coastal provinces. In all cases, this percentage has risen between 1985 and 1990, along with the rise in the provincial share of FDI.

Provincial share of FDI provides an indication of the spatial distribution of *realized* FDI, but it is also important to examine where the investments originated, in order to examine the importance of business and ethnic networks. Unfortunately it is not possible to obtain comprehensive published data on realized FDI by country of origin and by province. Nevertheless, an overall understanding of the sources of FDI and how they have changed can provide some ideas about the spatial impacts.

Distinctive patterns can be identified through an examination of the available data on the origins of the investors and their investment locations in China. Up to the mid-1980s, Japanese and US investors favoured the traditional industrial centers of

Beijing, Tianjin and Shanghai, while Hong Kong and ASEAN[5]-based investors favoured Fujian and Guangdong (table 5.3). Since the Japanese and US investors were chiefly large corporations, it seems they wished to invest in the tried and known locations — locations that have historical links with the West. The investors from Hong Kong and ASEAN, predominantly small and medium-sized investors, were investing in areas familiar either because of proximity or kinship ties. The notable absence, for obvious reasons, of investors from Taiwan and South Korea, is also a feature of the pattern of foreign investments up to the mid-1980s.

Table 5.3
Comparison of foreign investment (1979-1986) in major centers
(percentage of total)

	Three Industrial Centers	Fujian/Guangdong
Hong Kong	17.82	72.32
Japan	66.36	4.80
USA	68.69	3.10
ASEAN	26.81	50.28

Note: The three industrial centers are Beijing, Tianjin and Shanghai.
Source: Wu (1989, p. 57)

By 1991, the dominance of the Asian connection with regard to FDI was even more pronounced. Whereas Asia provided 59 percent of the *committed* FDI between 1979-1985, it represented just over 83 percent of the total committed FDI in 1991. The situation with *realized* investment is not too different.

By examining *realized* foreign direct investment in China for the period 1979 to 1995, it is possible to gain further insights into the origins of foreign investment in China. A large number of factors influence the annual fluctuation of realized FDI so it is prudent to examine the cumulative investments since 1979 (with the implementation of the economic reforms) to gain a better understanding of the overall impacts of FDI. Considering the cumulative investments over the period 1979 to 1995 (table 5.4), it is clear that Hong Kong dominates throughout the entire period and that Asia-based investors contributed close to three-quarters of the total realized foreign investment. North America accounted for 8 percent and the European countries (including UK) accounted for about 4 percent of the total. Given the rapid growth of investment from South Korea and Taiwan in the 1990s, investments from the Asian nations continue to dominate.[6]

If the foreign investment pattern of the first five years (1979-83), after economic reforms were implemented, is compared with the eleven years from 1984 to 1995, a number of changes could be identified. The cumulative investments from Hong Kong

84

amounted to over 54.4 percent of the total foreign investment during 1984 to 1995 and that from Japan averaged just 8.3 percent. Other countries showing increases included Taiwan, South Korea and Singapore.[7] Investments from several countries, including the United Kingdom, Italy, Australia and Canada have declined during the same periods.[8] This emphasizes the increasing dominance of the Asian countries as the key investors in China.

Table 5.4
Source of realized foreign direct investment in China, 1979-1995
(percentage of total)

	1979-83	1984	1985	1986	1987	1988	1989	1990
Asia								
HK/Macao	57.96	52.69	48.85	60.40	69.08	65.60	61.24	54.87
Japan	12.81	15.83	16.11	10.74	9.50	16.11	10.50	14.44
Philippines	0.06	0.16	0.16	0.06	0.16	0.11	0.04	0.05
Thailand	0.00	0.00	0.45	0.49	0.49	0.19	0.37	0.19
Malaysia	0.00	0.00	0.01	0.02	0.01	0.04	0.01	0.02
Indonesia	0.00	0.00	0.00	0.03	0.00	0.01	0.04	0.03
Singapore	0.73	0.08	0.52	0.69	0.93	0.87	2.48	1.45
S. Korea	0.00	0.00	0.00	0.00	0.00	0.00	0.00	0.00
Taiwan	0.00	0.00	0.00	0.00	0.00	0.00	0.00	0.64
North America								
USA	11.54	18.06	18.26	16.80	11.36	7.39	8.38	13.08
Canada	0.88	0.00	0.48	0.00	0.44	0.19	0.50	0.23
Europe								
Germany	0.49	0.53	1.23	1.03	0.14	0.47	2.40	1.84
France	2.85	1.42	1.66	2.26	0.67	0.71	0.14	0.60
Italy	1.38	1.27	0.99	1.24	0.70	0.96	0.89	0.12
UK	4.31	6.90	3.65	1.43	0.20	1.07	0.84	0.38
Australia	1.17	0.03	0.73	3.21	0.21	0.13	1.31	0.71
Others	5.83	3.02	6.89	1.63	6.11	6.15	10.85	11.36
Total	100.00	100.00	100.00	100.00	100.00	100.00	100.00	100.00

Table 5.4
Source of realized foreign direct investment in China, 1979-1995
(continued)

	1991	1992	1993	1994	1995	1979-95	1984-95
Asia							
HK/Macao	56.96	70.04	64.93	53.23	43.30	54.53	54.36
Japan	12.20	6.63	4.90	5.46	10.62	8.48	8.26
Philippines	0.13	0.15	0.44	0.37	2.20	0.88	0.92
Thailand	0.45	0.75	0.84	0.61	0.60	0.59	0.62
Malaysia	0.04	0.22	0.33	0.53	0.54	0.38	0.39
Indonesia	0.05	0.18	0.24	0.30	0.23	0.21	0.22
Singapore	1.33	1.12	1.77	3.09	3.87	2.57	2.66
S. Korea	0.00	1.06	1.37	1.90	2.47	1.56	1.64
Taiwan	1.07	9.33	11.30	8.88	6.58	6.99	7.34
North America							
USA	7.40	4.60	7.45	6.52	6.51	7.47	7.26
Canada	0.25	0.52	0.49	0.57	1.29	0.75	0.74
Europe							
Germany	3.69	0.81	0.22	0.69	1.10	0.88	0.90
France	0.23	0.42	0.51	0.51	1.49	0.96	0.86
Italy	0.65	0.24	0.36	0.54	1.14	0.74	0.71
UK	0.81	0.34	0.79	1.80	2.10	1.67	1.54
Australia	0.34	0.31	0.40	0.49	0.65	0.58	0.55
Others	14.40	3.30	3.64	14.50	15.32	10.77	11.02
Total	100.00	100.00	100.00	100.00	100.00	100.00	100.00

Source: China Statistical Yearbook (various issues)

NIEs in China

The previous section identified the increasing importance of Asian-based investors to China. The difference could be partly explained by the rise of investments of those based in Taiwan and South Korea that together provided 14.7 percent of the total FDI in 1995. In fact, in the same year, the NIEs provided 56.2 percent of the total FDI in China.

Before taking a closer look at the investments from the NIEs, it is important to understand the limitations of the available information and the quality of the data.

Prior to the establishment of diplomatic relationships in August 1992, there was no official sanction for trade or investments between South Korea and China. Much of the trade and investments were undertaken through third parties, such as investment vehicles based in Hong Kong, a state of affairs well-known to both sides but officially unacknowledged. Hence, the official statistics about investments and trade between China and South Korea are understated due to this official 'blind eye'. This is also true of the trade and investment flows between Taiwan and mainland China although there is tacit recognition in that both the trade flows and investment flows have proceeded for a much longer period. The Taiwan government finally had to recognize the significant outflow of capital from Taiwan to the mainland by establishing first of all a registration of investments and then a vetting process for investments which supposedly sanctions the type of sectoral investments which are permitted in the mainland. The latter is represented by the statistics provided by the Investment Review Board of the Ministry of Economic Affairs.[9] In the case of Singapore, 'China fever' was brought on partly by the political leaders deciding in 1992 that Singapore was far behind other nations in cultivating the China opportunities. It threw itself into a frenzy trying to drum up investments between Singapore and China. There are at present no comprehensive data on what investments there are between Singapore and China but this can be partially remedied through a careful examination of newspaper reports in Singapore. One full year's newspaper clippings were scrutinized to survey the range of investments that have been reported as being made by Singapore-based firms in China.[10] Since 1993, Singapore has decided to invest in a major industrial estate in Jiangsu province (just outside of Shanghai) and this is reflected in the rapid climb of its percentage share of total FDI in 1994 and 1995.

Table 5.5
FDI outflow from the NIEs (US$ million)

	Source			
	Hong Kong	Singapore	S. Korea	Taiwan
Southeast Asia	1143	2095.13	124.07	3905.16
		(28.3)	(38.18)	
China	3160	139.87	55.34	753.89
		(1.87)	(11.23)	
Realized Sum Reported by China	1913.42	50.43	0	0

Notes: data on Hong Kong refer to 1989, all other data refer to 1990. Figures in brackets refer to the percentage of total FDI from that country. Data on Hong Kong and Taiwan are on approval basis.

Sources: Maruya (1992); Ministry of Trade & Industry, Republic of Singapore (1993), p. 105; National Bureau of Statistics, Republic of Korea (1991); China Statistical Yearbook (various years).

China as a destination of investment must compete with other alternative investment opportunities for entrepreneurs based in the NIEs. This is best examined through the outward-bound investments from the NIEs to the rest of the world. Table 5.5 shows that except for Hong Kong, China, even as recently as 1990, did not loom large in the investment plans of other NIEs-based investors. Southeast Asia, referring chiefly to the ASEAN countries, has attracted investments several times those directed to China. This is perhaps understandable. In the case of Singapore, the other Southeast Asian nations are close by and their economies, their business sectors, and ways of doing business, are familiar to those based in Singapore.[11] More likely than not, they would have multiple business linkages developed over decades either through kinship ties or through mutual interest in similar or related sectors. In the case of Taiwan, the government and trade associations assiduously encouraged systematic examination of investment possibilities during the late 1980s by organizing study missions to various Southeast Asian nations and publicizing the results of the missions (*Common Wealth*, Aug., 1987, Oct. 1989). Consequently, Taiwanese investments in various Southeast Asian nations, notably Thailand, Malaysia and Indonesia, boomed.

The case of China is very different. First, there were the political barriers for South Korea and Taiwan. While it is possible to obtain data from South Korea on investments to China for the period since 1988, the Chinese continued to report nothing — until just before and after normalization of relationships — and the reports are at best patchy.[12] The obvious presence of Taiwanese investors in China finally led to recognition in the published statistics from a few provinces but the data probably refer to a fraction of what is actually invested.[13]

It is well known that Hong Kong-based investors have been active in China for many years and certainly since the declaration of the open policy in 1979. By the early 1980s, Hong Kong investors have penetrated every province and have continued to dominate as the single most important source of FDI for China. It is also widely acknowledged that Hong Kong is chosen by many investors from other countries who have found it convenient to use Hong Kong as the base to invest in China for a whole variety of reasons, including taxation, politics at home and convenience. Available studies of Hong Kong investments in China tend to focus on the Pearl River Delta or the Shenzhen and Zhuhai Special Economic Zones (Federation of Hong Kong Industries, 1992; Liew et al., 1992). Investments from Hong Kong can be treated as endemic throughout China though as table 5.9 shows, the Hong Kong-based investors also have distinct regional preferences.

Sectoral emphasis

There are distinct sectoral and regional patterns associated with the investments from the NIEs. Tables 5.6 and 5.7 compare these patterns for South Korea and Taiwan.[14] Labour-intensive manufacturing activities dominate both Korean and Taiwanese investments. One surprising feature is the lack of reported Taiwanese investments in the service and/or tourism sectors. This is probably due to the highly selective nature of the published data about Taiwanese investment in China. Information gained via a variety of sources indicates that there is indeed a great deal more interest in the tourism sector. A recently published survey of major Taiwanese backed projects (both planned and under implementation) gives a more realistic spread of sectoral emphasis (*Forbes*, Feb. 1993). Due to the nature of the information, much caution has to be exercised when interpreting the sectoral emphasis. If this set of data is any indication, there is a great deal more participation in the non-manufacturing sectors, particularly real estate and tourism, than is indicated in the officially published data.

Table 5.6
South Korean and Taiwan investment in China

	South Korea	Taiwan
Manufacturing (% of total) (by value)		
Food & Beverages	3.80	4.30
Textile & Apparels	19.20	13.14
Shoes & Leather Prod.	12.00	9.71
Timber & Furniture	3.80	4.18
Paper & Printing	1.40	3.42
Rubber & Plastics	0.00	7.58
Petroleum & Chem. Prod.	0.80	2.11
Non-metal Products	4.10	4.42
Metal Products	1.81	7.52
Electronics & Components	17.20	17.23
Machinery & Instruments	4.60	15.40
Other	23.10	10.89
Non-Manufacturing (value in US$ million)		
Construction	..	169.723
Non-Metal & Quarry Products	1.302	144.866
Agriculture & Poultry	1.900	21.38
Forestry	0.614	0.00
Services & Hotels	22.898	56.47
Transportation & Warehousing	0.500	0.00
Trading	0.300	6.39
Non-classified	0.000	0.98

Notes: S. Korea data refer to cumulative investments to the end of 1992 and data on Taiwan refer to the situation at the end of April 1991. * items refer to June 1993.
Source: Korean Institute of Economic Policy (1992); *China Times*, July 12, 1993

89

The information available on Singaporean investments in China is even less complete but it is possible to identify both location and sectors by the descriptions gleaned from an exhaustive survey of one year's newspaper clippings.

Table 5.7
Recent major projects with Taiwan investments

Sector	No. of projects
Agriculture & Poultry	1
Food Processing	24
Mineral Products	3
Textile & Apparel	8
Footwear	4
Paper Products	3
Chemical Products*	9
Rubber Products	2
Metal Products**	9
Electrical & Electronics	8
Hotels	2
Real Estate	6

* includes plastic products.
** includes 4 auto parts projects
Source: Forbes (Hong Kong), February 1993

Due to the fact that the projects are of varying sizes and not all the reports indicate clearly the total amount of investments, it is not possible to provide an average project value or even a total value of the investments represented by the projects listed in table 5.8. Mindful of the fact that newspaper reports include projects at various stages of development — those that are still under consideration, those that are already under implementation, and those that are in operation — the above information should be treated at best as an imperfect guide to the locational and sectoral choices of some Singaporean investors. This set of information indicates that Fujian Province, although one of the major destinations of investments, is really only one of about four major destinations which include the provinces of Jiangsu, Guangdong and Shandong. While the newspapers do report that some of those who have chosen to invest in Fujian Province did attest to the importance of kinship ties for their decisions,[15] most investors do not necessarily regard that as the most important factor. On the contrary, a number of investors indicated that they were deliberately seeking opportunities in other provinces because too many investors have concentrated in Guangdong and Fujian and both are seen as too competitive. The Singaporean government has played an important role in pointing out the opportunities elsewhere in China and organizing officially led investment missions to other provinces, in particular the provinces of Jiangsu and Shandong.

The evidence suggests a preliminary conclusion that both kinship ties and interventions from the state have been instrumental in channeling investments from Singapore. The extent of these influences in terms of the size of the total investments in any one location or in particular sectors, is difficult to establish at this time. The available information also indicates that there is a fairly even split of Singaporean investments amongst the major sectors. Real estate development and services and tourism are well represented and this pattern mirrors the type of investments in which Hong Kong-based investors first engaged in China.

Table 5.8
Singaporean investment projects in China (newspaper reports)

Province	No. of Projects	Real Estate	Services/ Tourism	Manu- facturing	Others or unknown
Jiangsu	28	10	2	10	6
Fujian	27	13	6	4	3
Guangdong	25	9	1	9	6
Shanghai	23	8	4	7	4
Shandong	14	3	4	2	5
Sichuan	12	4	4	0	4*
Anhui	6	1	3	0	2
Beijing	5	1	1	2	1
Tianjin	5	1	1	2	1**
Zhejiang	5	0	2	1	2**
Yunnan	4	0	1	0	3
Hainan	3	1	1	0	1
Liaoning	3	2	0	0	1
Total	171	53	30	37	39

* includes 3 infrastructure projects;
** includes one agriculture project.
Source: Straits Times and *Business Times* (July 1, 1992 to June 30, 1993 inclusive)

Regional choices

In terms of locations, distinct choices are evident. All the NIEs have concentrated their investments in the coastal regions. Hong Kong-based investors tend to have distributed their investments more widely, but the coastal region is still where most of the investments are located.

Table 5.9 reports the FDI agreements signed in 1991 for the twelve coastal provinces and identifies the major sources of investments due partly to the extended experience they have with investing in China.[16] Except for the province of Liaoning, all the other provinces have Hong Kong as their chief source of FDI (just over 71 percent for the coastal region) and always by a huge margin over the second major source.[17] That Hong Kong dominates as the source of investments at the provincial level should not be surprising since it dominates at the national level.

Table 5.9 also identifies Taiwan as the second most important source of FDI in eight of the twelve provinces and as the third most important in two other provinces. In all, Taiwan investors are reported to have contributed 12.74 percent to the total FDI agreements signed in 1991 among the 12 coastal provinces.[18]

Table 5.9
Coastal provinces and FDI (agreements signed) (1991)

Region	Province	FDI agreements No. % coastal total	Amt. % coastal total	Major sources (size of investment as % of province) Source	No. 1 % Amt.	Source	No. 2 % Amt.	Source	No. 3 % Amt.
Bohai	Liaoning	5.1	5.3	Japan	52.9	HK	34.3	USA	4.2
	Beijing	6.4	2.8	HK	7.0	Taiwan	16.1	USA	17.9
	Tianjin	3.1	1.9	HK	48.1	USA	16.4	Taiwan	9.5
	Hebei	2.6	1.9	HK	52.8	Taiwan	13.1	UK	7.7
	Shandong	7.1	6.7	HK	47.1	Taiwan	13.0	USA	12.5
	Subtotal	24.4	18.6	HK	43.3	Taiwan	9.4	Japan	6.2
East China	Jiangsu	10.1	7.2	HK	53.9	Taiwan	16.7	USA	7.2
	Shanghai	3.2	4.7	HK	n.a.	USA	n.a.	Japan	n.a.
	Zhejiang	5.2	3.1	HK	68.7	Taiwan	15.7	USA	5.8
	Subtotal	18.5	14.5	HK	n.a.	USA	n.a.	Japan	n.a.
South China	Fujian	10.8	14.2	HK	59.2	Taiwan	34.4	Singapore	1.4
	Guangdong	40.4	48.0	HK	79.9	Macao	4.7	Taiwan	5.3
	Guangxi	1.7	1.0	HK	54.0	Taiwan	27.4	USA	5.2
	Hainan	4.2	3.8	HK	30.4	Taiwan	5.7	Japan	4.3
	Subtotal	57.1	66.9	HK	72.3	Taiwan	28.5	USA	1.3
Total	Coastal	100.0	100.0	HK	71.3	Taiwan	12.7	USA	1.3

Source: Wu (1997) adapted from Mitsubishi Research Institute (1993), 'Amt.' refers to US$ value of agreements

From another source it is possible to identify that close to 70 percent of the cumulative Taiwan investments preferred Guangdong, Fujian and Hainan (KIEP, 1992; Tung, 1993) (table 5.10). Perhaps unexpectedly, Guangdong Province attracts close to double the Taiwanese investments compared with Fujian Province.[19] Conventional wisdom suggests that because of the common dialect and kinship ties, Fujian would be the preferred location for Taiwan investors. Indeed, many localities and investors, hoping to take advantage of Taiwan investors' interest in China, are developing industrial estates and other properties based on the assumption that Taiwan investors would favour locations in Fujian.

Table 5.10
Comparison of investments from Taiwan and Korea by region
(percentage of total investments)

	South Korea	Taiwan
Bohai region	54.73	7.36
Shandong	34.97	2.40
Beijing	10.43	3.32
Tianjin	7.02	1.17
Hebei	2.29	0.47
Northeast	30.32	1.69
Liaoning	18.41	1.34
Jilin	3.11	0.32
Heilongjiang	8.81	0.03
South China	8.69	69.30
Guangdong	6.02	43.49
Fujian	2.44	23.82
Hainan	0.22	1.99
East China	6.13	16.79
Shanghai	1.58	11.54
Zhejiang	2.50	1.97
Jiangsu	2.06	3.28
Other	0.13	4.86

Source: Korean Institute of Economic Policy (1992). Korean data cumulative to Dec. 1992. Taiwan data cumulative to April 1991.

Taiwan investments in China, though numerous, are on average relatively small in value. In Guangdong and Fujian, where the great majority of the projects and investments are located, the average value of each project is below the overall average, reflecting the labour-intensive type of industries, such as athletic shoes

93

manufacturing, that have shifted from Taiwan. The size of investments in Shanghai are the exception, being close to four times the average but this may reflect the small number of projects.

For the Korean investors, the most favoured area is the Bohai region that attracted 55 percent of the cumulative investments up to the end of 1992. The second most favoured region is the northeast region that commands another 30 percent of the Korean investments. Thus the areas most proximate to Korea gained the lion's share of the Korean investments. The northeast region includes areas such as the Changbai Korean Autonomous Counties (Yanbian) which include many villages that are inhabited almost entirely by Korean ethnic people who speak the Korean language and have common cultural ties with South Korea. Any investments in these areas would have the advantage of no language barrier and shared cultural values. These general impressions mask many details though. When the data are examined more closely, a more focused pattern emerges.

In the Bohai region where close to 55 percent of the investments and half the projects are located, the largest projects by value are located in Beijing. In Shandong Province, where the largest share of the total investments is located, the project values are just above the overall average and they are concentrated in Qingdao, Weihai and Yantai,[20] all three of them being 'open' coastal cities. In Hebei Province, the projects are concentrated in two transportation hubs, Qinghuangdao, a major port city and Chengzhou, a major railway center.

In the Northeast region, most of the investments are located in Liaoning Province focusing on three industrial centers, Shenyang, Dalian and Yangkou. The largest projects are however located in Heilongjiang Province, in the provincial capital Harbin, and in the border city of Mudajiang. In Jilin Province, almost all the investments are located in the border region of the Changbai Autonomous Xians, the area inhabited by ethnic Koreans. Average investments in this region are less than half the average project value, indicating perhaps that many of the investments are in tourism and the service sector, catering to the increasing number of South Korean visitors.

In southern China, although the number of projects and the total value of the projects are small, the average size of the projects in Guangdong and Fujian are comparatively large. In Guangdong, the investments are concentrated in the three Special Economic Zones (SEZ) of Shenzhen, Shantou and Zhuhai, and in the provincial capital Guangzhou. In Fujian, where the average investment size is double that of the national average, the South Korean investments are concentrated in Xiamen, location of the SEZ, and in the provincial capital Fujian. The largest average project by value is reserved however for the province of Zhejiang, focusing on the port city of Ningbo.

From this set of data on Korean investments in China, the following conclusions can be made about their locational preferences. First, the investments are largely concentrated in major industrial or transportation centers and almost exclusively in the coastal region. Second, the average value of projects varies greatly from region to region. The region that has the highest average value is South China which paradoxically has the second smallest share of the total Korean investments. Third, Korean investors have invested significantly in the SEZs where some of their largest projects are located. Fourth, the focus of Korean investments in the Bohai and Northeast region does exhibit some possibility that the coastal areas closest to Korea have enjoyed a disproportionately large share of the total Korean investments. Fifth, there is some evidence that kinship ties influence a small proportion of the projects and value of investments, notably in the border regions of Jilin and Heilongjiang, but that these investments, though numerous, have a low value on average.

Since South Korean investors have a relatively late start compared to investors from other parts of Asia, the regional location and the sectoral concentrations may change with time. Signs of such potential changes are the recent agreements on high-technology cooperation and infrastructure projects. Given investments from Taiwan and Korea are supposed to be recent and rapidly rising, a comparison of where these investors invest and how much they have invested may throw some light on what differences, if any, investors from different NIEs have. Even though the available information is limited, the locational differences of the investments from these two countries are glaring (table 5.10). Whereas the Korean investors favour the Bohai region (Shandong Province in particular), the investors from Taiwan overwhelmingly favour southern China, in particular Guangdong, Fujian and to a lesser extent, Shanghai.

The value of Korean investments is, on average, much larger than those from Taiwan. It does not follow that the regions with the largest share of investments have the projects with the highest values. The reverse is the case. In both cases, the regions with the largest share of investments do not have projects with the highest project values.

The number of projects and total investments from Taiwan far exceed that from Korea, but this could be partly explained by the late start of Korean investors and their comparative lack of previous ties in China. Because the two sets of data cover slightly different periods, they are not exactly comparable but the vast regional differences would not be changed in the space of over one year so the relative distribution amongst the provinces should be about the same.[21] It is possible to examine Korean investments in one region of China in more detail.

The Korean diaspora

The rapid economic growth of South Korea has made it a significant investor in Asia and this is reflected in the rapid rise of South Korea as a source of foreign investments in China (see table 5.4). One Chinese region that has received significant attention from South Korean investors is Yanbian.[22]

Yanbian Prefecture, bordering North Korea, has a total population that has increased from 830,000 in 1950 to 2.14 million by 1993. While ethnic Koreans are still the largest ethnic group in Yanbian, as a proportion of the total population, it has steadily declined from 63 percent of the total in 1949 to 40 percent in 1993 (*Yanbian*

95

Statistical Yearbook, 1994, p. 41).[23] The spatial distribution of the ethnic Koreans is also uneven, with the majority concentrated in cities such as Yanji and Tumen. About 60 percent of the 1993 population of these cities is ethnic Korean (*Yanji Statistical Yearbook*, 1994, p. 80).

The economy of Yanbian Prefecture, the Korean Autonomous Region in Jilin, is very much based on agriculture and light industries with tobacco, cigarettes and timber as the major products. International interest in the Yanbian area has been heightened since 1990 when under the auspices of UNDP, China, the Democratic People's Republic of Korea, the Russian Federation, South Korea and Japan met to discuss plans for the development of the Tumen Region Economic Development Area. Since then, a number of meetings have been held between these nations, more recently with the inclusion of Mongolia. This has culminated in May 30, 1995 when China, DPRK, Mongolia, Russia and South Korea met in Beijing to initial three agreements to set up the Tumen River Area Development Coordination Committee (China, North Korea and Russia), the Consultative Commission for the development of Tumen River Economic Development Area (TREDA) and Northeast Asia (all five nations) and a memorandum of understanding 'on an environmental principle promising to give full consideration to environment protection and the conservation of natural resources' (*Asian Wall Street Journal*, May 31, 1995).

Table 5.11
Utilized foreign investment in Yanbian Autonomous Region, 1993

Country	Cumulative	percent	1993	percent
Hong Kong	225	7.47	225	9.66
Japan	40	1.33	28	1.20
Taiwan	263	8.73	79	3.39
N. Korea	170	5.65	147	6.31
S. Korea	1605	53.30	1143	49.06
Russia	258	8.57	258	11.07
Canada	30	1.00	30	1.29
USA	287	9.53	287	12.32
Australia	133	4.42	133	5.71
Total	3011	100.00	2330	100.00

Source: Yanbian Statistical Yearbook (1994, p. 491)

The TREDA scheme has so far produced a great number of reports and a lot of scholarly as well as commercial interest, but few substantial developments on the ground.[24] Works such as those by Kim et al. (1992), Manguno (1993) and Rimmer

(1994) as well as numerous articles in publications such as the *China Economic Review, China Trade Report, Beijing Review* and the *Far Eastern Economic Review*, have ensured much scholarly as well as business sector interest. On the ground, the reality is somewhat different.

In spite of several years of promotion by the UNDP, the only real achievement is the signing of the three agreements at the end of May in 1995. These agreements do not seem to bind the nations involved to anything more than further discussions because no specific actions were mentioned. The lack of progress in this major scheme has not deterred the South Koreans from investing in Yanbian.

The major cities in Yanbian are Yanji, the Prefecture capital, Tumen and Hunchun that is fast becoming the gateway to Far East Russia. As part of the international agreements signed in May 1995, China has also specified the geographic area included in the Tumen Economic Development Area (TEDA) which now includes the entire Yanbian Prefecture, thus making it clear to those in the Yanbian Prefecture the central government's reliance on the Prefecture government to promote the success of its regional development strategy. Available information clearly indicates that South Korean investors are the ones that have lavished their attention on the Prefecture and its towns.

Table 5.12
Foreign direct investment in Yanji, 1994

	Number	Total US$ '000	Foreign US$ '000	% Foreign	Avg. Project
S. Korea	189	231,884	112,983	48.72	1,226.90
Hong Kong	45	57,221	33,733	58,95	1,271.58
N. Korea	20	11,634	6,883	59.16	581.70
Japan	18	14,277	7,380	51.69	793.17
USA	22	27,170	19,806	72,90	1,235.00
Taiwan	6	3,400	1,912	56.24	566.67
Canada	5	3,175	1,289	40.60	635.00
Russia	4	2,164	1,360	62.85	541.00
Singapore	1	5,255	1,320	25.12	5,255.00
Philippines	1	3,510	1,105	31.48	3,510.00
Australia	2	1,144	493	43.09	572.00
Malaysia	2	1,355	825	60.89	677.50
Germany	1	800	400	50.00	800.00
Burma	1	500	500	100.00	500.00
Total	317	363,489	189,989	52.27	1,146.65

Source: Yanji Economic Relations Commission, unpublished data

Diaspora investors and their motivations

In another study, Wu (1997) characterized the advantages of the diaspora Chinese and their investments in China as global networks and local linkages. Global networks refer to the business and financial networks of diaspora Chinese overseas, their business consortiums and joint projects and the international business cross-ownership and family or kinship ties that many Chinese overseas entrepreneurs have. Local linkages refer to the kinship ties and common dialects that give them distinct advantages when negotiating with local and even national leaders.

In spite of the recent and increasing participation of large firms, the majority of Hong Kong and Southeast Asia-based investors in China are small and medium sized firms that seek the advantages of low wage labour, inexpensive land and local officials willing to cooperate. These small and medium sized firms thrive on their ability to respond to changing markets, are reliant on low overhead to thrive and cannot afford lengthy negotiations or long delays with their projects. Hence the investors seek out localities within easy access, where they tend to know who to negotiate with and where the local officials tend to be cooperative and willing to negotiate (Leung, 1993). The Pearl River Delta area is physically close to Hong Kong, where many of the Hong Kong investors originated and where the provincial officials pride themselves on being innovative and ahead of the rest of China to attract foreign investments (Vogel, 1989). Both parties found their ideal match.

The Hong Kong-based Chinese or the Southeast Asia-based Chinese investors tend to conduct business in quite different ways than the large multinational corporations though a few of the family conglomerates would rival some multinational corporations in terms of size of market, financial resources and their network of production and investment. The diaspora Chinese entrepreneur can take on different roles and identities in order to gain social and political stability and business advantages. In their home base, the diaspora Chinese entrepreneurs would have gained citizenship, perhaps even localized their names to emphasize their assimilation and local identity. Using their international networks, they would emphasize their international role in promoting their home country's development, their ability to bring international capital and investment and to mobilize capital through their own or well-connected international financial institutions. In short, in their home base, the diaspora Chinese entrepreneur is careful to cultivate an image of a responsible citizen, an international entrepreneur mindful of the economic welfare of their home base (adopted or by birth) and cautious to take steps to bolster their political standing in order to conduct business locally and overseas.

To their counterparts in Southeast Asia or other parts of the world, they may act as willing partners in business ventures or consortiums either in third countries or in the home base of the consortium members. Their capital allows them to choose to be partners of varying importance in particular projects, or even lead a consortium if the opportunity arises. Their need is to maintain business contacts and partnerships, to be seen as leaders who are willing to share opportunities with other diaspora Chinese entrepreneurs so that they will reciprocate, that they appreciate the main investors taking the up-front risks but are willing to offer them opportunities to share in a variety of projects. The astute key entrepreneurs would tend to take the lead in what may otherwise be seen as perhaps too risky ventures by negotiating favourable terms with the Chinese officials who may accede since they are keen to get a major international investor to invest.

The diaspora Chinese entrepreneur will subsequently parcel out the project to other clans or business associates. Ultimately, the consortium leader may in fact hold a minority of the original project, having made significant profits by parceling out the projects and then minimizing his own exposure. In this role, the diaspora Chinese entrepreneur is seen to be making use of his business and financial networks to form consortiums, minimizing risks but at the same time is seen as taking a leadership role in providing his lesser brethens the opportunity to participate in large projects in China, a major emerging market.

In China, the diaspora Chinese entrepreneur takes on a different role again. He now wishes to be seen as the patriotic diaspora Chinese bringing to his 'motherland' the benefits of international commercial experience, industrial expertise and international networks. To acquire entry or maximize concessions, the diaspora Chinese entrepreneur tends to secure a foothold in his home village, be seen as a patron, so as to better secure concessions on land prices, override any planning restrictions and even obtain monopolies in infrastructure projects.[25] Local officials, usually some close or distant kin, are willing partners to assist in these respects since they are aware of the potential local and personal gains and the increased credibility they may gain with the provincial and central governments because they are dealing with a well known diaspora Chinese entrepreneur. The above basically describes the mode of operation of the large overseas Chinese entrepreneurs but the ethnic Korean investors are likely to behave in a similar manner.

This brief sketch of the variety of identities that the diaspora entrepreneur can take on underlines the importance of first starting with one's own home base, then reaching out through kinship and business networks to invest in China. These practices tend to have initial spatial focus in order to maximize the initial advantages and from there branch out to other parts of China where other advantages could beckon.[26] The diaspora Chinese business networks bring to China not merely the financial clout of businesses based in one country but they have the potential to bring together the combined financial strength, investment skills, technical expertise and marketing skills from a vast array of possible combinations of localities and countries around the globe. This is the global network of the diaspora Chinese at work. Thus through the diaspora Chinese, a group that local officials are often culturally empathetic, sharing a common language and possibly a local dialect, local officials have access to the rest of the world without going through the provincial or central governments. The benefits of global networks are quickly brought to localities.

The previous sections outlined the importance of Asian investments in China. Although the total amount of investment is still very much dominated by Hong Kong and then by Japan, the rising importance of the investments from Taiwan, Korea and Singapore, particularly for specific regions, cannot be denied. For a country such as

China, which is short of capital, foreign investment is welcome but what are the possible motivations of investors based in the NIEs? There is little doubt that foreign investors are motivated by a host of factors. Among these are push factors largely due to the process of economic restructuring at home, rising labour costs, shortage of labour, labour activism, rising land costs, loss of export quota and the realization that it is important for a small economy to develop a large external economy. The pull factors that China provides are the various incentives provided by the open policy and local authorities, a potential to gain a foothold in China's large domestic market, a business environment lacking in regulations and potential windfall gains in the context of a large untried market.

For any one individual investor, there is probably a unique set of factors or combination of factors that prompts the investor's decision to invest in China. This is probably particularly true for the decision where to invest. In spite of the economic reforms, investors are faced with a host of difficulties when doing business in China, especially in locations other than the large provincial capitals. There are few clear regulations published, observed and implemented. Those that are published can be changed abruptly without notice. The decision-making system is at best opaque and it seems that the context is one of rule by those in power rather than rule by law. Infrastructure is often nonexistent and when present is often poor. There is also usually uncertainty about supplies. In this context, the kinship network is paramount for a number of reasons:

1 *to ease the way*: kinship ties and language and/or dialect familiarity are important links to ease the way, to establish channels for discussions and to reduce uncertainties. For example, being one of the kin or from the same village, where one could immediately establish rapport and a sense of common background and common values, could ease obtaining permission to establish a particular type of manufacturing establishment. Access to the top officials can be fast tracked.
2 *to gain a better bargaining position*: by appealing to common ties and decades of relationships, investors can appeal to the desire to re-establish long term ties and this is the way many entrepreneurs tend to negotiate about land prices and utility rates.
3 *to obtain special assistance*: due to poor infrastructure and shortages, it is sometimes necessary, for example, to alternate the supply of electricity to different parts of a city in order to avoid overloading the system. Kinship links can ease the way to guarantee a regular supply. During both normal and abnormal situations, there is a line of communication with those in charge through kinship ties.

The data from China indicate that investors from the NIEs, at least during the initial investment stage, have strong locational preferences. This is due partly to the ethnic and kinship links that the investors perceive to provide advantages for their initial investments. The data from Hong Kong indicate that investors do move away from the beach heads they established once they gain experience with investing in an environment that is largely unknown and, to them, full of uncertainties. Both the overseas Chinese and the ethnic Korean investors have shown similar tendencies in China.

The literature on ethnic businesses and business networks do not specifically deal with the spatial implications. It is the argument of this chapter that by understanding where the diaspora capital may tend to first invest, we could better understand the development of regions that may be expected to attract large diaspora capital. Whether other ethnic groups tend to exhibit the same regional preferences or strategies when they make investment decisions in similar settings — settings that are highly uncertain and full of unknowns — is yet to be researched. For example, do the diaspora Vietnamese tend to exhibit the same regional preferences as they return to Vietnam to invest? Do the Polish American investors tend to do the same when they go back to Poland to invest? In other words, does diaspora capital exhibit certain characteristics that are very different from the more corporate-based capital? Is there a diaspora logic that is different from the corporate logic and how does regional development benefit from understanding the differences?

Notes

1. One major problem is that S.Korea and Taiwan are usually not identified among the list of investors. For example, even in the 1995 Statistical Yearbook of Fujian Province, there is no separate identification of Taiwan as a source of FDI when it is well known that FDI from Taiwan is the major source for that province.

2. See data contained in the *1994 Foreign Trade and Economic Relations Yearbook*. Foreign investments are sub-divided into three categories: (1) foreign loans and international bank credits; (2) foreign direct investments; (3) others (including compensation trade, outprocessing and international leases). Data in this chapter pertain only to foreign direct investments and all references to foreign investments refer to direct foreign investments.

3. A much more serious flaw in the data is pointed out by Liew et al., (1992, p. 27). They reported often the data on utilized foreign investment do not include machinery and installations which are considered to be owned by the foreign investor. This accounting method is particularly true for compensation trade agreements. Liew et al., calculated that in the case of Guangdong Province, the distortions introduced by this accounting method may mean an understatement of about 35 percent of the actual total foreign investments.

4. During the 1970s, the manufacturing sector in Hong Kong had the highest contribution to GDP and the highest percentage of total employment of close to 50 percent in 1976. Since the early 1980s, Hong Kong's manufacturing sector employment has declined in relative importance to other sectors of the economy. In 1987, it was surpassed by the wholesale and retail sector in terms of contribution to the GDP and by 1990, it was again surpassed in terms of percentage of total employment.

5. Here, ASEAN refers to Malaysia, Thailand, Singapore, Philippines, Indonesia, Brunei and Vietnam.
6. Data obtained from Taiwan and South Korea indicate significant investments since the late 1980s.
7. There is a time lag between the signing of an agreement and the actual investment. This may partly explain the small size of investment reported from Taiwan.
8. Investments from Taiwan probably existed previously but were channeled via third parties. For example, Xiamen reported that its first investments from Taiwan occurred in 1983 (*Ta Kung Pao*, Aug. 31, 1993). Liaoning reported that its first Taiwan investment came in 1984 (*Ta Kung Pao*, Aug. 25, 1993).
9. There is an acknowledged wide gap between what is officially reported in Taiwan and the reports coming from China on the amount of investments from Taiwan (*China Times*, June 12, 1993). Tung (1993) cites a report in the *Free China Journal* (Feb. 26, 1993) which reports that Taiwan's indirect trade with the mainland amounted to US$7.4 billion in 1992 and indirect Taiwanese investment in the mainland totaled more than US$3.8 billion.
10. The news clippings were culled from the *Straits Times* and the *Business Times* from June 1, 1992 to June 30, 1993. The number of clippings from 1993 is almost twice the number from 1992.
11. The Malaysia, Singapore and Indonesian triangle involving development of Batam island in Indonesia and Johore in Malaysia is such an example.
12. Shandong and Guangdong are the only two provinces which published data on South Korean investments in 1991.
13. The Taiwan government was at first quite opposed to the idea of Taiwan-based investors investing in the mainland. As investors found a myriad of ways to get around the official prohibition, the government asked for the voluntary registration of investments in China as a way of preparing a scheme for official sanctions and as a way of finding out the extent of investments in China. Finally an approval body was established in the Ministry of Economic Affairs.
14. Since the normalization of relations, China and South Korea have entered into a number of agreements, including agreements in high tech R&D and joint development of a optical fibre network (*Electronics*, Oct. 26, 1992 and Feb. 23, 1993).
15. For example, the Hokkien Clansmen Association of Singapore announced that it would build a shopping center in Jinjing, Fujian (*Straits Times*, May 19, 1993).
16. Note that table 5.9, based on official Chinese data, does not include investments from South Korea.
17. In 1990, Hong Kong was the chief source of FDI for all coastal provinces.
18. Most of the data is from the provincial Foreign Trade and Economic Relations Committees cited in Mitsuibishi Research Institute (1993).
19. This preference is also clearly shown in table 5.9. Over one third of Taiwan investments in Guangdong are located in the Shenzhen SEZ. In Fujian, just over 51 percent of the Taiwan investments are in Xiamen.

20. Yantai reports that there are about 20,000 overseas Chinese in South Korea, of whom about half hailed from Yantai. Yantai also reports a 2.7-fold increase of investments from South Korea for the first six months of 1993, to about 3.6 million yuan worth of investments from South Korea (*Ta Kung Pao*, Sept. 1, 1993).

21. Much of course could have changed since the publication of these data. Taiwanese and Korean investments in China are supposed to have risen even more rapidly during 1993. The data for individual cities give a hint of the rapid increases in selected locations in China. The individual data suggest that there may be a spatial diversification of investments from Taiwan and South Korea.

22. In terms of the size of investments, Shandong Province, which is the part of China closest to South Korea, has received the lion's share of the investments from Korea.

23. South Korea pays a great deal of attention to the ethnic Koreans in China and their potential roles in promoting economic links between the two countries; see Kim and Kim (1994).

24. Between 1991 and 1994, US$5 million was spent by the UNDP on various consultant reports on various aspects of the TREDA.

25. Many diaspora Chinese made their moves immediately after the Tiananmen Incident in 1989, many immediately negotiated investment projects with the Chinese officials while the West condemned the government's actions, thus earning for themselves the gratitude of the Chinese government for coming to the aid of the 'motherland' while other investors were regarded by the Chinese officials to have tried to isolate China. There are of course many diaspora Chinese who are genuine about their desire to assist the development of the land of their ethnic origin. Their contributions should not be diminished by the less altruistic motives of others.

26. A similar strategy is used by the Singapore government to coordinate Singapore's moves into China. The government ensured that consortiums are formed, that the consortiums make use of the excellent contacts made by the government and select a few locations to concentrate their investments.

References

Alonso, W. (1968), 'Location Theory', in Friedmann, J. and Alonso, W. (eds), *Regional Development and Planning*, MIT Press: Cambridge, MA, pp. 78-106.

Alonso, W. (1975), 'Industrial Location and Regional Policy in Economic Development', in Friedmann, J. and Alonso, W. (eds), *Regional Policy: Readings in Theory and Applications*, MIT Press: Cambridge, MA, pp. 66-96.

Asian Wall Street Journal, May 31, 1995.

Business Times (Singapore) (various issues).

China Statistical Yearbook (various years), Statistical Publications: Beijing.

China Times (Taipei) (various issues).

Common Wealth (Taipei) (various issues).

Federation of Hong Kong Industries (1992), *Hong Kong's Industrial Investment in the Pearl River Delta*, FHKI: Hong Kong.

Forbes (Hong Kong) February, 1993.

Goldberg, M.A. (1989), *The Chinese Connection: Getting Plugged into Pacific Rim Real Estate, Trade and Capital Markets*, University of British Columbia Press: Vancouver.

Hamilton, G.G., Zeile, W. and Kim, W.J. (1990), 'The Network Structures of East Asian Economies', in Clegg, S.R. and Redding, S.G. (eds), *Capitalism in Contrasting Cultures*, Berlin: De Guyter, pp. 105-130.

Hamilton, G. (ed.), (1991), *Business Networks and Economic Development in East and Southeast Asia*, Centre of Asian Studies, University of Hong Kong: Hong Kong.

Hsing, Y.T. (1995), *Blood, Thicker than Water: Networks of Local Chinese Bureaucrats and Taiwanese Investors in Southern China*, Centre for Human Settlements, School of Community and Regional Planning, University of British Columbia: Vancouver.

Isard, W. (1975), 'Comparative Costs and Industrial Location', in *Introduction to Regional Science*, Prentice Hall: Englewood, pp. 80-111.

Kim, W.B., Campbell, B., Valencia, M. and Lee, J.C. (eds) (1992), *Regional Economic Cooperation in Northeast Asia*. East West Center: Honolulu.

Kim, T.H. and Kim, S.J. (1994), *Korean-China Economic Cooperation: The Role of Ethnic Koreans in China*, Korean Institute of Economic Policy: Seoul (in Korean).

Kotkin, J. (1993), *Tribes: How Race, Religion and Identity Determine Success in the New Global Economy*, Random House: New York.

Korean Institute of Economic Policy (1992), *The Evolution of China's Policies of Inducing Foreign Investment and Korea's Investments*, KIEP: Seoul (in Korean).

Kunio, Y. (1988), *The Rise of Ersatz Capitalism in Southeast Asia*, Oxford University Press: Singapore.

Lever-Tracy, C., Ip, D. and Tracy, N. (1996), *The Chinese Diaspora and Mainland China: An Emerging Economic Synergy*, Macmillan: London.

Leung, C.K. (1993), 'Personal Contacts, Subcontracting Linkages and Development in the Hong Kong-Zhujiang Delta Region', *Annals of the Association of American Geographers*, Vol. 83, No. 2, pp. 272-302.

Liew, P.W. et al., (1992), *Reform and Openness in China and the Economic Development of the Pearl River Delta*, Nanyang Commerce Bank: Hong Kong (in Chinese).

Manguno (1993), 'A New Regional Trade Bloc in Northeast Asia?', *The China Business Review*, March/April, pp. 6-11.

Maruya, T. (1992), 'Economic Relations Between Hong Kong and Guangdong Province', in Maruya, T. (ed.), *Guangdong: 'Open Door' Economic Development Strategy*, Institute of Developing Economies: Tokyo.

Ministry of Trade and Industry, Republic of Singapore (1993), *Economic Survey of Singapore 1992*, SNP Publishers Pte. Ltd.: Singapore.

Mitsubishi Research Institute (1993), *China: Information Compendium (1993 edition)*, MRI:Tokyo.

National Bureau of Statistics, Republic of Korea (1990), *Korea Statistical Yearbook*, Economic Planning Board: Seoul.

Rimmer, P. (1994), 'Regional Integration in Pacific Asia', *Environment and Planning A*, Vol. 26, pp. 1731-59.

Sato, Y. (1993), 'The Salim Group in Indonesia: The Development and Behavior of the Largest Conglomerate in Southeast Asia', *The Developing Economies*, Vol. 31, No. 4, pp. 408-41.

Sesudason, J.V. (1989), *Ethnicity and the Economy: The State, Chinese Business and Multinationals in Malaysia*, Oxford University Press: Singapore.

Sieh, L.M.L. (1989), 'The Transformation of Malaysian Business Groups', in McVey, R. (ed.), *Southeast Asian Capitalists*, Oxford University Press: Singapore, pp. 103-126.

Straits Times (Singapore) (various issues).

Suehiro, A. (1989), 'Capitalist Development in Postwar Thailand: Commercial Bankers, Industrial Elite, and Agribusiness Groups', in McVey, R. (ed.), *Southeast Asian Capitalists*, Oxford University Press: Singapore, pp. 35-63.

Suehiro, A. (1993), 'Family Business Reassessed: Corporate Structure and Late-Starting Industrialization in Thailand', *The Developing Economies*, Vol. 31, No. 4, pp. 378-407.

Ta Kung Pao (Hong Kong) (various issues).

Tung, R. (1993), 'Taiwan and Southern China's Fukien and Kwangtung Provinces', Background paper for Taiwan in the Asia-Pacific in the 1990s Conference, ANU, April 1-2.

Vogel, E.F. (1989), *One Step Ahead in China: Guangdong Under Reform*. Harvard University Press: Cambridge.

Wu, C.T. (1989), 'Regional Impacts of Foreign Investment in China', *Asian Economic Journal*, Vol. 3, No. 1, pp. 35-71.

Wu, C.T. (1997), 'Globalization of the Chinese Countryside: International Capital and the Transformation of the Pearl River Delta', in Rimmer, P. (ed.), *Pacific Rim Development: Integration and Globalization in the Asia-Pacific Economy*, Allen & Unwin: Sydney, pp. 57-82.

Yanbian Statistical Yearbook (1994).

Yanji Statistical Yearbook (1994).

Zhou, Q. (1993), 'The Fluctuating and Selective Regional Distribution of Development Resources in China, 1953-1990', Paper presented to the Biennial Conference of Chinese Studies Association of Australia, Brisbane, Australia, July 1993.

6 Industrial Restructuring in the Asian NIEs, the Behaviour of Firms and the Dynamics of Local Production Systems

The Case of Audio Production in Singapore

Leo van Grunsven

Introduction

This chapter deals with the global-local dimension of the production system which characterizes one branch of manufacturing in the production complexes of one of the Asian NIEs, Singapore. Central in the discussion are the implications of industrial restructuring in the Asian NIEs. It will report on recent research into changing local production systems, specifically the global-local dimension, in Singapore under the influence of the triggers of restructuring. The production system, and the global-local dimension in particular, is understood here to refer to global procurement versus localization (as reflected in local sourcing and local content) and the local growth and role of supplier firms as an integral segment of industries. Before outlining the main propositions emanating from the analysis, it is useful to provide some background through a brief discussion of the evolution of 'the local' as a dimension of production systems in the Asian NIEs.

During the 1960s and 1970s, in the Asian Pacific Rim and Latin America production complexes emerged which rapidly became integrated in the developing system of international production. Globalization processes and the operation of MNCs, in tandem with impulses provided by export-oriented industrialization policies, led to the establishment of export-manufacturing processing and assembly activities in these complexes, embodied in MNC transplants as well as in local firms acting as producers in international subcontracting networks set up by enterprises from the core regions of the world economy. These complexes were soon designated as offshore export platforms.

The initial features of industrial production in these complexes under the influence of globalization have given rise to a debate on the merits of export-oriented production complexes in the 'semi-periphery', dominated by MNC transplants. A major issue concerned the production system, or the organization of production, employed in transplants in the dominant industries. It was observed that foreign transplants operating in export platforms showed little tendency towards 'local embedment'. Commonly, all materials used as input in the production process were imported (purchased intra-firm or extra-firm). The dominant viewpoint in the debate was therefore that the production system employed by MNC transplants brought few benefits to the host economies.

However, in the course of the 1980s a different situation emerged with respect to the global-local dichotomy in the sourcing patterns of MNC transplants operating in the established production complexes. Amongst the many changes in production characteristics, including the production system, triggered by a range of factors, both internal and external to the firm (Ho Kong Chong, 1993, 1994; Kim, 1993; Lui and Chiu, 1994; Park, 1994), a trend towards a larger degree of local sourcing became quite noticeable in a number of industries. Related to this is the emergence of a substantial number and range of supply firms, both local and foreign, in these production complexes. As a result, the characteristics of production in a range of industries evolved towards a larger degree of local integration.

It should be added, however, that this 'localization' trend has not emerged to the same degree in export platforms. It has progressed more rapidly in production complexes in Southeast and East Asia, compared with e.g. the US/Mexican border zone. In the latter case, local material input supply to the *maquiladoras* and thus 'local content' has remained extremely low. There is still a marked absence of a localized supply structure (Fuentes et al., 1993; Brannon et al., 1994), in contrast to many Southeast and East Asian cases (Ki Suk Lee and Chung Tong Wu, 1993). A range of factors accounts for these differences. These seem to include first of all the nature of production and the position of the operations in the particular transplants in the commodity chain within the firm. A second factor is the local or regional industrial structure and labour market conditions or, more broadly stated, the local manufacturing infrastructure. Third, the role of government is quite significant. Governments are more or less active in the development of local manufacturing infrastructure. Specifically also, governments have in differential degree exerted pressure on foreign transplants to increase local content. To some extent, institutional and international trade arrangements have an impact. Fifth, the degree of localization also seems to reflect the extent to/rate at which production arrangements and organization of production have changed in response to changes in market demand and increased global competition. Sixth, it also reflects corporate strategies and managerial attitudes towards local sourcing. Another factor, related to the previous one, refers to the role and — strategic — behaviour of Japanese companies. In the internationalization process, many of these companies have — given favourable local conditions — actively engaged in the transfer of the 'Japanese model' of work and production organization and the supplier system to the offshore production complexes. This has not only occurred in offshore export platforms in the semi-periphery favoured by Japanese companies, but also in Europe and the United States (Kenney and Florida, 1993). Where it has evolved, conditions in both the host economies and home economies have frequently contributed to a system whereby not only local firms are part of the supplier system. Often, these have been supplemented by Japanese supply firms setting up operations near the plants of the client firms. Not only is the Japanese presence in Southeast and East Asian production complexes stronger compared with e.g. the US/Mexican border zone, but also the local conditions in the former complexes have generally been more favourable for the transfer of the specific 'Japanese production organization' (Kenney and Florida, 1994). As has recently been argued by Fujita and Hill, 'local development' here derives in part from the 'localizing more of the production process' characteristic of 'global toyotaism' (Fujita and Hill, 1995).

As far as the Asian NIEs are concerned, the literature on recent industrial development trajectories in these countries suggests a relationship between the further growth of local supply systems (not necessarily accompanied by a further increase in localization) and the necessity to restructure imposed on transplants by changes in the set of local conditions. In the early to mid-1980s, the Asian NIEs have adopted industrial restructuring policies in response to fundamental changes in their internal and external environments. Industrial restructuring is understood to refer to 'a process of deliberate or planned structural reconfiguration in response to changing conditions' (Park, 1994). Thus, these policies were aimed at and involved the 'reworking' of their competitive advantage and the redefinition of their hitherto function as export platform. The triggers of restructuring as well as the specific strategies adopted by governments in response to these, are already well documented in the recent literature (see e.g., the various contributions in special issues of *Environment and Planning A* on industrial restructuring and regional adjustment in the Asian NIEs; Clark and Kim, 1995) and will therefore not be dealt with here. Both MNC transplants and local firms have responded to the triggers and the restructuring efforts — as well as to a host of other changes, including those in the wider regional environment in the Asia-Pacific — in a number of ways. One should be cautious about generalization, since the process of restructuring and its outcomes or implications are quite differential, depending on domestic institutional and organizational arrangements (Lui and Chiu, 1994). Yet, the research reported in the recent literature reveals common elements in the responses of plants and/or firms in each of the four Asian NIEs. These can be categorized in sectoral and spatial responses. The former include (1) process automation, (2) changes in product structure towards high value-added and quality products through product substitution, (3) flexibilization of the labour process and the input of labour as well as more emphasis on job training, and (4) subcontracting of production. The spatial responses include (1) intensifying the spatial division of labour within the nation, and (2) internationalization through the relocation of production. Thus there are multiple dimensions to the implications of restructuring, including organizational, employment or labour market, and spatial (locational) dimensions (Park, 1994; Le Heron and Park, 1995). As to the organizational dimension, externalization of production operations by transplants and large local main producers is reflected in an expanding local supply network.

Like in the other NIEs, significant alterations in local production systems in Singapore have occurred as a result of the changes in firm behaviour, propelled by the imperatives of restructuring (Ho Kong Chong, 1993, 1994; Natarajan and Tan, 1992).

These alterations are found in a range of industry branches. Restructuring is very much an ongoing process as the imperatives appear to become stronger over time and are spreading in the economy. In this chapter the focus is on the spatial and organizational aspects of the behaviour of firms, in the process of adopting strategic responses to the imperatives of restructuring, and the implications for the global-local dimensions of the production system. These are highlighted for a very dynamic industry branch, the production of audio equipment.

In discussions about the global-local (and internalization-externalization) dimensions in the organizational aspect of production systems employed by firms, implicitly the focus often seems to be on main producers in industries and large establishments, be they transplants or local firms. This seems to be unwarranted and too limited in scope in situations where production systems in the recent past have undergone substantial change (associated with a localization trend) resulting in the growth of a substantial local supplier segment. This holds even if it is acknowledged that this segment can be associated also with the onset of restructuring in the recent past. There seems to be no *a priori* reason why the supplier segment in the course of time should not also feel the imperatives of restructuring. As will become clear in the discussion which follows, the production of audio equipment in Singapore is currently characterized by a substantial local supplier segment. The research which is reported in this chapter indeed departed from the assumption that in Singapore at this stage this segment might very well be also involved in a restructuring process. For this reason surveys have been conducted among both the main producers and supply firms. The adoption of such a perspective proved to be very fruitful. As will be shown below, the findings pertaining to the main producers confirm changes in the activities carried out in the Singapore plant and strategic responses to changing local conditions, which are in line with findings reported in the recent literature. In addition, however, fundamental changes are also observed in the patterns of operation of the supplier firms. The findings reveal that these patterns currently are quite dynamic. They also indicate that this dynamics is such that it may result in the gradual disintegration of the localized supply segment. A more regionalized structure seems to be in the making. After a brief look at the position of audio equipment production in Singapore's electronics industry and the nature of audio equipment production, the survey findings will be discussed.

Audio equipment production in Singapore

Over the years, the electronics industry in Singapore has shown substantial growth. By the early 1990s it was the top contributor in terms of output, employment, net value added and net fixed assets in the manufacturing sector. Their contributions in 1991 were 38.8 percent, 34.4 percent, 35 percent and 20 percent respectively (Economic Development Board, 1993). During the 1980s, the branch has undergone substantial change. Introduced in the early 1980s, the production of disk drives in the early 1990s emerged as the segment having the highest share of electronics' output, employment and direct exports (see table 6.1). The available statistics also show a significant position and contribution of component-producing establishments in terms of number of establishments, output and employment. Because direct exports as a proportion of output are substantially less than in other segments, it can be derived that many of these establishments are engaged in local supply. This lends substantiation to the observations as to the emergence of a local supplier segment in the course of industrial development in production complexes in the Asian NIEs.

Table 6.1
Principal statistics of the electronics industry in Singapore, 1991

	Establish-ments	Workers	Output	Direct Exports	Value Added
				S$ million	
Computers & Data Processing Equipment	18	2,875	2,127	1,944	302
Diskdrives	12	27,691	7,064	6,391	1,224
Computer Peripheral Equipment	18	9,285	2,967	2,636	1,286
Office Machinery & Equipment	4	2,518	441	388	105
Communication Equipment	9	8,199	1,134	982	398
Television Sets & Subassemblies	6	5,946	1,607	1,449	144
Microphones, Loudspeakers & Amplifiers	5	3,430	348	204	104
Audio & Video Combination Equipment	11	13,561	3,387	2,887	510
Semiconductor Devices	22	15,096	3,542	3,177	627
Capacitors	8	3,804	442	305	166
Resistors	7	1,029	75	54	23
Printed Circuit Boards without Electronic Parts	21	5,552	641	229	194
Printed Circuit Boards with Electronic Parts	66	14,064	2,838	1,888	734
Other Electronic Products	36	10,308	2,344	1,141	402
Total	243	123,358	28,958	23,676	6,217

Source: Research and Statistics Unit, Economic Development Board (1993)

Audio equipment production has a modest position in the electronics industry in Singapore. Table 6.1 indicates for 1991 a share of less than 5 percent of the total number of electronics establishments and a share of approximately 12 percent of output, direct exports and employment. Careful investigation of available sources resulted in the identification of 13 establishments. As table 6.2 shows, these are dominated by MNC transplants, particularly by transplants of Japanese firms. All but one of the transplants were established in Singapore in the 1970s. In the majority of cases, the parent companies have additional subsidiaries in Singapore where other types of products are manufactured and/or where other types of activities are carried out (e.g. marketing). Most parent companies also have other (in a number of cases more than one) subsidiaries elsewhere in the region where production related to audio equipment is carried out. Most countries in the region feature in the location pattern, though Malaysia, Thailand and China are the most prominent locations. For example, Philips Electronics also has subsidiaries in Malaysia, Hong Kong and China where audio equipment is assembled. In addition, four of the transplants in Singapore have set up their own subsidiary elsewhere in the region (mostly Malaysia) where operations related to audio equipment are carried out.

Table 6.2
Main audio equipment producers/establishments in Singapore (assemblers)

Name	Origin
Aiwa Singapore	Japan
Asahi Electronics	Japan
General Motors	USA
Hitachi Consumer Products	Japan
JVC Electronics	Japan
Mitsumi Electronics	Japan
Matsushita Electronics	Japan
Pioneer Electronics	Japan
Philips Electronics	Netherlands
Trio-Kenwood	Japan
Sanyo Electronics	Japan
Mitsubishi Electronics	Japan
Thomson Audio	France

The 13 establishments which were identified can be considered or 'defined' as the main producer or assembler segment of the audio equipment branch in Singapore. Associated with localization processes in the recent past, a range of local supply firms, both local firms and foreign transplants, are integrated in the audio branch. These constitute the second segment of the production system. In the research, through information obtained from the main producers as well as from other (secondary) sources, a list could be compiled of 35 firms which are in this segment (these are firms whose main activity is related to audio and which have one or more of the 13 main producers as client). Of these, 29 were included in the research, in addition to the 13 main establishments. A brief profile of this segment will be given in a later section of the chapter.

Table 6.3
Current production of the audio transplants

Est.	Current production
A	Portable radio cassette players (1974), Midi-sets (1978), Mini-sets (1990)
B	HiFi, Cassette players (1973), Mini-sets (1990)
C	PCBs & other components, Radios (1981), Car audio (1987)
D	Radio cassette players, Amplifiers, Car audio, CD players, HiFi, Mini-sets (1988)
E	Car audio (1978)
F	Radio cassette players (1972), CD players (1989), HiFi (1993)
G	Portable radio cassette players, HiFi (1977), CD players (1992)
H	Car audio, HiFi (1979)
I	Radio cassette players (1977), Midi-sets (1978), CD players (1988)
J	Radios (1972), Car audio (1979)
K	Car audio (1978), HiFi (1990), Mini-sets (1992)
L	-
M	-

As table 6.3 shows, a substantial variety of audio equipment is manufactured by the main producers. In most plants, new products or product lines have been added to existing ones or product lines have been replaced by new ones. With respect to most plants, the managers stated that some of their products or product lines (e.g. radio cassette players) had been manufactured in this particular plant already for a long time, since the 1970s. However, as to these products, new models have been introduced regularly and the current products bear little resemblance to the ones which were originally manufactured (only the designation of the product has remained the same). In table 6.3, two establishments do not have any products/product lines listed. These establishments have recently ceased manufacturing in Singapore. In one case, the product lines were transferred to other subsidiaries of the parent company in the region. In the other case, the product lines were contracted out to independent firms outside Singapore. This brings us to a consideration of some aspects of the recent behaviour of the main producer transplants.

112

The main producers: company behaviour

From the interviews which were conducted with plant managers, it is clear that substantial changes have occurred in the transplants in the recent past. In all cases, products have been substantially upgraded and the products currently manufactured are generally considered to be in the high-end range of the audio equipment produced by the company. Nine of the eleven plants reported the use of 'state-of-the-art' product and process technologies. In addition, in the majority of the transplants product lines are now highly automated. The main motive for process automation was to alleviate the growing constraints as to the availability and cost of labour. In some cases, the labour force has declined as a result. In most cases, process automation has resulted in a substantial change of the composition of the labour force. The share of unskilled and low-skilled workers has declined, while the share of (semi-) skilled production workers and technically trained personnel has increased. The share of males in the labour force has increased also.

Spatially, in tandem with the upgrading process most companies have relocated product lines out of the Singapore plant. Table 6.4 shows the broad findings as to the decanting process. This process appears to have gained momentum in the second half of the 1980s and early 1990s. As expected, most of the relocation concerned lower end products. In a few instances it also concerned in-house production of components. As mentioned earlier, two establishments have transferred production altogether out of Singapore. Most of the relocation has occurred to other countries in the region, significantly to Malaysia. Some of the transplants expect the relocation of additional production activities in the years to come. The two establishments referred to above now concentrate on other activities, i.e. R&D and technical support. Though in the other transplants production is still the main activity, towards the end of the 1980s or in the early 1990s in the majority of cases other corporate functions have been added. As table 6.5 shows, these are R&D, marketing & sales, purchasing and/or technical support functions. This reflects the deepening of internationalization, in which new elements have emerged in the 1980s, in response to increased global competition, corporate expansion in the region, market shifts and a number of other factors (van Grunsven, 1994). This constitutes a significant aspect of the changes that have occurred as it indicates that offshore transplants in some locations have assumed additional roles in the value/commodity chains. Two of the establishments are now operating under OHQ (Regional Headquarter) status, which implies that they are also overseeing production which is carried out elsewhere in the region. In this context it may be noted that in some additional cases the parent companies of the transplants have an OHQ in Singapore which is physically separated from the production plant(s). In one of the two cases listed in table 6.5 the OHQ status also derives from the fact that the parent company has recently shifted the global headquarter of the audio product group (a subdivision of the consumer electronics division of the company) to the particular establishment in Singapore.

Table 6.4
Relocation of production by the audio transplants

Est.	Product	Year	Location
A	Components	1994	Indonesia
B	Portable CD players	1991	Thailand
	Portable audio, radios	1994	Indonesia
C	-	-	-
D	Low-end audio	1988	Malaysia
E	Magnetic tape heads	1982	Malaysia
	Components	1984	Malaysia
	PCBs	1990	Malaysia
F	Portable radio cassette players	1988	China
G	-	-	-
H	Low-end HiFi	1988	Malaysia
I	Low-end radio cassette recorder	1985	China
	Portable audio	1987	Malaysia
	Car audio	1989	Malaysia
J	Car audio	1990	Malaysia
K	Radios	1977	Malaysia
	Portable audio	1990	Malaysia
	Portable audio	1995	China
L	Portable radio cassette players	1980	Malaysia
	(Portable) CD players	1990	Indonesia
	Portable audio	1990	Indonesia
M	Cassette players/recorders	1993	Malaysia
	CD players	1993	Malaysia
	Amplifiers	1993	Malaysia

While production remains the main activity in most cases, as observed, the transplants increasingly have narrowed or confined production activities to final assembly. This is reflected in the pattern of sourcing. Only one of the establishments currently still produces part of the material input in-house (table 6.6). This is a US transplant. Component production earlier carried out in-house in the other transplants, in all cases has been relocated or externalized. Table 6.6 shows the overall findings as to the current pattern of sourcing. Virtually all Japanese transplants procure part of the material input from the the home country (generally around 20 percent or less). This involves intra-firm, extra-firm or both types of sourcing and usually concerns key components. In some cases inputs are procured intra-firm from 'the region', meaning one or more

114

of the ASEAN countries. This is related to relocation and/or the transfer of component production by the parent company to some of the ASEAN countries. On average, some 25 percent of material inputs are obtained intra-firm (in most cases outside Singapore).

Table 6.5
Non-production activities performed by the transplants

Est.	Nature of activity	OHQ	Main activity
A	R&D (1988), Sales (1993)	No	Production
B	Product Adjustment (1973), Technical Support (1989)	No	Production
C	R&D (1989)	No	Production
D	Purchasing (1987), R&D (1991)	No	Production
E	-	No	Production
F	-	No	Production
G	R&D (1988), Marketing & Sales (1988)	No	Production
H	-	No	Production
I	Purchasing (1972), R&D (1989)	No	Production
J	Quality Control (1972), R&D (1980)	No	Production
K	Product Adjustment (1968), Purchasing (1968), R&D (1978)	Yes	Production
L	Technical support (1968), R&D (1970)	Yes	R&D
M	Technical support (1988)	No	Technical Support

The percentage of input materials procured locally and extra-firm varies considerably, from 20 percent to 90 percent, with an average of 48 percent. The findings appear to substantiate the observations made earlier in the chapter concerning localization. Components which are sourced locally include stuffed PCBs, encasings, ICs, CD and cassette mechanisms, capacitors, resistors, magnetic heads, plastic parts and metal parts. These are either purchased at arm's length or the production has been subcontracted/contracted out to local suppliers. Contracting out arrangements are most common for the production of stuffed PCBs, encasings, and CD and cassette mechanisms. Such arrangements have grown substantially during the 1980s. It may be noted here that in a number of cases the assemblers provide part of the inputs needed to produce the components. These do not necessarily originate from Singapore and are often obtained through the sales and purchasing offices of the company. The suppliers which receive inputs from the clients (less than half) do however still source a substantial part of the inputs which are needed themselves. More than half of the suppliers do all sourcing which is needed themselves. Procurement is from Singapore, Japan, USA, Europe, Malaysia and other countries in the region.

Table 6.6
Pattern of sourcing of the audio transplants

Est.	Intra-Est. %	Extra-Establishment Intra-Firm %	Location	Extra-Firm %	Location	% Local	Total
A	-	10	Japan	40	Singapore	40	100
		20	Indonesia	10	Japan		
				20	Region		
B	-	-	-	80	Singapore	80	100
				20	Japan		
C	45	3	USA	30	Singapore	30	100
				20	Region		
				2	USA		
D	-	20	Japan	20	Singapore	20	100
		60	Region				
E	-	30	Malaysia	70	Singapore	70	100
F	-	30	(Singapore)	70	Singapore	70	100
G	-	16	Japan	70	Singapore	70	100
		9	Malaysia				
		5	Taiwan				
H	-	30	Japan	20	Singapore	20	100
				50	Region		
I	-	10	Japan	90	Singapore	90	100
J	-	-	-	20	Singapore	20	100
				80	Japan/Korea/		
					Region		
K	-	62	Japan/USA/	20	Singapore	20	100
			Region	18	Region		
L	-	-	-	-	-	-	-
M	-	-	-	-	-	-	-

Some of the assemblers have recently also engaged in the contracting out of the final assembly of finished products to independent firms in Singapore, under an OEM agreement. In this way capacity problems are solved and/or problems with respect to labour, which would have been encountered in case of expansion 'in-house', can be avoided. Also, it increases the flexibility of production. Increasingly, the contracting out of the production of components like stuffed PCBs and encasings, as well as the assembly of finished products under OEM, is also to supply firms outside Singapore, particularly in Malaysia. This is done for the reason of costs. Hence, noteworthy in table 6.6 is the number of instances in which part of the material input is procured extra-firm in 'the region', as well as the percentages involved. This indicates that besides from/to suppliers in Singapore material inputs which require substantial input of labour to produce are also purchased from or subcontracted/contracted out to — independent firms in — Malaysia, Thailand or Indonesia. This indeed seems to indicate that the suppliers in Singapore are experiencing cost problems (i.e. have started to feel the triggers of restructuring). This makes it relevant to pose the question whether any strategic responses by these establishments are discernible. In the next section we will present some of the research findings pertaining to the supplier segment.

The supplier segment: characteristics and dynamics

The suppliers included in the research are quite diverse in terms of origin, status and period of establishment. As table 6.7 shows, half are Singapore establishments and the other half are foreign. Given the predominance of Japanese establishments among the assemblers, it is not surprising that most of the foreign suppliers are of Japanese origin as well. Logically, all the foreign establishments are subsidiaries. This also holds true for one-third of the Singapore establishments. The majority of the latter were set up during the 1980s, in contrast to the Japanese and other foreign establishments which have been operating in Singapore since the second half of the 1970s. Most of the parent companies of the subsidiaries (including three of the five parent companies of the subsidiaries of Singapore origin) have other subsidiaries in the region, in number ranging from one to eleven. Besides Singapore (six cases), these are located in Malaysia, Thailand, China, Indonesia, Korea, Taiwan, and Hong Kong.

As to production carried out by the suppliers, one can distinguish between production in the narrow sense (that is non-assembly) and assembly. The activities of 70 percent of the establishments are in the former category and include injection moulding, painting, printing, stamping, and wire harnessing. The latter category comprises 30 percent of the establishments and is predominantly PCB assembly. Table 6.8 shows the products manufactured by origin of the establishment. More than two-thirds of the Singapore establishments are in PCB assembly or the production of encasings. The Japanese establishments carry out a wider range of component manufacturing. A small number of the establishments also carry out final testing and R&D. Most establishments have departments dealing with marketing/sales/purchasing, technical support, and operational management. Many of the suppliers have a range of clients, though in many cases the 'market' is restricted to Singapore. Eleven of the 15 Singapore establishments and eight of the 12 Japanese establishments only produce for clients in Singapore (the 13 assemblers). Only nine establishments export a usually small part of the output to clients outside Singapore, commonly located in one of the other countries in the region. For most of the

117

establishments it is not profitable to expand in foreign markets through export from the Singapore facility. As we will see later on, a number of establishments use alternative strategies to achieve that.

Table 6.7
Origin, status and period of establishment of supply firms

| | Subsidiary | | Period of Establishment | | | | |
	Yes	No	- 75	76-80	81-85	86-90	Total
Japan	12	3	8			1	12
USA	1			1			1
UK	1			1			1
Singapore	5	10	1	4	6	4	15
Total	19	10	4	14	6	5	29

Table 6.8
Production by origin of the suppliers

	Japan	USA	UK	S'pore	Total
PCB	1			5	6
Encasing	4			4	8
Speakers/parts	1				1
PCB/product assembly				1	1
PCB/CD & cassette mechanisms				2	2
Metal parts			1	1	2
Mechanical parts				1	1
Magnetic heads	1				1
Cassette mechanisms	1				1
Car stereo	1				1
Plastic parts				1	1
Electrical parts	1				1
Capacitors/ceramic filters	1				1
Connectors		1			1
Packaging	1				1

This reflects one of the main problems the suppliers are confronted with: the ever-increasing production costs, which is very much related to the availability and cost of labour. Though about half of the establishments have engaged in process automation

118

to alleviate this problem, production processes are in many cases still characterized by high labour intensity and low value-added. The size of the establishments in terms of number of workers varies substantially (from as low as 24 to as high as 990, the average number of employees was 235 and about three-quarters of the establishments employed less than 300 workers), but all made use of foreign workers (mostly guest-workers from Malaysia) and all had reached the maximum allowed (40 percent). In view of the labour situation, most of the establishments were not expanding the facility. Rather, the opposite is already occurring in some cases and may become a trend in the near future.

In relation to this, the research revealed some significant phenomena. Firstly, besides attempts by a number of establishments to upgrade their operations by substituting products, the adoption of new process technologies and going into R&D, a substantial number of establishments (17 out of the 29, two-thirds of the Singapore establishments and half of the foreign establishments) in the course of the 1980s have engaged in contracting out activities. This involves either part of the production process or specific product lines. Operations performed by second tier subcontractors include injection moulding, subassembly, plating, metal cutting and manufacture of subcomponents. The second tier subcontractors are overwhelmingly located in Singapore.

Secondly, many suppliers have started to relocate operations out of Singapore. Table 6.9 shows that, so far, half of the total number of establishments (a majority of the Singapore establishments and somewhat less than half of the foreign establishments) have relocated production out of Singapore. This gained momentum in the early 1990s and, as table 6.9 shows, more establishments will adopt this strategy in the years to come. Malaysia, Indonesia and China are the favoured countries for the relocation of production. The products are shipped back to Singapore for further processing and/or delivery the clients. However, in a number of cases the products are also delivered to local clients. This is related to the relocation of production by main producers and puts the remarks made above as to expansion strategies in context. We will return to this below.

Related to relocation, it can be observed that a significant number of establishments have set up one or more subsidiaries outside Singapore (table 6.9). The subsidiary establishments also make use of other subsidiaries of the parent company in the region for the purpose of relocation. So far eight of the 15 Singapore establishments and three of the 12 Japanese establishments have set up one or more subsidiaries outside Singapore, mostly in Malaysia and Indonesia. As relocation will continue in the years to come, it is to be expected that more establishments will internationalize. Subsidiary establishments have been set up even though no relocation of production has taken place yet. This most reflects the fact that internationalization is an outcome also of expansion strategies which (necessarily) have assumed a regional scope. In relation to this, it was observed that the factors underlying internationalization are twofold. One factor, mentioned in the majority of cases, is similar to the main reason why the main producers engaged in relocation, the limited availability and increasingly prohibitive cost of labour in Singapore (cost push).

Table 6.9
Relocation of production and internationalization of suppliers

ID	Origin	Subsidiary	Own subsidiaries No	Location	Relocation Product(s)	Year	Location	Future relocation Product(s)	Year	Location
1	S'pore	yes	-	-	Cassette mechanisms	1991	Malaysia	Injection moulding	1997	China
2	USA	yes	-	-	-	-	-	-	-	-
3	S'pore	no	1	Malaysia	PCB ass.	1994	Malaysia	-	-	-
4	S'pore	yes	1	Malaysia	PCB ass.	1991	Malaysia	-	-	-
5	Japan	yes	-	-	-	-	-	-	-	-
6	Japan	yes	-	-	-	-	-	-	-	-
7	UK	yes	-	-	Metal components	1993	India	-	-	-
8	S'pore	no	-	-	-	-	-	-	-	-
9	S'pore	yes	1	Malaysia	-	-	-	-	-	-
10	S'pore	no	-	-	-	-	-	-	-	-
11	Japan	yes	2	Malaysia Indonesia	Speakers	1988 1991	Malaysia Indonesia	Speakers	1995	China
12	S'pore	no	4	Malaysia Indonesia Japan	Cassette mechanisms	1988	Malaysia	-	-	-
13	Japan	yes	-	-	-	-	-	PCB ass.	1995	Malaysia
14	Japan	yes	1	Singapore	Injection moulding	1994	China	-	-	-
15	Japan	yes	-	-	-	-	-	-	-	-
16	S'pore	no	1	Malaysia	Audio ass.	1994	Malaysia	-	-	-
17	Japan	yes	-	-	Ceramic capacitors	1993 1994	Thailand Malaysia	-	-	-
18	S'pore	yes	1	Malaysia	PCB assembly	1989	Malaysia	PCB/audio assembly	1995	China
19	Japan	yes	-	-	-	-	-	Assembly electrical parts	1995	Malaysia
20	S'pore	no	-	-	-	-	-	Injection moulding	1995	Malaysia
21	S'pore	no	-	-	-	-	-	-	-	-
22	Japan	yes	1	Indonesia	Assembly car audio parts	1991	Indonesia	-	-	-
23	Japan	yes	-	-	-	-	-	-	-	-
24	Japan	yes	3	Malaysia	Assembly parts home audio	1988 1993	Malaysia Malaysia	-	-	-
25	Japan	yes	-	-	Magnetic heads	1992	China	-	-	-
26	S'pore	no	-	-	-	-	-	Metal parts	1995	China
27	S'pore	yes	1	Indonesia	PCB ass. testing	1990 1993	Indonesia Indonesia	-	-	-
28	S'pore	no	-	-	-	-	-	Injection moulding	1995	Malaysia
29	S'pore	no	3	Singapore Malaysia Vietnam	encasings	1993	Vietnam	-	-	-

The second factor is market expansion and the following of clients in order to stay in the market, maintain market share, or on request of the client (market pull). Thus, as suggested above, relocation by the main producers — and the fact that the expansion of the branch now takes place elsewhere in the region — has an impact on the spatial strategies pursued by the suppliers in Singapore. To illustrate this point we may briefly refer to some findings of a different study carried out recently in the southern State of Johor, West Malaysia, which borders Singapore. This study pertained to the local linkage patterns of recently established MNC operations. Two cases can be brought to the fore here as examples: Aiwa Electronics and Matsushita Audio Video. Both transplants are relocation cum expansion facilities, in relation to the transplants in Singapore. Though these transplants had started operation only a few years ago, they had already developed substantial linkages with local suppliers.

A. Aiwa Electronics

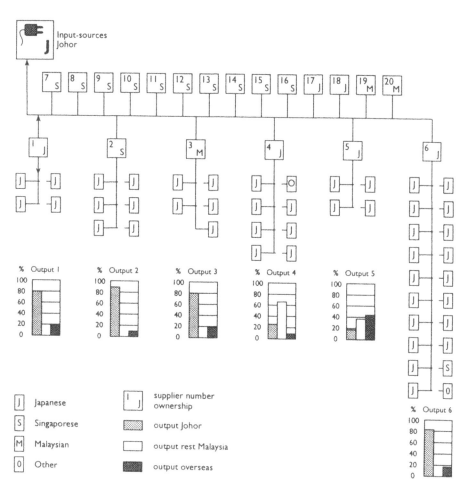

B. Matsushita Audio-Video

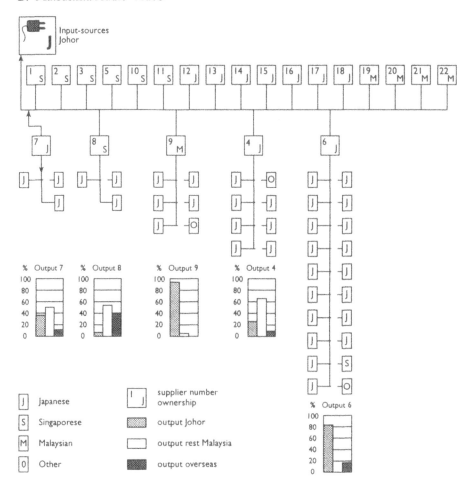

Figure 6.1   **The local backward linkage structure of two audio main producers in Johor, West Malaysia**

Source: van Grunsven, L., C. van Egeraat & S. Meijsen (1995)

As figure 6.1 shows, Singapore companies played a significant role in the local
supply structure (the bottom half of the figures shows the other clients of some selected suppliers). They were all branch plants of local supply firms in Singapore. They
had come to Johor after the shift of the main producers, in order to maintain supply
links. At the same time they are able to supply to other main audio producers in the
region as well as ship supplies to clients in Singapore. Thus, the cost factor is not
totally irrelevant to the market-pull type of relocation/internationalization.

The interviews made clear that in some cases relocation had resulted in a significant scaling down of operations in the Singapore facility. This may become a trend too, given the expectations for the future expressed by the plant managers. Most of them stated that in the near future the neighbouring region will be much more important for the operations of the establishment and company than Singapore. If expansion does take place, this will occur outside Singapore. Only a minority of the managers (eight out of the 29) stated that production in Singapore would definitely be continued. Thus, the focus of operational strategy in the future will be regional rather than local. In the last section of this chapter some possible or likely implications of the findings presented above as well as of the observations which have been made will be indicated. This will be followed by some concluding remarks on the position and role of the national state.

Some comments on implications

The findings presented above with respect to main producers of audio equipment in Singapore (all of which are transplants of MNCs) appear to be in line with what has been postulated in the recent literature on strategic firm responses to the triggers of restructuring. Additional insights have been obtained by including the supplier segment of the industry branch in the analysis. The research which is reported in this chapter departed from the assumption that in Singapore at this stage this segment might very well be also involved in a restructuring process. This has proven to be the case.

In addition to the changes observed with respect to the main supplier segment, fundamental changes are also observed in the patterns of operation of the supplier firms. The findings reveal not only that these patterns currently are quite dynamic but also that they will remain dynamic for some time to come. Thus, indeed there seems to be no *a priori* reason why the supplier segment in the course of time should not also feel the imperatives of restructuring. What implications can be derived from the dynamics observed?

In this chapter the focus is on the spatial and organizational aspects of the behaviour of firms, in the process of adopting strategic responses to the imperatives of restructuring, and the implications for the global-local dimensions of the production system. It has been argued in the introduction that production systems in the recent past have undergone substantial change, associated with a localization trend, resulting in the growth of a substantial localized supplier segment in the production system. It appears, or at least seems, that currently both the main producer segment and the supplier segment of the production system are affected. The main producer segment is involved in a process of upgrading, yet lacks any capacity for local expansion. Expansion implies operation on a regional basis, as reflected in the regionalization trend which enables more cost-effective operation through relocation. A similar observation can be made with respect to the supplier segment. The findings indicate that the dynamics within this segment is such that it becomes less localized.

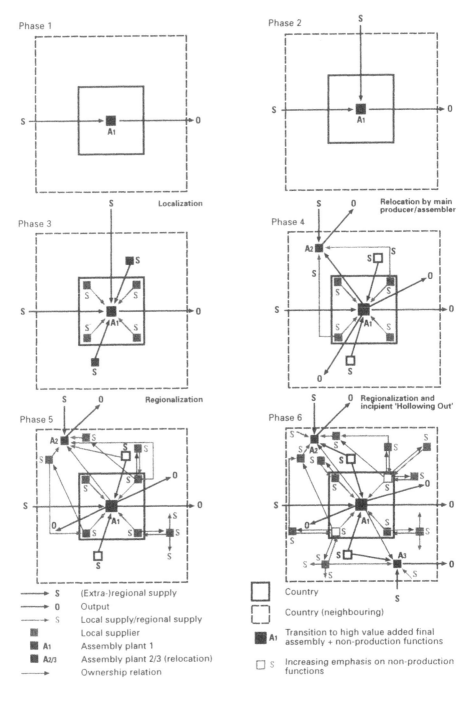

Figure 6.2   The regionalization of Singapore's audio production

Regionalization is a striking new course the supplier segment has taken. Whether the dynamics will result in the gradual disintegration of the localized supply segment remains to be seen. However, a more regionalized supply structure seems to be in the making, after a phase of the development of a localized supply structure. The overall process is depicted schematically in figure 6.2. The global dimension remains, and the global-local configuration seems to be transformed into a global-regional-local configuration (from the perspective of the main producers). This may not necessarily have any consequences for 'local content'.

Thus, in the process of restructuring, the production system and localization appear to be reshaped. However, possible implications for the patterns of production organization are not so clear-cut. More research is needed on this, though it might be postulated that, since much of the spatial shift is to cross-border locations in relative proximity, patterns of production organization are not significantly altered as yet. Indeed, the fact that many supply establishments which have set up operations in Malaysia have done so in the southern state of Johor might have been 'inspired' by the necessity to maintain supply arrangements and contact. However, this has yet to be firmly established.

The relocation by main producers and the market pull responses of suppliers, coupled with the main prospect of contraction of local production in the supply segment (rather than stability) also because of the cost push, may imply that for the near future hollowing out of the branch as a whole is a possibility which may turn into reality. It may be noted here that, overall, the findings reveal changes which conform to those observed in other segments of the electronics industry in Singapore (Natarajan and Tan, 1992). Likewise, the observations with respect to the supply segment of audio production appear to be applicable to local supply firms in other electronics branches. This can be derived from the 14 case descriptions of the internationalization of Singapore companies presented by Lee Tsao Yuan in a recent publication (Lee Tsao Yuan, 1994). In other words, the findings appear to conform to what is occurring elsewhere in the electronics industry (and the other way around). However, the most recent data available do not as yet, at the macro level (the industry), indicate a hollowing out (going by employment trends etc.). This may change in the near future as tendencies towards hollowing out already discernible at the micro level (particularly it seems in the supplier segment) are becoming more widespread.

It is questionable whether this will, in any way, concern the Singapore government who in the late 1980s explicitly endorsed and started to encourage the strategic responses of — local — firms by adopting a regionalization policy (the regionalization phenomenon itself however predates this policy and it is questionable whether the process would have evolved differently without the policy). The government considered that on the positive side local companies would increasingly concentrate their Singapore operations on higher value-added activities, in line with the objectives of its overall economic policy, and its policy towards the manufacturing sector in particular. As argued by Lee Tsao Yuan (1994), a successful outcome of this strategy may well be constrained by human resource limitations. It is one of the tasks of the state to remove these constraints. There are other implications for the economy and nation state involved on the negative side which the government may not have fully considered. Restructuring is a process, the course and outcome of which should — in the view of the Singapore state — be positive and confirm its ability to 'engineer' and 'control' processes of change. As to the implications for the economy, the course and outcome of restructuring may leave Singapore with a diminished level of integration within and between industries. This would be an outcome which is the opposite of the cluster development which the industrial policy in the 1990s aims to achieve. As to the implications for the nation state, it is clear that — given also the autonomous character of much of the regional behaviour of firms — control of and giving direction to the processes of change more and more require policies and actions at supranational level by agencies suited for this task. However, while national clusters of industries may gradually be hollowed out, this does not necessarily mean that the nation state faces the same prospect.

References

Brannon J.T., James, D.D. and Lucker, G.W. (1994), 'Generating and Sustaining Backward Linkages Between Maquiladoras and Local Suppliers in Northern Mexico', *World Development*, Vol. 22, No. 12, pp. 1933-45.
Clark, G.L. and Kim, W.B. (eds) (1995), *Asian NIEs and the Global Economy: Indus trial Restructuring and Corporate Strategy in the 1990s*, The Johns Hopkins University Press: Baltimore.
Economic Development Board (1993), *Report on the Census of Industrial Production 1991*, Economic Development Board, Research and Statistics Unit: Singapore.
Fuentes, N.A.F., Alegria, T., Brannon, J.T., James, D.D. and Lucker, G.W. (1993), 'Local Sourcing and Indirect Employment: Multinational Enterprises in Northern Mexico', in Bailey P., Parisotto, A. and Renshaw, G. (eds), *Multinationals and Employment. The Global Economy of the 1990s*, International Labour Office: Geneva.
Fujita, K. and Hill, R.C. (1995), 'Global Toyotaism and Local Development', *International Journal of Urban and Regional Research*, Vol. 19, No. 1, pp. 7-22.
Ho, K.C. (1993), 'Industrial Restructuring and the Dynamics of City-State Adjustments', *Environment and Planning A*, Vol. 25, No. 1, pp. 47-62.
Ho, K.C. (1994), 'Industrial Restructuring, The Singapore City-State, and the Regional Division of Labour', *Environment and Planning A*, Vol. 26, pp. 33-51.
Kenney, M. and Florida, R. (1993), *Beyond Mass Production. The Japanese System and its Transfer to the US*, Oxford University Press: New York.
Kenney, M. and Florida, R. (1994), 'Japanese Maquiladoras: Production Organization and Global Commodity Chains', *World Development*, Vol. 22, No. 1, pp. 27-44.
Ki, S.L. and Wu, C.T. (1993), 'Industrial Linkages Within an Export Processing Zone: A Case Study of the Masan EPZ in Korea', *Journal of Geography Education*, Vol. 29, No. 6, pp. 1-10.

Kim, W.B. (1993), 'Industrial Restructuring and Regional Adjustment in the Asian NIEs', *Environment and Planning A*, Vol. 25, No. 1, pp. 27-46.

Lee, T.Y. (1994), *Overseas Investment: Experience of Singapore Manufacturing Companies*, Institute of Policy Studies/McGraw-Hill: Singapore.

Le Heron, R. and Park, S.O. (eds) (1995), *The Asian Pacific Rim and Globalization*, Avebury: Aldershot.

Lui, T.L. and S. Chiu (1994), 'A Tale of Two Industries: The Restructuring of Hong Kong's Garment-Making and Electronics Industries', *Environment and Planning A*, Vol. 26, pp. 53-70.

Natarajan, S. and Tan, J.M. (1992), *The Impact of MNC Investments in Malaysia, Singapore and Thailand*, Institute of Southeast Asian Studies: Singapore.

Park, S.O. (1994), 'Industrial Restructuring in the Seoul Metropolitan Region: Major Triggers and Consequences', *Environment and Planning*, Vol. 26, pp. 527-41.

Van Grunsven, L. (1994), 'Industrial Change in Southeast Asia: New Spatial Patterns of Division of Labour', in Custers, G. and Stunnenberg, P. (eds), *Processes of Incorporation and Integration in Developing Countries*, Nijmegen Studies in Development and Cultural Change 16, Verlag Breitenbach Publishers: Saarbrücken, pp. 65-103.

Van Grunsven, L., C. van Egeraat & S. Meijsen (1995), New Manufacturing Establishments on Industrial Estates in Johor and Regional Economy: Labour Characteristics and Linkages. Final Report of Research Findings. Department of Geography of Developing Countries, Faculty of Geographical Sciences, Utrecht University, The Netherlands.

7 Paths of Development in the Japanese Automotive Industry

Changing Competitiveness and the Just-in-Time System

Bo Terje Kalsaas

Introduction

A rich literature has emerged addressing social and industrial development connected to Japanese automotive transplants in Western countries, especially those in the USA and the UK. There are also several reports on how Western manufacturers — have to — adapt to the Japanese way of organizing the labour process, whether it is termed just-in-time production, lean production, agile production or something else (Sugimori et al., 1977; Sheard, 1983; Sayer, 1986; Womack et al., 1990; Kenney and Florida, 1993; Kalsaas, 1995). However, over the last decade there has been less research providing a geographical and social perspective on the present situation and likely trends in this area in Japan, while broadly speaking US and maybe also European car makers have caught up with Japanese productivity (*Financial Times*, 20 April 1995; Ingrassia and White, 1994). Moreover, costs in Japan have risen significantly due to the further appreciation of the yen since 1990 (*The Economist*, 4 March 1995). Also, imports of cars made by non-Japanese producers are increasing. And what about the question of globalization? The largest Japanese car makers have probably the necessary economic strength to reap the benefits of globalization. Such a strategy, however, is in conflict with the spatial organization of just-in-time production, as we know it from Toyota City, if globalization also includes production of OEM (Original Equipment Manufacturing) parts and components. In addition, there is a surplus domestic production capacity for cars in Japan. Already in 1995, the surplus domestic production capacity of Toyota Motor Corporation alone amounted to 700,000 to 800,000 units (*Financial Times*, 11 May 1995).

There are certainly changes that threaten jobs in Japan and encourage Japanese car makers and other export industries to go abroad and increase their production in existing overseas plants. Toyota raised car production in the USA by almost 50 percent in 1996, and will double the capacity of its Burnaston plant in Derbyshire by 1998. Nissan's Zama plant was closed in 1995 and has been turned into a pre-delivery inspection centre for imported Ford vehicles. Nissan has also closed down an engine factory in Kyushu (*Financial Times*, 6 October 1995). In 1995, Toyota considered its first permanent domestic plant closures (*Financial Times*, 11 May 1995). New Toyota plants have been started up in Australia and Turkey, and expansion is planned for Taiwan and Thailand.

A main question that presents itself — and highlighted in this chapter — is how this new situation is being addressed by the Japanese automotive industry in Japan itself and whether the just-in-time production system is affected. This chapter presents findings of empirical research which entailed a detailed study and analysis of eight automotive plants, namely (1) Toyota Motor Corporation (TMC): the Tsutsumi plant, Toyota City, Aichi Prefecture; (2) Nissan Motor Co. Ltd.: the Oppama plant, Oppama, Kanagawa Prefecture, Tokyo urban region; (3) Toyoda Tekko Co. Ltd. (Toyoda Iron Works): the Honsha plant, Toyota City, Aichi Prefecture; (4) Aisin Keikinzoku Co. Ltd., Shinminato-City, Toyama Prefecture; (5) Ikeda Bussan Co. Ltd., the Oppama plant, Oppama, Kanagawa Prefecture, Tokyo urban region; (6) Kansei Corporation: the Omiya Plant, Omiya, Saitama Prefecture, Tokyo urban region; (7) Unisia Jecs Corporation: the Atsugi plant, Atsugi, Kanagawa Prefecture, Tokyo urban region; (8) F-Tech Inc., the Kuki Plant, Minami Saitamagun, Saitama Prefecture, Tokyo urban region. Plants 3 and 4 are affiliated with the Toyota group, plants 5 to 7 are affiliated with the Nissan group, and plant 8 is a Honda supplier. The location of the plants is shown in figure 7.1.

Table 7.1
Domestic production by the selected Japanese automotive producers, 1994

	Cars	Trucks & Buses	Total
TMC	2,769,359	739,097	3,508,456
Nissan	1,341,406	216,715	1,558,121
Honda	849,799	147,927	997,726

Source: JAMA (1995)

The final assembler cases differ as to production volume, and thus also in terms of market strength in relationship to the end user and supplier markets. The domestic production volumes of Toyota, Nissan and Honda in 1994 are shown in table 7.1. Data collection, through in-depth interviews conducted by the author in the period January-March 1995, focused on paths of development, relationships between subcontractor and final assembler, competitive strategy, time compression in production chains and locational aspects. These aspects reflect the frame of reference which was developed and employed to study the question referred to above. The presentation in this chapter draws heavily on Kalsaas (1995).

Figure 7.1   **Location of the automotive plants studied**

Framework

Possible path of development

Leborgne and Lipietz (1992) argue that there are two principal pathways of development of industrial relations out of the crisis of Fordism. The first pathway is a transition from the rigidity of Fordism to the flexibility of 'neo-Taylorism' (external labour market), while the second pathway evolves from direct control in Fordism towards involvement in 'Kalmarism' (internal labour market). 'Toyotism' is a third pathway that allows for a coexistence of the two principal pathways within a dualistic labour market. Toyota's production system is the paradigmatic example of Toyotism.

130

Direct control of labour represents a pattern that does not fully take advantage of worker skills and learning capability. Direct control therefore contrasts with autonomy of workers, a necessary condition for involvement and full use of talent. A rigid labour market is characterized by strict labour regulations, imposing limitations on exploiting overtime, temporary workers, etc., and compliance with national regulations as to job security, length of vacation, minimum wages, etc. This contrasts with a flexible external labour market, where capital has greater freedom to exploit labour.

Kalmarism represents the solution to involvement negotiated at society level, as exemplified by the Scandinavian welfare-state model of development. In Toyotism and in Japan, workers' involvement is negotiated at the firm level. The flexibility of capital in the neo-Taylorism path implies a low level of job security for workers, an obstacle to collective involvement. However, individual involvement is possible although it contradicts with the collective nature of a labour process. It can only be enhanced if the individual is regarded as a producer. The principal path of neo-Taylorism is associated with the political ideology of liberalism, as found in countries such as the USA, UK and France.

It is claimed that involvement negotiated at the firm level is gaining ground. It appears to be optimal for capital as the intelligence of workers on the shop floor is used, while at the same time external flexibility, e.g. a co-existence of core workers enjoying life time employment and temporary workers, is achieved. There is little room for capital to create a path combining flexibility in capital-labour relationships with collective involvement. Workers in a normal situation are not likely to cooperate in devising new arrangements which will render them in part redundant. In a just-in-time oriented production system, workers' involvement is crucial in order to cope with the highly time-compressed labour processes and the crucial dependence on quality.

Supplier-principal firm relationships

In the relationships with their OEM suppliers, final assemblers have to make a choice between subcontracting and quasi-integration based on partnership and trust, or a top-down relationship based on direct orders.[1] Partnership assures involvement by subcontractors, which is less likely to be achieved by direct orders, at least in a Western cultural context.

There is a similarity in the dimensions of quasi-integration, external flexibility and internal involvement in industrial relations. Vertical quasi-integration and external flexibility in the labour market are means for the principal firm to increase surplus value on the basis of direct control over workers and suppliers. The horizontal dimension represents some autonomy for workers and suppliers, which is a prerequisite for involvement and higher functional flexibility and efficiency. Moreover quasi-integration is cost minimizing à la Williamson, while vertical quasi-integration is revenue-maximizing only for the principal. Oblique and horizontal quasi-integration (partnership) are revenue-maximizing for the whole network.

131

The option chosen is also influenced by the cultural context within which the firm operates. For instance it is more likely to find relationships based on partnership in Scandinavia than in the USA due to differences in political culture (i.e., social democracy versus liberalism). A principal firm in the Toyotism path of development is likely to subcontract routinized work to flexible firms based on just-in-time supply and thus needs strong involvement by suppliers in order to succeed. There is no doubt that partnership constitutes the basis for involvement over time, even though the principal firm is the dominating agent and the subcontractors are the dominated ones.

The capital-capital relationship and competition

Competition requires firms to employ strategies aimed at improving their competitive position. Competition is regarded to be a fundamental factor driving the technology dynamism of capitalism (Asheim, 1985). Schoenberger (1987) identifies three important elements in competitive strategies. The first element is product design. The second — related — element is the firm's approach to the market. This may be perceived as either stable, homogeneous and standardized, or as unstable and highly differentiated. The third element is where firms seek to locate production, emphasizing either price or non-price factors.

The element of design is undoubtedly a feature of just-in-time production, where rapid change of models is emphasized. Moreover, a perception of the market as differentiated, emphasizing relatively flexible consumption, goes to the very heart of just-in-time in post-war Japan, characterized by shortage of capital and a domestic demand for a large number of different motor vehicle brands and models (Cusumano, 1985). A emphasis on non-price factors as to location of basic operations also appears to be a feature of just-in-time production and is consistent with the historical tendency to put economies of scope above economies of scale in Japanese automobile production.

Time has increasingly become more significant in strategies of firms. This is the case in turnover of car models, in the process of developing new models, and in production. In the concept of competition time may be incorporated into the value of the product, and thus some firms are not selling a tangible product but rather the logistics of it. Just-in-time production is noted for the general time compression of activities in the production chain, e.g. measured by throughput time and supply lead time in the relationship between producing agents.[2]

Furthermore, customer response is an important parameter of competition in the automobile industry. In the concept of manufacturing to order, customer response refers to the time span between the order placed by the end user and delivery of the product with the requested specifications. Again, this implies that all the linkages in the production chain have to be time-compressed, and in the case of just-in-time without keeping stock that drives up costs. This grows in importance in a production chain offering a large variety of product compositions, since the diversity leads to a rapid growth in the number of components with the same function.

132

In the JIT-production paradigm two superior operative perspectives are perceived. Social organization, or methods and techniques, are geared towards reduction of all types of waste (reduction of costs, e.g. working hours, capital for machines and tools, inventory in stock, buffer and process, manufacturing space, etc.); and flexible response to changing demand of diversified products, i.e. customer orientation (Kalsaas, 1995). Derived from these two main operative principles is the principle of fast, continuous and small lot production with the continuous search for best practice, which requires collective involvement of workers, as well as integration of suppliers in the principal firms' production system. In addition, one expects to find increased outsourcing of non-core production and services in order to cut costs, reduce risk and enhance flexibility. Increased outsourcing is also a strategy that increases capacity in existing plants without huge new investments. At the same time, in order to cut transaction costs, the principal firm is expected to put effort into reducing the number of suppliers by designing vehicles with fewer components (increased subassembly) and by making more parts interchangeable across models (increased standardized platforms). For the same reason, a tendency towards organizing the supplier base in tiers is expected.

Attributes regarded as core aspects related to the principle of fast, continuous and small lot production are (1) small batch production of diversified products and customer orientation; (2) time compression of all linkages and processes in the production chain, including response time to end users; (3) minimized stock and buffers; (4) increased quasi-integration and integration of suppliers with principal firms' production; (5) emphasis on total quality control; (6) priority for suppliers that are located in the area.

Location

The Japanese automotive industry is renowned for its just-in-time production system. It is widely argued in the literature that this has increased the agglomeration forces between final assemblers and subcontractors:

The new relative importance of short time distance in goods transport as a locational factor in just-in-time production is confirmed in the investigated cases. The locational forces are thus increasingly gravitating towards the main customers. This is particularly the case for component systems required to be supplied in sequence and synchronized with final assembly. (...) Establishing terminals and buffers in the proximity of final assemblers to substitute for too remote location for sequential just-in-time supply is confirmed to be commonly utilized. Nearby location of either terminal or production is a necessary condition for sequential just-in-time supply. How close is close is a relative question though. The time distance in this regard does not seem to be limited by the technical relationships in production, but rather by the need to being able to handle minor or larger disturbances to assure stable supply to final assembly. Disturbances do occur despite the routinized pattern in the relationship between subcontractors and final assembler (Kalsaas, 1995).[3]

TMC's production complex in Toyota City is particularly famous in this regard. Here several final assemblers are agglomerated (Takeuchi, 1971). A strategy which emphasizes neo-Taylorism in industrial relations is consistent with a strategy of putting standardized production above diversified production since the former does not require the same level of involvement of labour. Standardized production is consistent with a strategy that emphasizes price factors over non-price factors in location. Moreover, neo-Taylorism is consistent with a strategy of principal firms that gives priority to vertical quasi-integration above horizontal relationships with subcontractors. The latter aspect is in line with a global sourcing strategy that puts price before anything else, as long as the quality of parts is sufficient. Manufacturing to order from end users is difficult in a neo-Taylorism path since the production chain is likely to be organized globally. This imposes severe restrictions on the ability to compete in the area of fast customer response of customized products (Kalsaas, 1995). Transport of finished vehicles by sea transport across continents might add 30 extra days in customer response. This implies that final assembly should be located on the same continent as the market place.

Kalmarism and Toyotism in industrial relations are consistent with a competitive strategy which perceives the market as differentiated and emphasizes non-price factors to price factors in location. In these paths the principal firm is likely to favour horizontal quasi-integration to vertical integration in their relationships with subcontractors. These also are the preconditions for competing on the basis of production of customized products.

In the case of Toyotism in industrial relations, which combines involvement of core workers with numerical flexibility through temporary workers, it is possible for final assemblers to combine vertical and horizontal quasi-integration. This can be done for different parts according to the required involvement of subcontractors, e.g. in components where subcontractors have a leading edge in terms of technology. The supplier base thus can be divided into a group of development partners (specialist and supplier subcontracting) and a group which serves the role of capacity subcontracting (Chaillou, 1977; Holmes, 1986). Following on from this, it is possible for final assemblers to adopt strategies that combine local sourcing of components, developed in co-operation with development partners, with global sourcing, exploiting differences in costs across space.

Global sourcing implies that location of suppliers, in terms of logistics and time distance, is rather irrelevant. However, such a sourcing strategy can be employed within a framework of internationalization, which is qualitatively different from globalization. Internationalization refers to the extension of production activities across national borders, whereby the international economy is primarily based on nation states as the main organizing units (i.e. territorial integration). Globalization refers to a change towards functional integration of dispersed activities organized by and within TNCs, which implies a globalized economy (Asheim, 1994; Dicken, 1992). According to Lamming (1989), true global operations are a reality only for a handful of assemblers while component suppliers often have very comprehensive global operations, both in manufacturing and parts distribution. This leads Lamming to conclude that it is likely that commercial benefit from use of low cost countries is derived mainly from the achievements of the first tier suppliers, not the assemblers themselves.

Possible pathways of development

Functional flexibility on the factory floor appears to be present in the investigated cases, but is not as comprehensive and systematic as expected. Nissan's Oppama plant has no system for job rotation to create multi-skilled workers. Instead, the Nissan respondent referred to an annual procedure whereby employees are promoted and transferred to new tasks, partly based on their talent. Upper management has to circulate in the company to gain experience in production, sales, design and engineering. This is a criterion for promotion. Aisin Keikinzoku, a subcontractor in TMC's production chain, moves workers to busy lines from less busy ones, but does not apply job rotation.

For some of the lines at the Oppama plant, an arrangement has been introduced whereby workers follow the same car for part of the line and thus perform several operations. The arrangement was implemented in an effort to diversify the work on the lines. Regarding skills, it takes three weeks' training to become a specialized assembly worker, according to the respondent at Nissan's Oppama plant. It was expected that TMC would be the case that most systematically creates multi-skilled workers by job rotation, as this is crucial for varying the number of workers on the lines according to demand. The data confirm that TMC trains the workforce to handle several operations, but rotation of jobs take place 'basically one time per year', but this is 'very flexible'.[4]

All cases use shifts and overtime to achieve numerical flexibility. Nissan's Oppama plant operates two shifts (day and night) six days a week. Between the two shifts there is a break of three hours at both ends; the agreement between the union and management allows two hours overtime at each side. This enables production according to schedule, but is important also for absolute increase of production. Nissan's Tochigi and Kyushu plants operate two shifts as well, but the night shift ends at 2.00 a.m., with two hours available for overtime. This is explained by less demand for the models produced in these plants.

TMC operates day and night shifts more or less in the way Nissan's Oppama plant does. It has opted for a continuous shift system during day and night. This means a loss of numerical flexibility, but 'saves extra pay for night' as the respondent put it. The night shift is scheduled to stop at 1.00 a.m. According to the respondent at TMC's headquarters in Tokyo, this was explained by reduction in demand and of activity in Japan. In response to international criticism of long working hours, TMC decided to cut annual working hours to 1,891 from 1,952. According to the *International Herald Tribune* (14 February 1995), the reduction does not affect production since the 15 minutes reduction per day is achieved through shorter lunch breaks.

As a rule, subcontractors follow the shift system and pattern of work of their main customer(s). In the investigated subcontractor cases, utilization of overtime varies from virtually none to 50 hours per month. In one case where overtime was at a maximum, the respondent stated that workers make 50,000-80,000 yen extra per month from this. Further, it was claimed in another case that overtime is welcomed by the workers. One young white collar respondent believed that if he refused to work overtime this might hurt his career sometime in the future.

Both Nissan and TMC have an extensive welfare system for their employees. Nissan operates a hospital in Yokohama that is open to the public when there is capacity. The Oppama plant has accommodation available in the form of 400 flats for families and 1,000 for single persons. The monthly rental for a family flat is 11,000 yen, which is comparable to the market price. The subcontractors investigated have their own welfare systems, independent of final assemblers. However, in one case, a Nissan subcontractor shared the welfare system with that of Nissan. The headquarter and one of the branch plants of this subcontractor, Unisia Jecs, are located in Atsugi, one of Nissan's R&D hubs. The welfare systems of most other subcontractors are probably less developed than that of final assemblers.

In all cases workers are paid a fixed salary; bonuses and seniority play a crucial role in the wage system. Nissan tried to change the system based on seniority into one emphasizing individual capability and productivity. However, in this it met with strong resistance from the union. Reduction of the salary paid to the eldest workers has a severe impact on pensions. These could be reduced by as much as 50 percent, since these are calculated on the basis of earnings at maximum seniority. At Nissan wages do not increase anymore after 55 years of age, the retirement age in Japan before it was increased to 60. Seniority accounts for 70-80 percent of wages at TMC, the remainder is remuneration of capability and productivity. Toyota also wants to put more emphasis on individual skill in determining wages. However, in the case of blue collar workers it is difficult to measure. At Unisia Jecs, salary consists of a fixed component based on seniority and a variable component determined by individual capability. Kansei has recently changed its system, reducing the seniority share of salary to 40 percent and increasing the individual capability share to 60 percent. For Aisin Keikinzoku 90 percent of salary is paid out on the basis of seniority. Four of the investigated suppliers pay their employees a bonus each year, varying between 5 and 6 months of salary. Bonuses are determined by the profit of the company.

Regarding job security, both TMC and Nissan offer life time employment. The system appears to be under pressure from management. This is possible as employees do not have an official contract garanteeing life time employment. However, in practice this is difficult to change. When Nissan closed down the Zama plant in 1995, none of the employees were laid off. TMC operates with a large surplus capacity, as referred to earlier, without laying off employees. All subcontractor cases provide life time employment for core workers, no changes in the system are envisaged.

Nissan stopped hiring temporary or seasonal workers some years ago. Also TMC does not employ temporary workers because of the recession in the Japanese economy and as it wants to increase overseas operations. Several of the cases utilize temporary workers to achieve numerical flexibility which is necessary because of demand fluctuations. Thirty percent of the work force of Honda supplier F-Tech are workers from Brazil and Peru, employed on 6-month contracts. All Japanese workers have life time employment contracts. In many cases, the contracts were extended, some several times.

In both Nissan's Oppama plant and TMC's Tsutsumi plant, workers on the assembly lines are males, and they appear to be young, in their so-called 'best age'. However, the average age of the 5,400 employees in the Tsutsumi plant is 37.3 years. On average, they have 15.8 years of service. This could express the loyalty of workers to the company. According to Takeuchi (1990), it does not indicate a closed employment system. TMC warmly welcomes employees previously employed at other companies. In contrast to TMC, Nissan historically has a closed employment system. Employees recruited from other companies have difficulties in making a career: "*No matter how eagerly they work, they are just ninja under the elite of samurai*" (Takeuchi 1990, p. 178). For this reason, Nissan has a chronic lack of talented employees and therefore intends to change the employment policy.

To conclude this section, the necessary involvement related to numerical flexibility is confirmed, but the level of functional flexibility of workers was not as expected. The seniority basis of salary (conceived to be crucial for involvement) was under pressure, with larger emphasis on individual performance. Moreover, the findings indicate negative changes in another factor impinging on involvement, namely job security. Nissan has ended the system of using temporary workers to increase numerical flexibility, but other cases do exploit this to the fullest. In several cases, South American workers make up the temporary work force. It is clear that the scale on which temporary workers is used is affected by the macro-economic situation of Japan. However, differences in this respect are also related to the competitive position of cases and of the capital groups to which they belong. The pattern of Toyotism, with a mix of internal and external flexibility, is confirmed but the case data indicate a movement in the direction of external flexibility and less weight being put on what is conceived to be crucial for involvement. Thus a movement in the direction of neo-Taylorism has become apparent.

Subcontractor — final assembler relationships

Sourcing strategy

Nissan and TMC outsource extensively, both to affiliate subcontractors (in which the final assembler has an equity participation of 20 percent or more) and to independent firms. Nissan has about 400 suppliers for all its models, the Oppama plant has 150 suppliers for the three models manufactured. TMC's Tsutsumi plant has 130 first tier suppliers for the six models which are assembled here. Moreover, several second tier suppliers deliver directly to the plant. A total number of 240 direct suppliers was mentioned by the respondents. It was observed that one of the three receiving areas was designated to 64 suppliers, with specific timetables for delivery. In the case of Aisin Keikinzoku, 4 percent of output is supplied directly to TMC's automotive operations and 71 percent via a first tier supplier. All parts are invoiced via the first tier supplier.

TMC confirmed that the number of suppliers has increased over the past few years. This is due to overseas imports; the number of domestic suppliers has remained virtually constant. According to TMC's purchasing department, the increase is not substantial. When the number of suppliers increases, so does the complexity of the production chain. TMC tries to avoid this. The increase of the number of suppliers was explained by the trade dispute between the USA and Japan. TMC describes its sourcing strategy as 'value sourcing' which refers to integration of several car parts into components.

Both Nissan and TMC close sourcing contracts for the duration of the lifetime of car models. Kansei and Unisia Jecs unambiguously confirmed this. Ikeda Bussan's respondent stated that contracts are negotiated every year and that costs are the most important factor in the negotiations. Aisin Keikinzoku has lifetime contracts. The Honda supplier F-Tech negotiates all contracts annually.

In the process of selecting subcontractors, Nissan requests about five companies to produce parts for testing on the basis of its specifications, and selects one or two of these. The testing of parts goes all the way to line production before the final selection is made. Some Nissan subcontractors carry out R&D. Nissan, like TMC, also requests suppliers to participate in the development of new components.

When Ikeda Bussan is assigned new subcontracting work by Nissan, it arranges meetings at an early stage prior to model change. After Nissan has given a target cost, Ikeda Bussan makes an offer. It is not an open competition, but Ikeda Bussan's respondent pointed out that Nissan has three suppliers capable of producing and delivering complete seats. The respondent thought there might be open competition in the future when the *keiretsu* supplier networks are dismantled. In the case of Kansei, personal relations play an important role in the negotiation of contracts. Some contracts involve competitive bidding, others are negotiated without competition. Unisia Jecs takes part in the development of new components from the design stage by proposing solutions to technological issues. Other suppliers are involved at this stage as well. After Nissan has selected the technology, supply shares are negotiated. These negotiations are very important as economies of scale are involved. TMC also uses a sort of competition, whereby two or three firms are invited to submit proposals for producing new components. Price negotiations take place at an early stage in the process. F-Tech and Honda jointly carry out R&D for components. In-house testing is carried out by F-Tech, while outdoor testing in cars is carried out by Honda. F-Tech carries the costs of R&D as it knows it will get the business in the end.

Nissan has no fixed policy as to using single, double or multiple sourcing. This is decided on a case by case basis. In the case of Ikeda Bussan, external single sourcing is practised at the Oppama plant, but in combination with in-house production. Unisia Jecs is the sole supplier of pistons for Nissan's passenger car engines, but for most of Unisia Jecs' products Nissan practises dual sourcing. In contrast to Nissan, TMC has an official policy of purchasing identical parts and components from two or three suppliers. This encourages competition in terms of costs, production time and creativity. Regarding overseas suppliers, TMC started off by having at least one domestic supplier in addition to overseas suppliers, to guarantee delivery. This policy has since been abandoned. TMC now has over 140 subcontractors in the USA (Toyota Motor Corporation, 1994).

To some extent, outsourcing is still combined with in-house production. For example, as to Nissan's Oppama plant the production of seats for one of three lines is outsourced, while the other two lines are supplied by in-house production. A respondent of Nissan claimed this to be a special case motivated by the need to provide employment to part of its female workers. The seat subcontractor's version of this arrangement is that Nissan wants to maintain hegemony in seat technology. This subcontractor, Ikeda Bussan, also supplies Nissan with parts for its in-house production of seats; in turn, Nissan purchases parts from some of the firms which supply Ikeda Bussan. Ikeda Bussan is the sole external supplier of complete seats to the Oppama plant, as mentioned. In the case of the other Nissan assembly plants there are additional suppliers. Ikeda Bussan and one of its competitors supply Nissan's Kyushu assembly plant with seats from a joint venture facility located in the vicinity of Nissan's operations. Ikeda Bussan uses imported leather for some seat covers. Nissan coordinates the import from the USA and thus some of the material supply of the subcontractor.

Keiretsu supply network

One hundred and twenty of 150 subcontractors to Nissan's Oppama plant have a capital relationship to Nissan. Besides capital relationships, there is the confirmed practice of Nissan and TMC to make engineers and managers available to the subcontractors. A respondent at Nissan's headquarters claimed that the *keiretsu* supplier network no longer exists, and that partnerships are now based on technological capability and personal relationships. However, the manager of one of Nissan's subcontractors perceived his company to be included in Nissan's *keiretsu* supplier network, emphasizing cultural features of loyalty, control and power in the relationship between suppliers and final assembler (Brøgger, 1993; Kalsaas, 1995).

Nissan generally deploys managers and engineers to its subcontractors. This was not perceived by the subcontractors as the client exercising control, but rather as support from a partner. The same occurs further upstream the actual production chains. Nissan owns 60 percent, 30 percent and 30 percent of the equity of Ikeda Bussan, Kansei and Unisia Jecs respectively. Subsidiaries or affiliates of Nissan own an additional 43.5 percent of Kansei's equity. In the case of Unisia Jecs, 55 percent of the equity is owned by relatively small shareholders (1.9-3.0 percent each) who

139

maintain a friendly relationship with Nissan. Five percent is owned by another Nissan supplier. Furthermore, 9 of 12 members of the board of Kansei and half of the members on Unisia Jecs' board are affiliated with Nissan.

Regarding dependence on one or few customers, 90 percent of Ikeda Bussan's output is sold to Nissan; Kansei and Unisia Jecs sell 89 percent and 80 percent respectively of the output to Nissan. The remaining 10 percent of output of Ikeda Bussan is purchased by Honda and Mitsubishi. Kansei has Isuzu, Mazda, Mitsubishi and Honda among the customers of its operations in Japan, while Unisia Jecs has Mitsubishi, Isuzu, Suzuki, and several other Nissan companies in the customer base. The data for Toyoda Tekko are more limited in this regard, but it was confirmed that the company is controlled by TMC through ownership, and the president is a former TMC employee. Ninety-eight percent of output is purchased by customers in the Toyota group; TMC purchases 80 percent. The subcontractor is participating in a Toyota study group with the aim of implementing *heijunka*.[5] Fifty subcontractors have signed up to participate in the group.

Aisin Keikinzoku is owned by the Toyota group; TMC's equity participation is 40 percent. Aisin Seiki, member of the Toyota group, and TMC purchase 81 percent of output. Most of the other customers are also members of the Toyota group or affiliates of TMC, but the customer base includes Mitsubishi, Mazda and Suzuki as well. Aisin Seiki is a first tier supplier to TMC plants of parts supplied by Aisin Keikinzoku. Of total output, 10 percent is supplied directly to TMC, even though Aisin Keikinzoku is a second tier supplier of these parts.

Honda purchases 90 percent of F-Tech's output, Mitsubishi 5 percent and Suzuki less than 1 percent. F-Tech is a sole supplier to all of Honda's operations overseas and in Japan. Honda owns 20 percent of the equity, the founder family 50 percent, employees 10 percent, the remainder is held by several small shareholders. Honda wants to reduce its equity share in F-Tech. Though it has no members on the board, Honda participates in the meetings and two board members are retired Honda employees. Honda has no engineers or managers deployed at F-Tech, but one engineer is a retired Honda employee.

Generally, the history of the subcontractor-customer relationship goes back to the entry of these firms in the automotive industry. The same customers have been served throughout. However, several firms have a strong intention to capture new customers, across *keiretsu* boundaries, and to establish a foothold in other industries as well. Kansei is developing new products for other industry branches, an effort which is encouraged by Nissan's board members. Unisia Jecs aims to be a supplier to the Toyota group. The strategy is first to be a supplier to a Toyota first-tier supplier or to Daihatsu (a friend of Toyota). F-Tech, already a supplier of Honda, seems to succeed in becoming a second supplier of Nissan. Its goal is to be less dependent on Honda. A first step towards this aim is the reduction of Honda's share of output to 70 percent, leaving 15 percent for other car manufacturers and 15 percent for other production. The second step will be the reduction of Honda's share to 50 percent. F-Tech is supplied with some electrical parts by a Toyota subcontractor. This relationship will be terminated as it has to pay up to 10 times more than TMC for identical parts.[6]

It is easy to conceive that the *keiretsu* pattern of supplier network is a hindrance to doing business with competitors of the principal firm. Kansei tries to solve this by keeping the cost structure of subcontracted work for competitors of Nissan a secret. A respondent at TMC's headquarters in Tokyo strongly emphasized the mutual benefits to suppliers and TMC, pointing to the loyalty of TMC to its suppliers (and dealers). TMC makes no secret of which companies supply TMC as a whole. However, data are not available as to which suppliers do business with which TMC factory. This has to remain a 'black box' for the suppliers.

Tiering and wages

Suppliers offering lower wages compared to final assemblers was confirmed in some cases. Two of Nissan's first tier suppliers claim that their salary level is 90-95 percent of that of Nissan. This leads to social tensions. The respondent at Aisin Keikinzoku, a second tier supplier to TMC, estimated the indexed wage level to be 100, compared with 130 for first tier suppliers and 150 for TMC. Partly, this reflects differences in wage levels between regions in Japan. The first two cases referred to above are located in the same part of the Tokyo region as Nissan's main final assembly operations, while the latter is located on the Sea of Japan side.

To conclude this section, when analyzing the Japanese supplier-final assembler relationships in relation to the quasi-integration concept, the control exercised by the principal firm is apparent. It seems like the principal firm is in a position to fix a price that transfers the value added achieved by the subcontractor to the client. This is indicated by the strong control exercised through ownership, but also by the practice of the final assemblers to deploy key employees at the first tier subcontractors. Thus, costs and technology are transparent at all levels. The Honda supplier case is an exception in this regard. The findings indicate that dual rather than single sourcing is common in the relationship between subcontractors and final assemblers. Particularly TMC appears to exercise strong control over their suppliers. This is confirmed by TMC's claim of the necessity to be in control over all aspects of automobile technology. Despite the factors of control and dual sourcing, the subcontractors appear to be very involved, skilled and creative in supplying their customers. The subcontractors appear to have guaranteed orders, which fits well with the idea of partnership.

Based on the analysis above, the concept of partnership versus direct orders and quasi-integration does not seem to explain the Japaneses cases in a satisfactory manner. It seems as if Nissan and TMC are able to orchestrate their production chains in a way that increases control, partnership, and competition in a Japanese way within a *keiretsu* supplier network, which apparently still exists. In the case of Nissan, however, it seems that the network is under pressure. Some of the data collected from the headquarters indicate that Nissan wants to change it. The fact that Nissan's suppliers are encouraged to add new customers to their customer base will further diminish the *keiretsu* network features. Nissan's attitude can also be caused by its

141

relatively more difficult business situation, which has led to the closure of the Zama plant and the decision to close down an engine factory in Kyushu (*Financial Times*, 6 October 1995). The fact that the *keiretsu* type of supplier network constrains access to the technology of other final assemblers could also be a motive to dissolve it. Companies which do not have the leading edge technology are most interested in change.

Finally, it is confirmed that the aspect of exploiting cheaper labour through the supplier network is still valid. The differences between final assemblers and specialist first tier suppliers have narrowed in recent years. The data also indicate that the wage differences cause irritation when firms are closely associated and located in close proximity.

Competitive strategy

Model cycle time

Nissan wants to extend the life time of models from 4 to 5 years. However, another respondent at Nissan considered the 4-5 year life time too short, and claimed that the company is rethinking how it can be further extended (changes to models could for instance not be as fundamental as it has been until now). This development is opposed by Nissan's dealers in Japan. They rather would like a shorter life time to boost sales. TMC's policy is to maintain the present four year model life time for passenger cars and six years for commercial cars. Effort is focused on further compressing the lead time of the development of new models. A development period of 25 months was mentioned.

Manufacturing to order and customer response

In the domestic market, both Nissan and TMC only produce to order. Particularly TMC emphasized the aspect of only producing to demand. Nissan and TMC's customer response time depends on demand and capacity. Nissan mentioned that the response time ranges from two weeks to 45-60 days for a best selling car, three weeks is the 'normal' response time indicating balance between demand and production capacity. It takes twelve days from the moment a car is ordered by a customer from a domestic dealer until it is on the assembly line. A completed car leaves Nissan after two or three days, including inspection and certification. However, cars are most frequently sold from dealer's stock.

Nissan cars produced for export to the USA are manufactured to orders received from Nissan Motor Corporation (NMC) in the USA; the USA dealers place the orders with NMC. In this case there is a four month customer response time.[7] However, because of stock and advance orders based on forecasted demand, customers do not normally have to wait that long. In the case of TMC, domestic dealers keep stock of best selling cars, otherwise the customer response time ranges from two to four weeks. The respondent at TMC's headquarters in Tokyo claimed that the delivery time was not a problem for Japanese customers. TMC's export system as to orders and organization appears to be rather similar to that of Nissan, according to the data. The customer response time seems to be somewhat shorter for end users who order cars that are not in stock in the USA. Thirty days additional response time to that of domestic orders was indicated by the respondent. Neither of the final assembler cases put in efforts to further time compress the customer response time.

Relationship to dealers

Nissan's domestic dealers order cars every day. Orders are based on the one hand on forecasted sales and on the other hand on actual car sales. The dealers are economically responsible towards Nissan for both forecasted and actual sales. Dealers can adjust orders relative to sales in such a way that it is often possible to operate with relatively shorter customer response than otherwise would be possible given the ordering system and technical limitations. After the dealers have placed their orders no changes are possible, unless it concerns a very special customer. TMC closes annual contracts with dealers. These are obliged to submit orders on a three month, one month and ten day basis to TMC. The ten day order is binding, and the monthly order is generally reliable. TMC has confidence in the dealers. It was further claimed that the Toyota dealers know what the customers want, and that dealers are loyal to TMC because they make a profit.

Differentiation of product

Nissan divides options in two categories: dealer options and factory options. Typical factory options are colour, seat cover, engine and wheel, while dealer options are map monitoring display, television, CD ROM, and baby seat. For Nissan's Cefiro model, 16 dealer options and eight body colours are available.

Nissan's respondents could not confirm that the policy is to reduce the number of options offered to end users. Some options have become standard, such as airbags. However, according to Nissan's supplier of complete seats to the Oppama plant, the number of seat variants has been reduced in order to achieve lower costs. There is also a tendency to make less radical changes to new car models, such that the same seats are kept in a new model.

TMC is reducing the number of model grades[8], colours and component variants, as well as the number of options for customers. The reason for this is that some of the options attract few customers. TMC began cutting costs in mid-1990 through 'value analysis', i.e. reducing manufacturing costs, 'value engineering', i.e. paring costs throughout the development process, and greatly reducing model variations (*Asahi Evening News*, 9 February 1995). By 1994, TMC had reduced the range of parts it uses in its cars by about 30 percent and model variations by about 25 percent (*Financial Times*, 8 February 1995). The additional aim is that at least 70 percent of parts in each new Toyota model was also used in the previous model (*The Economist*, 4 March 1995).

Nissan does not offer many options for cars in export markets, while TMC offers packets of options in export markets. These are configured and marketed as power packets, safety packets, and exterior packets. Some models can be delivered with up to 5 different packets.

To conclude this section, the development path of competition towards shorter model life time seems to have halted, and is even being rolled back somewhat. The data indicate that the leading Japanese auto maker TMC is aggressively putting effort into further time compression as to the development period of new models. Comparative data are not available for Nissan in this aspect. Manufacturing to order is the rule in the domestic market. However, dealers rather than customers place the orders guiding production. Fixed orders about one month in advance assure final assemblers of a relative stable demand allowing efficient production scheduling and smooth production.

Particularly TMC is in a process of reducing the level of differentiation, in terms of model grades and customer options. This means that consolidation and standardization is pursued fitting the concept of economies of scale. It implies a step back towards Fordism, or towards neo-Taylorism. If Toyota is not conciously applying the economies of scale concept, the results of its cost cutting strategy appear to be rather similar. Yet there are several indications of TMC following a path of economies of scale rather than economies of scope.

Time compression of the production chain

Both Nissan's Oppama plant and TMC's Tsutsumi plant have mixed production schedules in final assembly. It is more mixed in the Tsutsumi case (seven models on two lines) compared to the Oppama plant (three models on three lines). Nissan's throughput time is one shift (about eight hours net), including body assembly, painting and final assembly. Throughput time in final assembly is four to five hours. The speed of the line is equivalent to approximately 55 cars per hour. Nissan uses 14 man-hours to produce a middle class car such as the Bluebird. Comparative figures for TMC are not available, but it was pointed out that throughput time is determined by the level of automation, models, and demand. The respondent particularly emphasized the demand aspect, which is related to the aspect of multi-skilled workers discussed earlier.

As to stamping of body parts, Nissan produces batches for one week of production. This fits with the production planning system whereby the production schedule is fixed one week prior to assembly. The stamping shops have a single *kanban* ordering point. Nissan and TMC keep no stock, except for imported materials. In the case of Nissan's Oppama plant, a three week stock of imported materials is kept.

The frequencies of delivery of outsourced parts and the length of time, parts and components are stored as line inventory, depends on how frequently particular items are used on the line which relates to the models and variants being assembled. For frequently used parts the supply frequency might be eight times per day and waiting time a few hours. At the other extreme rarely used components might be kept as line inventory for several days. TMC uses the *kanban* system for ordering parts and components. Nissan uses its own APS (Action Production System) for in-house material flow control. APS is comparable to TMC's *kanban* system. However, it is more computerized.

Related to the fixed production plans, Nissan's final assembly plants use a five-day supply lead time when ordering parts from subcontractors. The delivery schedules submitted to subcontractors stipulate which parts to deliver where and at which time(s) of the day. Nissan matches this relatively rigid MRP system by being flexible in assembly. In contrast to Nissan, TMC also applies *kanban* for external supply.

Both Nissan and TMC submit orders to first tier suppliers which, in addition to call-off by MRP or *kanban*, consist of forecasted need and notification or frame orders. Nissan's order system consists of parts showing expected demand for the next three months, the next month, and for the next ten days. This is updated daily. TMC's order system is also based on monthly and ten-day frames.

Just-in-time supply

Nissan and TMC practise sequential just-in-time only for complete seats and wheels. Earlier, batteries, windows, carpets and door trims, in addition to drive shafts and ceilings, were supplied this way to Nissan. In its terminology, this is the only just-in-time supply, even though the delivery frequency of the other categories could reach eight times per day. Nissan's seat supplier, Ikeda Bussan, earlier supplied the Oppama plant with ceilings in sequence. This ended in 1994 when Nissan decided to synchronize from in-house to save costs. Ikeda Bussan needed four persons on a full-time basis to synchronize the supply. Currently, Ikeda Bussan supplies ceilings eight times per day based on five-day orders. Also Unisia Jecs has ended its supply sequencing of drive shafts and suspension dampers to Nissan. During operation, Nissan issued a delivery order every 2.5 minutes. It was really hard work to handle these orders and rather impractical in view of the location of the Atsugi plant. It was thus forced to establish deposits in the proximity of the final assembly plants. Nissan is now also sequencing these parts from in-house. Ikeda Bussan is the only subcontractor among the investigated cases still supplying car assemblers sequentially. However, Kansei supplies the truck maker Nissan Diesel in sequence.

Except for sequential supply, Nissan's delivery frequency is individual according to parts and components. The bulk of actual supply frequency is two to eight times a day. Kansei's Omiya plant supplies Nissan's factories four times a day. Maximum frequency for components from Unisia Jecs' Atsugi plant is four times a day. Nissan has accepted a reduction of delivery frequency of materials that are utilized in small lots, as it cuts costs. The components are despatched from the Atsugi plant to Nissan half a day before assembly.

The delivery frequency to TMC's Tsutsumi plant is based on the demand signal communicated by *kanban*. However, when making up the numbers of *kanban* supplied in one batch, the basic idea is to fill up relatively small trucks. Some materials are delivered once a day three hours before they are needed. Some electrical parts from Nippon Denso and floor carpets could be delivered sixteen times a day, one hour before assembly.

TMC tries to increase the frequency of delivery in order to reduce the level of inventory. On the day of the visit to the Tsutsumi plant the maximum timetabled arrival frequency at one of the three receiving areas (comprising twelve platforms) was eleven times a day, minimum one and average five. The relevant data are presented in table 7.2. Each cell in the matrix represents the supply frequency for a particular subcontractor. The number of cells with data thus is equal to the number of suppliers designated to this receiving area. Sixty-five subcontractors were thus designated to the twelve platforms. The frequency data should not be confused with the frequency of individual parts, as not each truck load contains the same parts. The volume and number of variants of parts, and the sequence in which they are needed, determine this supply strategy. This was the case for both Nissan and TMC and is related to limited space at the lines.

Table 7.2
Time tabled supply frequency at TMC's Tsutsumi plant

# 1	# 2	# 3	# 4	# 5	# 6	# 7	# 8	# 9	# 10	# 11	# 12
8	4	1	6	6	1	10	8	4	8	4	6
8	6	4	4	4	1	10	8	4	12	1	6
4	4	4	5	6	6	2	4	11	4	1	2
4	6	4		2		2	4	4	6	4	1
1	8	4		2		1		6	2	4	1
6	1	4		4		6			1	10	4
						8					11

Variation in orders

According to a Nissan respondent, orders that do not follow routinized procedures are made about once per day at each factory. This happens because of misreading buffers, breakage at line, etc. The respondent at Kansei confirmed that emergency orders do occur, and for a batch of about 100 units the plant can handle a surplus of 20, since it always produces extra parts for stock. This was not identified as a problem by Unisia Jecs. It is able to handle a sudden five percent increase in demand. This is incorporated in the production plan. In the case of Aisin Keikinzoku, call-off deviates about ten percent from the three month notification. In the extreme, variance could be plus or minus 20 percent. Aisin Keikinzoku maintains stock in order to be able

146

to respond to fluctuations in demand. According to F-Tech's respondent, the orders that are not following the routine procedure are handled by maintaining some stock and by additional production which requires working overtime.

Suppliers' stock

Kansei is the only subcontractor case in the study that operates a warehouse and distribution centre. It was argued that this is necessary because of the flexibility and supply lead time demanded by Nissan, in relationship to thresholds in production. Kansei's Omiya plant on average maintains an inventory of finished components equivalent to the supply of 2.5 days. Ikeda Bussan has zero inventory of finished seats, but keeps an inventory of semi-finished parts. Unisia Jecs keeps stock of finished parts for one day of supply because of some remotely located customers operating with compressed supply lead time. Toyoda Tekko produces according to *kanban*, but the stamping shop at the upper end of the internal labour process runs batches that are larger than required for one shipment. The stock of finished parts at Aisin Keikinzoku varies from zero (complete aluminium windows) to more than a week's supply (castings in relatively small series). F-Tech operates with a stock of half a day supply.

JIT supply utilized by first tier subcontractors

Ikeda Bussan operates on just-in-time supply of most parts and materials. For example, rolls with material for seat covers are supplied two times a day. An exception is chemicals for seat foams which arrive in liquid bulk from Kyushu three times a month. Unisia Jecs issues call-off to suppliers two days prior to delivery. The bulk of parts is supplied once a day. This relatively low frequency is explained by small lots and an effort to keep transport costs low. The bulk of supply to Toyoda Tekko is delivered two to four times a day. Aisin Keikinzoku receives aluminium and aluminium alloys once a day based on *kanban* orders. In the case of F-Tech, delivery once a day is the maximum supply frequency. This involves four truck loads of steel from Nippon Steel in Chiba and two truck loads from a steel mill in Hiroshima arriving at F-Tech every morning on workdays. Other materials and parts are supplied with a frequency of two to three times a week.

To summarize, except for sequential just-in-time supply, there is a considerable difference between Nissan's Oppama plant and TMC's Tsutsumi plant as to the arrangement for ordering parts and components. Nissan operates on a five days' supply lead time, TMC operates *kanban*, implying a considerably shorter supply lead time. This is, however, dependent on how large *kanban* orders are. Supply lead time varies from a few hours in the case of the first tier subcontractor Toyoda Tekko, located nearby, to two to three days for the relatively remotely located and second tier subcontractor Aisin Keikinzoku.

The above difference seems to support the claim that — because of the traffic situation in Tokyo — Nissan is not utilizing just-in-time (Mair, 1992a, 1992b).

However, this claim is actually unfounded. Firstly, a supply arrangement that implies a frequency of small lots up to eight times a day is in accordance with the basic idea of just-in-time supply. Secondly, it is important to distinguish between the supply part of just-in-time and just-in-time production. Nissan is clearly practising just-in-time production, in view of the very limited line inventory. Thirdly, Nissan's ordering arrangement requires a delivery frequency comparable to that of TMC, irrespective of traffic density. A crucial point is that Nissan's arrangement offers more flexibility as to transport arrangements and reserve time for transport, in view of the relatively long supply lead time. This is also related to location, as Nissan's system allows the possibility of a more decentralized location pattern of subcontractors. Hence, remotely located agents may use a larger part of the five days' lead time for transportation, in which case production will be more time compressed.

Another important difference is, that Nissan's ordering system and the locational opportunities it provides to first and second tier subcontractors, exposes the final assembler to greater risk, even chaos, in case major external events lead to interruptions. The effect of the Great Hanshin Earthquake in Kobe-Osaka in January 1995 illustrates the point. A few days after the earthquake, Nissan's Oppama plant was substantially still behind production schedule, despite great efforts in catching up. The reason for this was that delivery to some first tier suppliers (from their suppliers in the Osaka area) was interrupted. The earthquake also led to disturbances in the EDI communication of orders to several suppliers. The Oppama plant tackled the problems by cutting overtime for a period. But due to what was in this sense a rigid ordering system, parts and components from unaffected subcontractors kept flowing into the plant. Piles of components could therefore be observed at the line a few days after the disaster. TMC's *kanban* system is more flexible under such circumstances as suppliers only deliver according to the phase in the final assembler's production.

The difference between Nissan and TMC, regarding the control of inward logistics, confirms that it is possible to apply several techniques in just-in-time supply. The data also indicate that sequential just-in-time supply has been rolled back in the case of both Nissan and TMC. One reason appears to be the costs associated with this supply arrangement. The data further indicate a change in the case of Nissan allowing less frequently used parts to be supplied at lower frequency and thus in larger lots. Subcontractors keep some stock for their customers. An important reason is the ability to meet unscheduled variations in demand, but remotely located customers and the available supply lead time are also reasons.

Locational aspects

Time distances in supply

Nissan requires subcontractors supplying in sequence to be located within ten minutes' driving time from the assembly plant.[9] The supplier of wheels to Nissan's Oppama plant has twenty minutes' driving time and the seat supplier, Ikeda Bussan, ten minutes. TMC's stand in this matter is that driving time should be within thirty to sixty minutes.

As tables 7.3 and 7.4 show, Kansei's Omiya plant is located 110 km from Nissan's Oppama plant (four hours' driving time), Unisia Jecs' Atsugi plant is located 50 km away (1.5 hours' driving time). The Omiya and Atsugi plants supply all of Nissan's final assembly plants and some other first tier suppliers of Nissan, since there is a high level of division of labour between the four and five plants of Kansei and Unisia Jecs. This differs from Ikeda Bussan, which produces complete seats in all their plants. There is, however, a specialization in particular seat parts which are distributed among the branch plants.

Table 7.3
Location of main consignees for Kansei's Omiya plant

Customer	Road distance (km)	Driving time by truck (hrs.)
Nissan Tochigi	70	3
Nissan Oppama	110	4
Nissan Murayama	55	1.5
Nissan Zama[1]	80	3.5
Nissan Kyushu	1,300	14
Nissan Shatai, Kyoto	540	9
Nissan Shatai, Shyonan	120	4

Note 1: closed in 1995

Table 7.4
Location of main consignees for Unisia Jecs' Atsugi plant

Customer	Road distance (km)	Driving time by truck (hrs.)
Nissan Zama	16	
Nissan Yokohama	59	1.5
Nissan Oppama	50	1.5
Nissan Murayama	139	2
Subaru Gunma	139	4
Nissan Tochigi	160	0.5
Aichi, Nagoya	350	5-6
Nissan Kyushu	1,121	12
Unisia Jecs Kyushu	1,200	12

The time distances shown in tables 7.3 and 7.4 should be seen in relation to the density of traffic in the Tokyo region. Kansei's Omiya plant's furthest customer is Nissan's Kyushu plant, which is supplied by trucks like the other customers. Unlike Kansei, Unisia Jecs has established a plant in Kyushu near Nissan. This plant is supplied by Unisia Jecs' plants in the Tokyo region, but Nissan's Kyushu plant is also supplied directly because of the division of labour and specialization among the branch plants.

Most of Toyoda Tekko's customers are located in Toyota City and the surrounding area. The driving time to TMC's Tsutsumi plant is ten minutes. For Aisin Keikinzoku, located on the Sea of Japan side, the main customers are located in Toyota City and Aichi prefecture. The road distance to Toyota City varies from 290 to 330 km depending on routing, which means 4 to 6 hours' driving time by truck.

Depots

Remotely located subcontractors have established depots in the proximity of final assembly, in order to prevent delays or interruptions in supply, e.g. a subcontractor of drive shafts and steering linkages, located in Akita, supplies the Oppama plant four to five times a day from a local depot. The maximum driving time in this supply category, acceptable to Nissan, is two hours. However, engines are supplied directly from a distance of six to seven hours' driving time, but this concerns a Nissan branch plant. About half of the suppliers to TMC's Tsutsumi plant are located within a 50 km radius (Toyota City and neighbouring area) of the plant; the remainder are located to the north and south along the expressways and highways. A few suppliers are located far away, such as in Tokyo, Kyoto and Kanagawa. Also some of TMC's subcontractors supply the assembly plants from depots, but this is discouraged as it increases costs and therefore the retail price for the customers. Neither Nissan, nor TMC concern themselves with the location of the subcontractors. They just require subcontractors to keep up with the delivery schedules. New subcontractors are selected on cost and quality considerations.

The location pattern of second tier suppliers

As to Ikeda Bussan's Oppama plant, half of the 100 subcontractors are located in the same prefecture. Some are located far away, e.g. harness components are produced by subcontractors located 300 km to the north of Tokyo and 1,000 km to the south. Remotely located suppliers are required to keep local depots, and three hours' driving time is considered to be the maximum distance for supply. Sixty percent of Kansei's subcontractors are located in the Tokyo region. Ten suppliers have established depots in the vicinity of the Omiya plant. The respondent regarded 200 km supply distance as unproblematic, especially when dealing with large companies. Half of Unisia Jecs' subcontractors are located in the same prefecture and almost all are located in the Tokyo region. Reliability in delivery and transportation costs are important considerations, besides quality, when selecting new suppliers. Toyoda Tekko has approximately 60 suppliers, almost all of which are located in Toyota City. Only raw materials are imported. Aisin Keikinzoku is further upstream in the production chain compared to the other subcontractors, and the location of suppliers is not considered to be important, only quality and cost. Almost all suppliers are located in the same prefecture as Aisin Keikinzoku, and all are domestic. The bulk of F-Tech's suppliers are located at a distance of 90 minutes' driving time or less. F-Tech has a few suppliers of small parts which are located on the Sea of Japan side. This is acceptable as the transportation costs of small parts is rather low. Generally, short distance is preferred in view of the importance of personal contact.

Increased import to Japan

Nissan confirmed that more materials would be imported in future, especially from the USA. The respondent stated that this is the policy of the Japanese government, not Nissan's policy. It is also caused by the appreciation of the Japanese currency. However, the respondent at one of Nissan's subcontractors claimed that Nissan wants suppliers to start purchasing from foreign countries. South Korea was mentioned as an possible country for setting up joint ventures. The respondent reasoned that this change follows from strategic considerations and that Nissan has the aspiration of becoming more global.

TMC has radically increased imports from the USA. It now imports about 150 different parts and components (Toyota Motor Corporation, 1994). The lead time is one to two months. Therefore, the ability to respond fast to changes in demand is very low. As to the impact of the import of components on the just-in-time system, in the case of overseas suppliers there is a rather low level of just-in-time supply. The increased imports are considered to improve quality and competitiveness in the US market. However, a respondent in the purchasing department also included the trade dispute between the USA and Japan in the explanation of the increased import. Several of the USA plants exporting parts to Japan from the USA are Japanese-owned. Increased import of parts is also confirmed to be the case for Honda Motors and Mitsubishi (Kalsaas and Takeuchi, 1996).

F-Tech has a plant in the Philippines where parts are produced for export to Japan. Forty percent of input material needed is shipped from Japan.

Location of final assembly

The location pattern of Nissan's assembly and engine plants and its suppliers shows a concentration in the Tokyo region, where the advanced machinery industry provides a resource basis (Takeuchi 1973, 1990). Until recently, Nissan had four car factories in the Tokyo region (Tochigi, Murayama, Zama and Oppama), plants for the production of engines and axle components in Yokohama and Kurihama, an engine plant in Iwaki, plants producing transmissions, transaxles, and steering components in Fuji and Kambara, and a plant for the production of axles and engine components in Tochigi. The Zama plant was closed in 1995.

Exceptions to the concentration in the Tokyo region do occur; Nissan has a joint venture car factory in Nagoya with Aichi Machinery Company, a branch plant in Kyoto (Nissan Shatai), and an engine and car factory in Kyushu, more than 1,000 km to the south of Tokyo. The establishment of the factory in Kyushu was motivated by the labour shortage in Tokyo, according to the respondent at Nissan's Oppama plant. In the late 1980s just seven percent of the parts were supplied to the Kyushu plant by local subcontractors.

The company town of Toyota City, thirty to forty kilometres to the east of Nagoya, is historically associated with just-in-time and the Toyota production system (Takeuchi, 1971). According to information provided by TMC, the company has ten plants and a head office in Toyota City. In three plants passenger cars are produced (Takaoka, Tsutsumi, Motomachi) and in one trucks and buses (Honsha). In the other plants, engines (Kamigo), chassis parts (Miyoshi), engine parts and chassis parts (Myochi), engines and exhaust emission control devices (Shimoyama), machinery, dies for casting and forging and moulds for plastics (Teiho), and electronic parts and components (Hirose) are produced. Furthermore, TMC has a car factory (Tahara) and wharf 60 km to the south of Toyota City. A considerable number of independent or affiliated automotive suppliers are located in the same area.

Toyota City is often referred to as a vertically disintegrated and spatially integrated production system (see e.g. Asheim, 1992). There can be little doubt about that, but it starts to be problematic if Toyota City is interpreted as the spatial configuration of Toyota's domestic production system. In 1992, TMC also established a car factory in Kyushu. Prior to this, in 1991 a branch plant was established in Tomakomai (Hokkaido) for the production of aluminium wheels, automatic transmissions, and transaxle cases. Thus, TMC's domestic production system is spread over a large part of the country. Furthermore, it was reported above that even the Tsutsumi plant in Toyota City receives only half of the outsourced parts from subcontractors located within Toyota City and Aichi prefecture.

Why has TMC spread its production system in this manner? It appears to create risk and uncertainty as to just-in-time supply, and thus to just-in-time production. According to TMC's respondent at the headquarters in Tokyo, the just-in-time solution for Kyushu is to keep line and transport inventory. It appears that the spread of investments to Kyushu and other areas outside the main cities is in accordance with the regional development policy of the Japanese government (Miyakawa, 1990). However, TMC's respondent denied that the Japanese government had played any role in the establishment of the Kyushu plant. It was stated that the main reason for the establishment was the shortage of labour in the Aichi prefecture. The findings regarding location for the domestic production system of TMC and Nissan are in accordance with a general pattern of an increasingly dispersed spatial pattern of car production in Japan (Kalsaas and Takeuchi, 1996).

To conclude the analysis in this section, except for the limited supply in sequence, the case data indicate a rather dispersed pattern of location of subcontractors and long transport distances. In the case of Nissan this is caused by the assembly plant in

Kyushu, located more than 1,000 km to the south of Tokyo. In many cases depots compensate for long supply routes. Nissan, and TMC in particular, are increasing imports of parts from the USA, which leads to rigidity in the just-in-time system because of the long transit time. This development moreover poses new challenges to TMC's logistics. It is not clear what role the Japanese government plays in this development, but it may be assumed that both the government (for political reasons) and the companies (for economic reasons) have an interest in increasing the import of car parts from the USA.

The data also indicate that Nissan is urging its subcontractors to import from countries such as South Korea. The underlying reason is the strategic importance of strengthening the global network. The Honda supplier F-Tech has established a plant in the Philippines to exploit cheap labour. This is in accordance with the firm's intensive exploitation of temporary workers, indicating a development path relatively close to neo-Taylorism, but based on involvement of a lifetime employed core work force.

Conclusion

The findings and analysis presented in this chapter indicate a development whereby the high level of job security for workers in Japan is under pressure, in combination with a pressure, as to remuneration, towards relatively less weight on seniority in favour of individual performance. This may constitute a threat to the involvement of workers and thus to TMC's pattern of the just-in-time concept.

The investigated first tier subcontractors are strongly controlled by the customers (final assemblers), but this appears to be combined with involvement and creativity. The control appears to be rather similar to that of branch plants. This can probably only be understood in the social context of the Japanese society. However, there is a potential fear that the dominating agents will pull the strings too tight in cost cutting at the expense of creative involvement.

Competition based on model life time has been halted and reversed somewhat in the case of Nissan, but time compression in model development appears to continue. The final assemblers are aggressively cutting costs and the differentiation of car models is rolled back; economies of scale is on the agenda. Dealers have to purchase cars on the basis of expected sales in the future, and there does not appear to be any serious competition on customer response time.

Nissan and TMC have significantly different concepts for ordering supply of outsourced work. Nissan operates with a relatively long supply lead time, and TMC uses time compressed *kanban*. Both have a supply frequency that is comparable and both apply just-in-time production. Nissan's system offers greater flexibility in terms of location and possible transport arrangements of the subcontractors. This does not appear to have been exploited so far; it is common that subcontractors keep some stock. Except for sequential supply, the findings indicate several relatively long transportation routes, which to some extent are compensated by operating depots in the vicinity of final assemblers. The import of car parts to Japan has increased significantly, and TMC operates huge warehouses for this purpose. It has also been established that subcontractors increasingly operate abroad, motivated by the desire to cut costs.

Available data show that production systems are increasingly dispersed across Japan. This is particularly the case for TMC. The main explanation seems to be the need to obtain access to new pools of labour. This started before the latest currency crisis, and might be halted by the forces leading to the moving of work and jobs abroad. The domestic spatial pattern may become even more dispersed depending on which factory or factories will be closed down in the future, for instance in Toyota City or in Kyushu.

Increased import of parts and increased spatial dispersion of the domestic production system leads to new challenges in logistics. The data indicate that more emphasis is put on cost effective transportation modes, such as sea transport, for relatively long and voluminous flows. This, and the tendency to globalize operations and increase imports from overseas, confirm that there are other relations and matters that are more important than keeping a just-in-time production system with zero stock intact.

Acknowledgement

It would not have been possible to conduct this study in Japan without the advice and assistance of Professor Takeuchi, Nippon Institute of Technology (NIT), the hospitality of NIT, and funding from the Sasakawa Foundation and the Research Council of Norway (Program for Transportation and Logistics Research — PROTRANS).

Notes

1. 'Quasi' in 'quasi-integration', refers to both the production process and valorization (Leborgne, 1987 and Laigle, 1989 quoted in Leborgne and Lipietz, 1992). Value added by the subcontracting firm is achieved by the principal firm via routinized interdependence between those two agents. Both forms depend on the productive complementary of their assets and skills. Quasi-integration minimizes both the costs of coordination, because of supplier's independence, and transaction costs, following from routinized just-in-time transactions between the firms. However, there are important differences between different types of quasi-integration. The two extremes are 'vertical quasi-integration' and 'horizontal quasi-integration', an intermediate type concerns 'oblique quasi-integration'. In the first case, the principal firm has the knowledge of the subcontractors at its disposal through a standardized (but OEM) product, or as a result of disintegration of the principal firm. Hence, the principal firm is in a position both to induce the

supplier to invest with little guarantee of continuous orders, and to contract at a price that transfers to it value, added by the subcontractor. In the second case, a supplier with specific technology establishes links through a strategic alliance with a regular customer of another sector in the division of labour. Oblique quasi-integration is most common, and the more horizontal the link, the better the bargaining power of the supplier, but also the more R&D in its product.

2. The throughput time, or total cycle time, in production of tangible commodities refers to the accumulated time for handling orders, production planning, internal transport, assembly, and shipment of finished goods. Within a production unit, this refers to the time which elapses from receipt of a production order until the product is dispatched to a customer. Supply lead time refers to the time which elapses from issuing a call-off to a supplier until the ordered materials are received at the defined location for unloading (Kalsaas, 1995).

3. Sequential supply refers to a supply arrangement whereby unique items are supplied in sequence and fully synchronized with the final assembly process. The Swedish term for this phenomenon is used here. In Japan, Nissan, Toyota, Honda and Mitsubishi denote the arrangement as synchronized supply. The other conceptual category of just-in-time supply refers to parts and components needed for one day of production, or less, according to demand. Compared to warehousing of parts, this just-in-time supply concept achieves an inward materials flow that is more in accordance with how the production is performed, though less synchronized than sequential just-in-time. In its most relaxed pattern, this is defined to include the concept of, for instance, European sourcing where just-in-time is somewhat diluted in order to accommodate suppliers within an extended trucking radius. However, this just-in-time supply concept may also include external supply with a frequency of several times per day, e.g. controlled by *kanban* as is the case for TMC (Kalsaas, 1995).

4. Letter, dated January 31, 1996, from TMC to the author.

5. Heijjunka means distributing volume and specifications evenly over the span of production (Toyota Motor Corporation, 1992).

6. Information provided in 1995 by Professor Takeuchi, Nippon Institute of Technology, Saitama-ken.

7. For a car to be delivered to a customer in the USA in the second half of month N, this car has to be ordered early in month N-4, included in the batch of cars ordered by NMC that month. Production is subsequently carried out by Nissan in Japan in month N-3. The product is shipped and transported in month N-2. The shipment is received in different ports in the USA in month N-1 and distributed to dealers in the first half of month N.

8. Grades refers to categories like IX, EX, X, etc., which mainly indicate differences to the interior.

9. See note 3.

References

Asheim, B.T. (1985), 'Capital Accumulation, Technological Development and the Spatial Division of Labour: A Framework for Analysis', *Norsk geogr. Tidsskr.*, Vol. 39.

Asheim, B.T. (1992), 'Flexible Specialisation, Industrial Districts and Small Firms: A Critical Appraisal', in Ernste, H. (ed.), *Regional Development and Contemporary Industrial Response: Extending Flexible Specialisation*, Belhaven Press: London.

Asheim, B.T. (1994), 'The Small Firm Squeeze: Globalization, Flexibilization and the Power of TNCs', Paper presented at the Workshop on 'The Changing Boundaries of the Firm', European Management and Organisations in Transition (EMOT), European Science Foundation, Villa Olmo, Como, Italy, 21-23 October 1994.

Brøgger, J. (1993), *Kulturforståelse: En Nøkkel til vår Internasjonale Samtid*, N.W. Damm & Søn A/S: Oslo.

Chailou, B. (1977), 'Definition et Typologie de la Sous Traitance', *Revue Economique*, Vol. 28, No. 2, pp. 262-85.

Cusumano, M.A. (1985), *The Japanese Automobile Industry: Technology and Management at Nissan and Toyota*, Council on East Asian Studies, Harvard University Press: Cambridge, MA.

Dicken, P. (1992), *Global Shift: The Internationalization of Economic Activity*, 2nd ed., Paul Chapman Publishing: London.

Holmes, J. (1986), 'The Organization and Locational Structure of Production Subcontracting', in Scott, A.J. & Storper, M. (eds), *Production, Work, and Territory: The Geographical Anatomy of Industrial Capitalism*, Allen & Unwin: Boston.

Ingrassia, P. and White, J.B. (1994), *Comeback: The Fall and Rise of the American Automobile Industry*, Simon & Schuster: New York.

Japan Automobile Manufacturers Association (JAMA) (1995), *The Motor Industry of Japan, 1995*, JAMA: Tokyo.

Kalsaas, B.T. (1995), *Transport in Industry and Locational Implications: 'Just-in-Time' Principles in Manufacturing, Generation of Transport and the Relative Impact on Location*, PhD Thesis, Department of Town and Regional Planning, Norwegian Institute of Technology, University of Trondheim.

Kalsaas, B.T. and Takeuchi, A. (1996), 'A Comparative Study of Developments in the Japanese and Scandinavian Car Industry', Paper presented at the 28th International Geographical Congress, Commission on the Organisation of Industrial Space, The Hague, August 5-10, 1996 (Reworked draft).

Kenney, M. and Florida, R. (1993), *Beyond Mass Production: The Japanese System and Its Transfer to the USA*, Oxford University Press: New York.

Lamming, R. (1989), *The Causes and Effects of Structural Change in the European Automotive Components Industry*, International Motor Vehicle Program, MIT: Massachusetts.

Laigle, L. (1989), *La Réorganisation du Réseau des Équipmentiers de l'Industrie Automobile: de la Sous-Traitance au Partenarit*, Diplôme d'Etudes Approfondies Univ., Paris VII, mimeo.

Leborgne, D. (1987), *Equipements Flexibles et Organisations Productives: les Relations Industrielles au Coeur de la Modernisation. Eléments de Comparison Internationale*, Mimeo, Centre d'Etudes Prospectives d'Economie Mathématique Appliquée à la Planification (CEPREMAP).

Leborgne, D. and Lipietz, A. (1992), 'Conceptual Fallacies and Open Questions on Post-Fordism', in Storper, M. and Scott, A.J. (eds), *Pathways to Industrialization and Regional Development*, Routledge: London.

Mair, A. (1992a), 'Just-in-Time Manufacturing and the Spatial Structure of the Automobile Industry: Lessons from Japan', *Tijdschrift voor Economische en Sociale Geografie*, Vol. 83, pp. 82-92.

Mair, A. (1992b), 'New Growth Poles? Just-in-time Manufacturing and Local Economic Development Strategy', *Regional Studies*, Vol. 26.

Miyakawa, Y. (1990), 'Japan Towards a World Megalopolis and Metamorphosis of International Relations', *Ekistics* 340, January/February.

Sayer, A. (1986), 'New Developments in Manufacturing: The Just-in-Time System', *Capital and Class*, Vol. 30, pp. 43-72.

Schoenberger, E. (1987), 'Technological and Organizational Change in Automobile Production: Spatial Implications', *Regional Studies*, Vol. 21, No. 3, pp. 199-214.

Sheard, P. (1983), 'Auto-Production Systems in Japan: Organisational and Locational Features', *Australian Geographical Studies*, Vol. 21, No. 1, pp. 49-68.

Sugimori, Y., Kusonoki, K., Cho, F. and Uchikawa, S. (1977), 'Toyota Production System and Kanban. The Materialization of Just-in-Time and Respect for Human Relations', *International Journal of Productivity Research*, Vol. 15, No. 6, pp. 553-64.

Takeuchi, A. (1971), 'The Automobile Industry in Toyota City', *Tohoku-Chiri*, 4-10, pp. 193-203 (in Japanese).

Takeuchi, A. (1973), *The Machinery Industry in Japan*, Taimeido: Tokyo (in Japanese).

Takeuchi, A. (1990), 'Nissan Motor Company', in De Smidt, M. and Wever, E. (eds), *The Corporate Firm in a Changing World Economy*, Routledge: London.

Toyota Motor Corporation (1992), *The Toyota Production System*, International Public Affairs Division, TMC: Toyota City, Japan.

Toyota Motor Corporation (1994), *Synergy: Toyota's Partnership with American Suppliers*, pamphlet, Summer 1994.

Womack, J.P., Jones, D.T. and Roose, D. (1990), *The Machine that Changed the World*, Rawson Associates: New York.

8 Local-Global Networks of High-Technology Industrial Districts in Korea

Sam Ock Park

Introduction

During the last three decades, the organization of industrial space in the global space economy has changed significantly due to technological changes, changes in production organization, and global shifts in competitive advantages (Piore and Sabel, 1984; Scott, 1988, 1992). The emergence of various types of new industrial districts whose industrial networks extend locally and globally has been one of the distinctive features of the changes in the organization of industrial space (Park, 1996). Several new industrial cities have developed in Korea during the last two decades. These new industrial cities can be regarded as certain types of new industrial districts in the context of the developing world. Major forces behind the formation of new industrial districts and competitive advantages in Korea are not based on the Western concept of industrial districts related to the flexible specialization school (Park and Markusen, 1995). Since the end of the last decade the new industrial districts in Korea have been restructuring by extending local and global networks in order to maintain or regain their competitive advantages.

In this chapter the industrial networks of the new industrial districts in Korea are analyzed: local networks in production, services, and technology on the one hand, and global networks through strategic alliances, direct investments, and joint R&D projects on the other. Two industrial agglomerations in Kyeonggi and Kumi are compared in terms of industrial networks. Interviews and questionnaire surveys were conducted with firms in the electronics industry in order to investigate their spatial industrial networks and industrial restructuring strategies.

New industrial districts and their competitive advantages

Based on the spatial linkages, three basic types of new industrial districts (NIDs) — Marshallian, hub and spoke, and satellite NIDs — have been identified in recent studies (Park, 1996). In the Marshallian NIDs, there are extensive local suppliers and customers' networks and only limited non-local networks. Small firms dominate, and are locally embedded and interconnected with each other as customer, on one hand, and supplier on the other. In the hub and spoke NIDs, the hubs dominate the local economy and they have both extensive local and non-local networks, while spoke and mainly small firms have strong linkages to hub firms. The transactions between hubs and local small firms are somewhat hierarchical. The satellite NIDs have extensive non-local suppliers and customers' networks with only limited local networks and can be easily found in developing countries or the peripheral regions of industrialized countries.

The three basic types are not static but change over time as networks become more complex and with changes in the production organization in order to maintain or enhance competitive advantage in the national and global market. This is possible because firms may restructure their organizations or change their network relationship with customer firms and supplier firms with the passage of time. Some of the small firms grow into large producers, some establish networks with large firms or are taken over, and some may face problems to survive, while new spin-offs or a generation of technological entrepreneurs can appear (Dunford, 1991). Moreover, through the ongoing process of industrialization and regional industrial strategies in order to gain or maintain competitive advantage, the characteristics of a local labor market and firms' behavior can be changed. These changes may contribute to the evolution of a local industrial culture which may direct firms' organizational culture. Such changes in the local industrial culture and firm' organizational culture can have an effect on the changes in networks and embeddedness of firms in the new industrial districts.

Marshallian industrial districts can develop into 'advanced hub and spoke' industrial districts with the rise of large firms which have global networks and embeddedness. External economies of scale and scope in the districts based on local production linkages, collaboration and cooperation are major competitive advantages of the Marshallian industrial districts. Savings in sunk costs with utilization of a flexible local labor market and local industrial environments can also be regarded as advantages of the Marshallian industrial districts. However, the competitive advantages of external economies based only on local networks can be vulnerable to external shocks and severely competitive global markets. It may be necessary for large firms in the district to maintain competitive advantages through the internal economies of scale and scope. Large firms can be formed by vertical or horizontal integration of small firms through mergers and acquisitions, or successful growth of innovative firms in the districts. The large firms can extend production networks and collaboration beyond the local boundary to the international level. As Appold (1995) suggests, the local agglomeration may be neither necessary nor sufficient to engender enhanced performance or competitive advantage. External economies also exist in the advanced hub and spoke new industrial districts with the development of close networks between large hub firms and small firms, and the continuation of interfirm relations among the existing small firms within the districts.

In the hub and spoke type, competitive advantages are mainly based on the internal economies of scale and scope of the hub firms because the industrial district type has only limited local external economies. This hub and spoke type can develop into the 'advanced hub and spoke' district when the reinforcement of competitive advantages are necessary by means of the external economies in the districts, resulting in the development of local networks and embeddedness. Consequently, spin-offs and local interfirm collaboration can be the main forces responsible for the change of the hub and spoke type into the advanced hub and spoke type. The participation of local entrepreneurship in spin-offs and collaborations among the small firms can be encouraged with the support of public and private organizations of the region. Collaboration among the small innovative firms as well as between large and small firms in the districts can change the local industrial culture, and can be a basis for regaining their regional competitive advantages. Satellite-type NIDs can also evolve into 'mature satellite' industrial districts with the increase of the intensity in local networks and embeddedness of new firms and spin-offs. The satellite industrial district, whose competitive advantages initially lay in factors such as cheap labor and land, may not continue to maintain its original competitive advantages with the advance of industrialization. The competitive advantages of the satellite industrial district also depend on economies of scale which are internal to firms but external to the district. The impact of the satellite industrial district on regional development is, however, limited because of insufficient local linkages. As such, local governments and public institutions will certainly promote local networks and embeddedness in order to increase regional development effects and to regain or maintain competitive advantages of the satellite industrial district. Spin-offs and contract-out activities of the branch plants can enhance interactions between large branch plants and locally embedded small firms. Collaboration between large firms and small firms in the districts can be a basis for maintaining or regaining competitive advantages.

Advanced hub and spoke industrial districts can progress into the 'pioneering high technology' industrial districts with the development of locally networked innovative small firms' industrial systems. In order to maintain or gain competitive advantages in the advanced hub and spoke industrial district, innovative firms should enhance local collaboration and production networks, on the one hand, and promote a global network of suppliers and customers with close collaboration in technology and marketing development, on the other. It should be noted that the competitive advantages of the pioneering high-technology industrial districts are related to technology innovation, innovative entrepreneurs, local and global networks and collaborations in production, and easy access to local producer services. Diversified demand conditions, agglomerations of related and supporting industries, and firms' strategy and rivalry in the districts affect the region's competitive advantages most of all.

However, it should be noted that not all industrial district types can develop into advanced types in their dynamic patterns. Marshallian industrial districts can decline without enhancing performances because of failure to restructure as regards competitive advantages. Many clusters of traditional industries in the developing countries have disappeared or declined without further progress of industrial districts. Without further progress of local networks and successful collaborations, the satellite and hub/spoke industrial districts can deteriorate and thus, cannot evolve into the advanced types. Without innovative collaboration at the local and global level, the advanced hub and spoke types cannot transform into the pioneering high-technology industrial districts. If we regard the Marshallian industrial district as a symbol of traditional canonical industrial district, the pioneering high-technology industrial district can be regarded as a symbol of the modern industrial district in the era of high technology and globalization.

Industrial policy and new industrial districts in Korea

Since the First Economic Development Plan was launched in the early 1960s, the national government has played a critical role in achieving industrialization and economic growth in Korea. The emergence of new industrial districts has been the joint product of the national government's industrial and regional development strategies.

The government's industrial strategy was fashioned to promote the most promising industries at any given stage. In the 1960s and early 1970s, labour-intensive industries such as textile and apparel were favoured, while in the 1970s heavy and chemical industries including shipbuilding, petrochemicals, automobiles, and consumer electronics were the target industries. Since the early 1980s, technology-intensive industries have been increasingly favoured. The pursuit of these sectoral policies has had significant effects on the spatial distribution of industries in Korea (Park, 1990). Export-oriented industrial policy focusing on labour-intensive industries up to the early 1970s resulted in overconcentration of industries and population in Seoul. In response, industrial dispersal policies were combined with sectoral policies. The establishment of industrial complexes outside Seoul city but within the Seoul metropolitan region in the early 1970s, the creation of large-scale heavy and chemical industrial complexes in the southeastern region in the 1970s, the development of large-scale high-tech parks outside the Seoul metropolitan region in the 1980s, and the establishment of large-scale industrial complexes in the western coastal regions in recent years are all related with the government's industrial and regional policies.

The development of major new industrial cities such as Ulsan, Pohang, Changwon, Kumi, and Ansan and the establishment of science parks in Taejon and Kwangju are thus concerted products of the national government's industrial and regional policies. These industrial cities have experienced rapid industrial and population growth, and have acted as generators of export in the 1970s and 1980s. However, the new industrial cities have been confronted with new challenges and problems such as labour disputes, wage increases, and intensified competitive pressures from abroad. Because of these problems and challenges, the new industrial complexes are now under the process of industrial restructuring.

Most of the new industrial cities in Korea can be regarded as satellite industrial districts or hub and spoke industrial districts. Pohang and Ulsan are typical of the hub and spoke type. The steel company is the hub in Pohang, while the initially petrochemical plant and now automobile plant are the hubs in Ulsan. In the 1970s and early 1980s, there were insufficient local networks in these new industrial districts. Kumi, Changwon and Ansan were typical satellite industrial districts (Markusen and Park, 1993; Park and Markusen, 1995). Most of the branch plants located in the districts had no inter-firm relations in the early development period. Even the Taeduck Science Park can be regarded as a satellite R&D district because R&D centers have few inter-establishment linkages within the science park and their linkages are mainly external to the science park.

Initially, the competitive advantages of the satellite new industrial districts in Korea arose from the national government's incentives such as tax exemption, provision of infrastructure, supply of cheap industrial land, and financial supports. In addition, the supply of cheap labour in the provincial regions was also an important factor for the creation of competitive advantages. In general, the initial competitive advantages of the satellite new industrial districts were related to factor conditions. Competitive advantages of the hub and spoke industrial districts in Korea mainly originated from economies of scale and factors such as availability of cheap labour, provision of cheap industrial land, and availability of capital through government financial support and foreign loans. The competitive advantages of the new industrial districts in the 1970s and 1980s were mainly related to basic factors advanced by Porter (1990).

However since the late 1980s the competitive advantages accruing from the abovementioned basic factors have ceased because of the rapid increase of wage rates, labour shortages, and other unfavourable conditions. In order to regain competitive advantages or to survive in the competitive industrial world, firms are undergoing industrial restructuring in recent years. Utilization of flexible labour, increase of subcontracting activities, direct foreign investments in China and Southeast Asia, and technological developments are the firms' major restructuring strategies (Park, 1995). Globalization as well as localization of industries have been the major trends resulting from the industrial restructuring in recent years. Furthermore, cooperation between large firms and cooperative small/medium supply firms, cooperation and competition among small firms, and government's support for small/medium firms are major factors behind localization and competitive advantages. DFIs and strategic alliances are the main elements in globalization and strategies to regain competitive advantages.

Industrial networks of firms in Kyeonggi and Kumi

Interviews and questionnaire surveys have been conducted in order to ascertain the distribution of industrial networks of Korea's major new industrial districts. Sixteen electronics or computer companies including Daewoo, LG, Samsung and Trigem have been interviewed in May 1995. Questionnaires were sent to about 500 firms located in Seoul-Suwon, Seoul-Inchon, and Kumi areas in June 1995, but only 12 firms responded. Because of the insufficient number of respondents, interviews with 30 randomly selected firms were conducted from August to November 1995. Out of 58 responses, industrial networks of 30 firms in Kyeonggi and 18 firms in Kumi were analyzed and compared. Ten responding firms in Seoul were not included in the analysis because of the focus on the new industrial agglomeration in Kumi developed by the national industrial policy, agglomerations in the axis of Seoul-Inchon, and the axis of Seoul-Suwon in Kyeonggi Province.

Table 8.1
Spatial supply linkages of firms

Type of supply	Percentage of firms which were supplied more than 30% from			Average % of supply of firms from		
	Local	National	Foreign	Local	National	Foreign
1. Kyeonggi						
Raw materials	68.3	46.2	38.5	37.4	36.0	26.6
Parts and components	67.1	42.9	21.4	47.8	32.5	19.7
Business services	72.7	36.4	9.1	65.5	29.5	5.0
Machinery equipment	38.5	38.5	38.5	32.4	36.4	31.2
Overall amount of supply	66.7	46.7	40.0	38.7	35.2	26.1
2. Kumi						
Raw material	50.0	62.5	37.5	34.6	45.2	20.2
Parts and components	85.7	47.6	23.8	55.5	32.1	12.4
Business services	64.7	58.8	23.5	45.9	42.4	11.7
Machinery equipment	36.4	77.3	31.8	22.7	50.7	26.6
Overall amount of supply	54.2	79.2	33.3	36.6	46.1	18.3

Note: 'Local' radius of 30km from a firm
Source: Data derived from interviews and questionnaire surveys

Local networks and embeddedness

The importance of local linkages in production and business services can be easily established in spatial supply linkages. In table 8.1, local linkages are considerably important in most of the supply activities, especially local linkages of parts and components as well as business services. In general, the degree of local supply linkages in Kumi is somewhat lower than that of Kyeonggi. However, the degree of local supply linkages in Kumi has significantly increased since the late 1980s (Park, 1990). Due to the concentration of high-order business services in the Capital Region and active subcontracting activities in Kumi, the degree of supply linkages of business services in Kyeonggi is higher than in Kumi, while the reverse holds true for parts and components. Overall, local supply linkages are more important than non-local supply linkages. The significance of local linkages is related to the development of local networks through cooperations between large firms and their supply firms, emergence of spin-offs, and cooperation and competition among small/medium firms in local areas.

During the restructuring period, there has been an increasing trend of intensifying linkages and cooperation between large firms and small firms. This trend of inter-firm relations is more important for the new industrial districts in Korea than the other restructuring strategies. Contract-out activities from large firms to small and medium firms have considerably increased since the 1980s (Park, 1994).

The increasing trend of local linkages and cooperation between large and small/medium firms has been promoted by both the national government's policy and large firms' restructuring strategies in recent years. The national government supports collaboration between large firms and small/medium firms in order to regain competitive advantages of the small/medium firms. The link between organization of cooperative supply firms to a specific large parent firm has been especially encouraged in order to provide stable customer markets, to promote technology development and specialization of the small firms, and to provide technical and managerial support for small/medium supply firms. Small/medium firms which belong to an organization comprising cooperative firms supplying a specific large parent firm are given priority in government aid such as financial assistance for plant automation and support for trust guarantee (Korea Federation of Small Business, 1995). In addition, where large parent firms involved in a cooperative network of small supply firms are concerned, the national government provides several incentives for the parent firm, to invest in cooperative firms in R&D facilities, skills training, technical guidance, etc.

From the viewpoint of large firms, subcontracting activities contribute to savings in production costs, reduce their vulnerability to a militant labour movement, and decentralize uncertainties. Many large firms have organized the cooperative group of small and medium-sized supply firms in order to save production costs and transaction costs and to guarantee the constant supply of materials from the cooperative group of firms. In 1995, 129 large parent firms were members of the organizations of the cooperative groups of small/medium supply firms, of which there were 6,788 small and medium firms. Large firms try to provide clusters of cooperative supply firms around their branch plants. The large firms have increased their cooperative supply firms and have intensified localization of the cooperative firms in the high-tech industrial districts over time. In addition, the large parent firms offer financial support; guidance in quality control, management, and manufacturing process; and various education and training services to the cooperative small and medium supply firms. The cooperative small and medium firms make up for about 30 to 35 percent of the total input supply to their large parent firms.

Accordingly, such collaboration and cooperation between large parent firms and cooperative small and medium-sized supply firms have significantly contributed to the formation of local networks and the dynamic development of the new industrial districts in Korea. Under the industrial restructuring process in recent years, because of these changes brought on by the national government's policy and firms' strategies to regain the competitive advantage, the satellite new industrial districts and the hub and spoke new industrial districts have the capacity to progress toward the advanced types.

Spin-offs from the large firms are also an important way to increase local networks and embeddedness in the new industrial districts. A considerable number of spin-offs from the large firms and new start-ups have appeared and maintain close relations with large firms in the new industrial districts. In our interview and questionnaire surveys, however, there are considerable differences between Kumi and Kyeonggi industrial districts in the ratio of spin-offs and new start-ups. In Kyeonggi 80 percent of the respondents were originally new start-ups and only 10 percent were spin-offs, while in Kumi the ratios of the new start-ups and spin-offs were 43 percent of the respondents, indicating that spin-offs are more important in Kumi. Formerly in Kumi, local networks and embeddedness were insignificant because there were only large branch plants. With the formation of spin-offs, however, local networks and embeddedness are developing in Kumi. In Kyeonggi, the potential for innovation and entrepreneurs is significant, and consequently the role of new start-ups is critical in the strengthening of local networks and embeddedness.

Overall, these spin-offs and new start-ups contribute towards an increase in local networks and local embeddedness in the new industrial districts. For example, in Taeduck Science Town, spin-offs began to appear after 1990 and more than 20 spin-offs, during the last four years, have developed from the institutions in Taeduck Science Park (Jeong, 1995). These spin-offs have close relations with research institutions in the Park and play a role in creating local linkages and embeddedness in Taejon city. Previously, there were few linkages between the research institutions in the Park and firms in Taejon city.

Cooperation among the local firms is also a significant factor in the increase in local networks. From table 8.2, it is clear that a considerable percentage of the responding firms have cooperative relationships with suppliers or customers. In Kyeonggi, more than 40 percent of the firms regard cooperation with local suppliers (within 30km) in training, shared equipment, technical assistance, shared personnel, and joint process development as 'important'. Cooperation with local customer firms in training, technical assistance, shared personnel, joint product development, joint marketing, and joint R&D investments is also regarded as 'important' by more than 40 percent of the firms. Cooperation with local competitors is also regarded as important by a considerable percentage of firms. Similar patterns can be found in Kumi, but, in general, the percentage of firms which have cooperative relationships with suppliers or customers in Kumi is lower than in Kyeonggi. Cooperation with local trade associations in all the cooperative activities is regarded as important by more than half of the responding firms in Kyeonggi. Cooperative relationships even

165

with competitors are regarded as important by about 20-30 percent of the firms. Such cooperation with suppliers, customers, competitors, and trade associations located in the local area is important for the evolution of local networks in the new industrial districts in Korea. Local networks are more intensive in Kyeonggi than in Kumi. However, it should be noted that inter-firm cooperation in the local area is a fairly recent phenomenon in Kumi under the industrial restructuring process.

Table 8.2
Importance of inter-firm cooperation

Type of cooperation	Cooperation with suppliers located in		Cooperation with customers located in		Cooperation with competitors located in		Cooperation with trade associations located in	
	local[1]	foreign	local	foreign	local	foreign	local	foreign
1. Kyeonggi								
Training	53.3[2]	26.7	50.0	12.5	35.3	17.6	85.7	14.3
Shared personnel	46.7	13.3	43.8	12.5	29.4	11.8	71.4	14.3
Joint product dev.	33.3	26.7	43.8	31.3	29.4	17.6	57.1	14.3
Joint process dev.	40.0	13.3	31.3	18.8	17.6	11.8	57.1	14.3
Other joint R&D	33.3	26.7	43.8	12.5	29.4	5.9	71.4	14.3
Shared equipment	53.3	20.0	31.3	12.5	23.5	5.9	57.1	14.3
Financial coop.	33.3	13.3	31.3	12.5	17.6	5.9	57.1	14.3
Joint marketing	33.3	13.3	43.8	18.8	17.6	5.9	71.4	14.3
Technical assistance	46.7	26.7	50.0	18.8	29.4	5.9	71.4	14.3
2. Kumi								
Training	45.8	20.8	42.3	19.2	29.6	22.2	50.0	14.3
Shared personnel	33.3	16.7	30.8	19.2	25.9	18.5	35.7	21.4
Joint product dev.	41.7	12.5	42.3	15.4	25.9	14.8	35.7	14.3
Joint process dev.	41.7	12.5	34.6	19.2	22.2	11.1	35.7	7.1
Other joint R&D	29.2	8.3	30.8	15.4	18.5	11.1	42.9	7.1
Shared equipment	20.8	8.3	30.8	15.4	18.5	11.1	28.6	7.1
Financial coop.	37.5	12.5	34.6	15.4	14.8	11.1	28.6	7.1
Joint marketing	16.7	8.3	26.9	15.4	22.2	14.8	28.6	7.1
Technical assistance	41.7	12.5	46.2	26.9	25.9	11.1	42.9	7.1

Notes: 1. 'Local' represents radius of 30km from a firm; 2. Values are the ratio (%) of the number of firms which regard each type of cooperation as 'important'.
Source: Interviews and questionnaire surveys

166

Cooperation with local universities and local government is considered important by most of the responding firms (tables 8.3 and 8.4). Cooperation with the local universities or higher education institutions in the training of scientists and engineers; continuing education for scientists, engineers, or managers; and other R&D projects/ventures are regarded as 'important' by more than 70 percent of the responding firms in Kyeonggi. Cooperation with the local universities is also regarded as important in Kumi, but the ratios are lower than those of Kyeonggi (table 8.3).

Formerly, local government was regarded as less significant than national government in the provision of support/incentives to industrial activities. However, with more local autonomy, the local government is regarded to be as significant as the national government. In some type of supports such as job training, real estate acquisition, finance, and R&D, many firms regard the local government to be more significant than the national government in both Kyeonggi and Kumi. Firms' recognition of the significance of the local universities and the local government in enhancing their competitive advantage promote cooperation and networks within the local areas. In general, cooperation between large firms and small/medium firms; the emergence of spin-offs; cooperation and collaboration among local firms of suppliers, customers, and competitors; and cooperation with local trade associations, local universities, and local government are the major forces which intensify local networks and embeddedness and, strengthen the dynamics of the new industrial districts.

Table 8.3
Significance of universities and other institutions of higher education

Types of activities	Kyeonggi		Kumi	
	Universities or other institutions of higher education located in			
	Local[1]	Foreign	Local[1]	Foreign
Supply of scientists/engineers	92.9[2]	35.7[2]	65.2[2]	30.4[2]
Continuing education for engineers & managers	78.6	28.6	69.6	39.1
Product technology	64.3	28.6	60.9	39.1
Process technology	64.3	21.4	56.5	39.1
Other R&D	71.4	28.6	39.1	30.4
Providing equipment	64.3	21.4	43.5	30.4
Training production workers	71.4	35.7	65.2	26.1
Technical assistance	64.3	21.4	56.5	34.8

Notes: 1. 'Local' radius of 30km from a firm; 2. Values are the ratios of the numbers of firms which regard each type as 'important'.
Source: Interviews and questionnaire surveys

167

Table 8.4
Importance of local and national governments

Types of support	Kyeonggi		Kumi	
	Local government	National government	Local government	National government
Tax incentives	86.7[1]	73.3[1]	71.4[1]	81.0[1]
Marketing	46.7	66.7	57.1	52.4
Trade fairs	46.7	53.3	52.4	52.4
Job training	73.3	53.3	76.2	47.6
Infrastructure	46.7	33.3	52.4	33.3
Real estate acquisition	53.3	40.0	57.1	47.6
Finance	73.3	66.7	71.4	52.4
R&D	60.0	53.3	52.4	42.9

Note: 1 Values are the ratio (%) of the number of firms which regard each type of support as 'important'
Source: Interviews and questionnaire surveys

Emergence of global networks and embeddedness

There has been an increasing trend of global network formation in production, research and development, and marketing in Korea in recent years. Strategic alliances, direct foreign investments, and subcontracting production beyond the national boundary are the major reasons attributed to the increase in global networks and embeddedness.

Large firms in the high technology sector have initiated strategic alliances in order to recapture competitive advantages. Samsung, LG, and Daewoo electronic companies have formed several strategic alliances in technology and marketing with firms in the United States and Japan. For example, Daewoo Electronics has forged technology alliances with Sony, National Electric, GE, etc. and LG Electronics is extending its strategic alliances from technology to marketing and joint R&D with GE. Even the small and medium firms have strategic alliances with foreign firms.

Based on our interviews and questionnaire surveys, in Kyeonggi 50 percent of the respondent firms have established strategic alliances for certain activities (table 8.5). In Kumi, the percentage is 40 percent. Firms in Kumi have more alliances with customer firms than with supply firms, while firms in Kyeonggi have more alliances with suppliers than customers. In general, technology transfer, direct investments, and joint R&D are relatively important types of strategic alliances. Strategic alliances are important for the formation of global networks. About 39 percent and 17 percent of the responding firms in Kyeonggi and Kumi, respectively, maintain certain types of strategic alliances with foreign firms (table 8.6). Even though the ratio of firms which have formed strategic alliances with foreign firms is relatively low in Kumi, the strategic alliances with foreign firms contribute to the process of global networks formation.

Table 8.5
Types of strategic alliances forged by firms (%)

| | Kyeonggi | | | | Kumi | | | |
Type of Alliance	1	2	3	4	1	2	3	4
Joint investment	5.6	5.6	0.0	11.1	13.3	3.3	0.0	13.3
Joint R&D investment	11.1	5.6	5.6	16.7	6.7	13.3	0.0	16.7
Direct investment	11.1	11.1	0.0	22.2	0.0	0.0	3.3	3.3
Technical exchange	22.2	16.7	0.0	27.8	10.0	20.0	3.3	23.3
Shared equity	5.6	5.6	0.0	11.1	3.3	0.0	0.0	3.3
Marketing alliances	11.1	11.1	0.0	16.7	6.7	6.7	0.0	10.0
Other	0.0	0.0	0.0	0.0	0.0	3.3	3.3	6.7
Total	38.9	33.3	5.6	50.0	16.7	26.7	6.7	40.0

Column 1: with suppliers; column 2: with customers; column 3: with competitors; columns 1, 2, 3: average number of alliances per firm; column 4: average number of alliances per firm with suppliers, customers, or competitors.
Source: Interviews and questionnaire surveys

An increase in DFI is significant with regard to global networks and embeddedness. DFI of larger firms is a strategy to reduce production costs in developing countries or penetrate the markets in developed countries. DFI is a relatively recent issue and the amount of DFI has increased dramatically in recent years. For example, Samsung Electronics had nine foreign branch plants in 1993, but the number will increase to 20 in a few years. Direct foreign investment from the large companies usually accompanies direct investment of small/medium supply firms. In addition, large firms tend to localize production linkages in host countries. Formation of intensive local networks of Korean large firms in Silicon Valley through direct foreign investment contributes to strengthening the global networks in information, technology and R&D. Direct foreign investment by the small/medium firms in Korea is not uncommon in recent years. Many cooperative supply firms invest in foreign countries: they are either firms which have their own technological advantages in some aspects or those which utilize cheap labour and other cost reduction factors in the host country. In general, the direct investment from the small/medium firms also contributes to the increase of global networks in information, services, and production.

169

Table 8.6
The regional percentage of firms which have strategic alliances by location

Location	Local[1]	National	Foreign
Kyeonggi	27.8[2]	22.2	38.9
Kumi	16.7	10.0	16.7

Notes: 1 'Local' = 30km radius from a firm; 2 values are the ratio (%) of the numbers of firms which regard strategic alliances as 'important';
Source: Interviews and questionnaire surveys

Outsourcing from foreign countries is the other important factor in the increase of global networks. In table 8.1, in Kyeonggi, the ratio of the number of the firms which were supplied more than 30 percent of the total input materials and services from foreign countries is 40 percent, which is relatively significant. Even though international linkages of business services are not strong, global linkages of machinery equipments, raw materials, and parts and components are quite important. Usually, in the high-tech or important parts and components sector, the level of foreign supply linkages is relatively high (Park, 1990). The overall level of foreign supply linkages in table 8.1 is somewhat lower in Kumi than in Kyeonggi. However, foreign supply linkages in Kumi are still significant.

Cooperative relationships with foreign firms are also important for the formation of global networks. About one-quarter of the firms surveyed regard most of cooperative activities with foreign customers and some of cooperative activities with foreign competitors as 'important' (table 8.2). This value is, of course, relatively low compared to that of local firms. However, it is important to note the fact that Korean firms have begun to consider it important to cooperate with foreign customers or competitors. Outsourcing activities and cooperation with foreign competitive firms may contribute to technology transfer and increase in competitive advantage. Foreign supply linkages and cooperation with foreign firms are surely significant in the increase in international networks and remaking of competitive advantages of the firms in the new industrial districts in Korea.

Conclusion

The purpose of the study reported in this chapter is to analyze industrial networks of new industrial districts in Korea. Interviews and questionnaire surveys were conducted in the Kyeonggi region and Kumi city in order to determine major characteristics of industrial networks formation in the major areas of the high-technology industrial agglomeration in Korea. Firms in the industrial districts restructure their network patterns in order to rebuild competitive advantages, on the one hand, and governments and public institutions promote and support industrial restructuring in the industrial districts, on the other. The six types of new industrial districts have their own competitive advantages for industrial growth in a given economic environment. Their competitive power, however, changes over time with the dynamics of the global space economy and their impacts on the local economic structure and local environments. Therefore, the basic types can develop into hybrid types in order to maintain or regain competitive advantages in the global economy.

There are only limited types of the new industrial districts and there are some limitations in the development of the dynamic new industrial districts in developing countries. In Korea, satellite and hub and spoke new industrial districts have been the basic competitive types of new industrial districts. Kumi and Changwon — new industrial districts in the 1980s in Korea — were good examples of satellite new industrial districts in developing countries (Markusen and Park, 1993; Park and Markusen, 1995). Pohang and Ulsan are the major cases of hub and spoke new industrial districts in Korea. The competitive advantages of these industrial districts comprised advantages in factor costs and national government's incentives. Firms in the new industrial districts in Korea, however, are undergoing industrial restructuring because the competitive advantages arising from the basic factors have ceased since the late 1980s with the rapid increase of wage rates, labour shortages, and other unfavourable conditions.

Firms in the new industrial districts in Korea are now remaking their competitive advantages by intensifying local and global networks. In recent years, cooperation between large firms and their cooperative small/medium supply firms; cooperation with suppliers, customers, competitors located in a local area; emergence of spin-offs, and cooperation with local trade associations, universities, and government have contributed to the increase of local networks and embeddedness and, subsequently then, to remaking competitive advantages. There has been an increasing trend of global networks in production, R&D, and marketing in Korea in recent years. Strategic alliances, direct foreign investment, subcontracting-out production beyond the national boundary, and cooperation with foreign suppliers and customers are the major factors for the increase in global networks. More active roles by local governments, universities, and trade associations are, however, required in order to secure the evolution of advanced types of the new industrial districts. Cooperation between large and small firms, provision of local innovative culture or technological infrastructure, support of spin-offs and new start-ups, formation of innovation networks, and public-private partnerships are the major strategies to maintain or remake the competitive advantages of the new industrial districts in Korea. It requires the formation of supportive bodies such as institutions for the evolution of the dynamic pattern of industrial districts. Some of the original basic types of new industrial districts in Korea may not regain competitive advantages and may decline without evolving into the advanced types, in the absence of supportive social structures or policies in the changing environments.

References

Appold, S.J. (1995), 'Agglomeration, Interorganizational Networks, and Competitive Performance in the U.S. Metalworking Sector', *Economic Geography*, Vol. 71, pp. 27-54.

Dunford, M. (1991), 'Industrial Trajectories and Social Relations in Areas of New Industrial Growth', in Benko, G. and Dunford, M. (eds), *Industrial Change and Regional Development: The Transformation of New Industrial Spaces*, Belhaven Press: London and New York, pp. 51-82.

Jeong, J.H. (1995), 'Spin-Offs Formation and Linkages in Taeduck Research Park', *Journal of Geography*, Vol. 25, pp. 57-80 (in Korean with English summary).

Korea Federation of Small Business (1995), *Directory of the Organization of Cooperative Supply Firms*, Korea Federation of Small Business: Seoul.

Markusen, A. and Park, S.O. (1993), 'The State as Industrial Locator and District Builder: The Case of Changwon, South Korea', *Economic Geography*, Vol. 69, No. 2, pp. 157-81.

Park, S.O. (1990), 'Government Management of Industrial Change in the Republic of Korea', in Rich, D.C. and Linge, G.J.R. (eds), *The State and Management of Industrial Change*, Routledge: London, pp. 74-87.

Park, S.O. (1994), 'Industrial Restructuring in the Seoul Metropolitan Region: Major Triggers and Consequences', *Environment and Planning A*, Vol. 26, pp. 527-41.

Park, S.O. (1995), 'Seoul (Korea): City and Suburb', in Clark, G. and Kim, W.B. (eds), *Asian NIEs and the Global Economy. Industrial Restructuring and Corporate Strategy in the 1990s*, Johns Hopkins University Press: Baltimore and London, pp. 143-67.

Park, S.O. (1996), 'Networks and Embeddedness in the Dynamic Types of New Industrial Districts', *Progress in Human Geography*, Vol. 20, pp. 476-92.

Park, S.O. and Markusen, A. (1995), 'Generalizing New Industrial Districts: A Theoretical Agenda and an Application from a Non-Western Economy', *Environment and Planning A*, Vol. 27, pp. 81-104.

Piore, M.J. and Sabel, C. (1984), *The Second Industrial Divide*, Basic Books: New York.

Porter, M.E. (1990), *The Competitive Advantage of Nations*, The Free Press: New York.

Scott, A. (1988), 'Flexible Production Systems and Regional Development: The Rise of New Industrial Spaces in North America and Western Europe', *International Journal of Urban and Regional Research*, Vol. 12, No. 2, pp. 171-86.

Scott, A. (1992), 'The Role of Large Producers in Industrial Districts: A Case Study of High Technology Systems Houses in Southern California', *Regional Studies*, Vol. 26, No. 3, pp. 265-75.

9   World City Futures: The Role of Urban and Regional Policies in the Asia Pacific Region

John Friedmann

"No matter how successful or unsuccessful, the future of Pacific- Asian societies and their cities will be determined as much by localized socio-economic and political processes as by global imperatives" (Douglass, 1996a, p. 2).

Introduction

I have chosen the title of this chapter with some care. To be candid, I have no idea what the future of any so-called world city will be in the next century. I do know that cities differ greatly among themselves, and that their *historical trajectories* are far from random: the past will shape the future of each city but not determine it. In addition, cities have always been parts of systems of cities, and today's global economy has brought into being a *global urban system*. This interdependent character of the urban dynamic will similarly shape the future of any given city, though not determine it. Finally, and this is what I would particularly like to stress in this presentation, urban outcomes are to a considerable extent a result of *public policies*. They are, in part, what we choose them to be. The cities of the next century will thus be a result of planning in the broadest sense of that much abused term. This is not to fall into the naive belief that all we need to do is to draw a pretty picture of the future, such as a master plan, or adopt wildly ambitious regulatory legislation as a template for future city growth. At best, such efforts remain in the realm of good intentions. Filling the gap between intention and reality is a good deal more complicated than that. Still, it is useful to think ahead to see what problems we face as we embark on the third millenium of the Christian era. There is no doubt in my mind that the coming decades will witness profound changes in the ancient civilizations of Asia, and that these changes will be made palpable in the cities, both old and new, of this vast region. Let us hope that these cities — unprecedented in scale as they surely will be — will also become a fitting home for the billions of people who will come to live in them.

The world city concept

The term 'world city' was introduced into the discourse on urban studies in the early eighties and has since been widely adopted (Friedmann and Wolff, 1982; Friedmann, 1986; Sassen, 1994; Knox and Taylor, 1995; Lo and Yeung, 1996), but a certain ambiguity has always attended its meaning. 'World city' can either refer to a class of cities that play a leading role in the spatial articulation of the global economic system, or designate a dimension of all cities that in varying measure are integrated with this system. These two meanings can be reconciled by positing a *global hierarchy — or hierarchical system — of cities*, where every city occupies a position that reflects its relative importance in the spatial articulation of economic and financial activities or, to put it more plainly, its relative economic power.[1]

At the top of this hierarchy we find a very small number of global financial centres: London, New York, and Tokyo (Sassen, 1991). Descending from these pinnacles of power, we can identify multinational financial centres (Miami, Frankfurt, Singapore among others), centres that dominate large national economies (such as São Paulo, Paris, Sydney, and Seoul), and important subnational or regional centres (Osaka-Kobe, Hong Kong, Vancouver, the Rhine-Ruhr conurbation, and Chicago are relevant examples). In all, some thirty 'world cities' fall into these categories which reflect the spatial reach of their economic and financial articulations (table 9.1). We can perhaps get a better sense of this 'reach' by looking at the dominant linkages of the global airline network. Figure 9.1, prepared by David J. Keeling of Western Kentucky University, clearly shows the triadic structure of the global cities network, with subsidiary roles performed by airports at Miami, Los Angeles, Singapore, Cairo, Frankfurt, and Paris.[2]

What is striking about the concept, but has rarely been singled out for comment, is that world city discourse is typically couched in the language of economics. Although this uni-dimensional character gives the world city concept analytical power, it hides from view other important dimensions of urban life. As a concept in economic geography, it aims at universal significance, highlighting what is common to all members of a class of world cities while ignoring everything that is uniquely emplaced in particular sites: the historical, socio-cultural, administrative, political, and environmental dimensions of urban life. But if the concept is going to be useful for public policy, the general and the specific must be brought together. This imperative is captured in the phrase 'the global-local nexus'. Articulating this nexus is the challenging task of urban policy, planning and design.

The geography of global capitalism

In a recent paper, Allen J. Scott defends the thesis "that world capitalism is moving into a phase of development marked by an intensified regionalization of production overlaid by — and rooted in — a global division of labour. In this process," he writes, "a significant reallocation of economic coordination and steering functions is occurring, away from the sovereign state, up to the international and down to the regional levels" (Scott, 1996).

Table 9.1
Spatial articulations: 30 world cities

---

1   Global financial articulations
  # London* A (also national articulation)
  # New York A
  # Tokyo* A (also multinational articulation: Southeast Asia)

2   Multinational articulations
  # Miami C (Caribbean, Latin America)
  # Los Angeles A (Pacific Rim)
  # Frankfurt C (Western Europe)
  # Amsterdam C or Randstad B
  Singapore* C (Southeast Asia)

3   Important national articulations (1989 GDP > $200 billion)
# Paris* B		São Paulo A
# Zurich C		Seoul* A
Madrid* C	#	Sydney B
Mexico City* A		

4   Subnational/regional articulations
Osaka-Kobe (Kansai region) B		Montreal C
# San Francisco C		Hong Kong (Pearl River delta) B
# Seattle C	#	Milano C
# Houston C		Lyon C
# Chicago B		Barcelona C
# Boston C	#	Munich C
# Toronto C	#	Vancouver C
# Düsseldorf-Cologne-Essen-Dortmund (Rhine-Ruhr region) B		

Population (1980s):
A 10-20 million   B 5-10 million   C 1-5 million
* national capital
# major immigration target
For European cities, I have benefited greatly from Kunzman and Wegener, *The Pattern of Urbanization in Western Europe 1960-1990.*

Source: Friedmann (1995, p. 24)

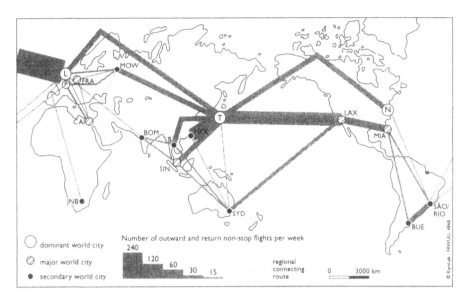

Figure 9.1   Dominant linkages in the global airline network

Source: Keeling (1995, p. 122)

I would like briefly to review this geography of global capitalism, because the 'regional level' to which Scott refers is precisely the level of world city formation with which we are here concerned. International organizations still collect data on a national basis, and this is perhaps as it should be. But what we call 'the economy' has burst its national container, as effective economic power has shifted both upward towards the global and downward towards regional world city levels. For our purposes, the relevant scale of economic life is the city region that extends outwards from core cities up to a distance that may be roughly represented by a commuting radius of one to (at most) two hours, covering a sprawling region which, in the Asian context, embraces populations that range from about five to over twenty million and which continue to expand at rates that may well lead to a doubling of population in less than twenty years (figure 9.2).

The chief sources of demographic growth for these mega-city regions come from rural migration (in Asia) and international migration (in Oceania and North America), though Asian world cities are beginning to experience international migration as well. Although agriculture, especially of the intensive sort — vegetables, fruit, small livestock — is still an important activity within these regions, it makes little sense to separate urban from rural in this context, especially in view of the fact that the income of many farm families increasingly depends on non-farm sources. Rural households in world city regions are now tightly integrated with an urban economy that is grounded in manufacturing and business services.

176

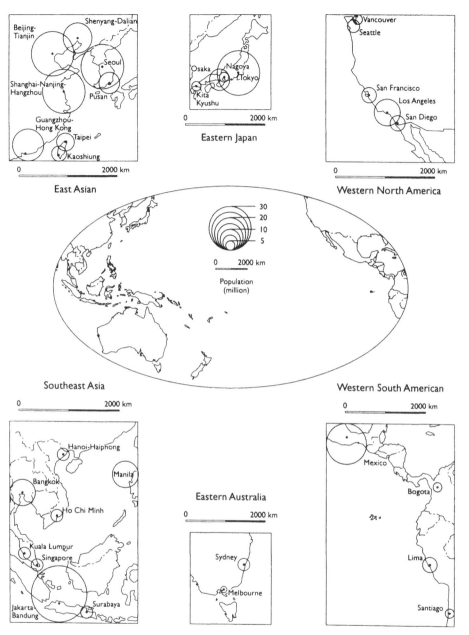

Figure 9.2   **The Asian-Pacific Rim: major extended metropolitan regions in excess of two million (2000 A.D.)**

Source: After Rimmer (1994). Map constructed by Dr. Mark Wang, Department of Geography, Melbourne University.

Each world city, as I suggested when discussing the concept earlier, integrates a larger region of which it is the economic and financial capital or, to use Saskia Sassen's apt phrase, the controlling center. How to draw the actual boundaries of these regions, if precision is desired, is often problematical, however. The case is fairly straightforward with primate cities such as Bangkok, whose unchallenged range of control is the entire national territory. But when you come to a regional city such as Hong Kong, difficulties arise, even though most people would agree that Hong Kong's primary region of influence whose economy it can be said to integrate is the Pearl River Delta, which includes Guangzhou as a secondary pole. Hong Kong-based financial interests, however, are found up and down the coast of China, and these linkages will undoubtedly intensify in the coming years. Or, to cite another example, Singapore's immediate hinterland includes parts of Johor in Malaysia and the Indonesian island of Riau, but for certain purposes this dynamic city state serves as a financial center for the entire Southeast Asian, multinational region.

Questions of measurement aside, I would now like to suggest, by way of a hypothesis, that *the economic power of a world city stands in direct relation to the productivity of the region it articulates.*[3] That is to say, the more productive its space of articulation, the greater will be its economic power. This hypothesis would help explain, in part, the low ranking of African cities in the world city hierarchy (no African city, for example, is included in table 9.1), compared to cities on the Asian-Pacific Rim, many of which are just beginning to rise into the top echelons of the global hierarchy. At the same time, we should remember that the productivity of this space is not necessarily pre-given but may be induced by the investment and, to be blunt about it, the colonizing activities of their respective core regions. The well-known examples of Singapore and Hong Kong again illustrate this proposition. Although these relations are based on economic and occasionally also political power, they need not be viewed as inherently exploitative, as my provocative reference to colonization might seem to imply. There is, indeed, a tradition in regional studies which automatically assumes a preponderance of so-called backwash effects — that is, effects negative for the economic growth — as a characteristic of core-periphery relation generally. We need to challenge this assumption in the light of present knowledge. In any event, in most Asian regions, so-called spread effects (which are positive for economic growth) seem to outweigh whatever backwash effects which may impact their fortunes.

The overall geography that emerges from this discussion is summarized in figure 9.3, which is borrowed from Scott (1996). On one hand, we see here an archipelago of wealthy city regions with their respective hinterlands, all tightly connected with each other. But we also see what Scott calls the extensive economic frontier of global capitalism with a few 'islands of prosperity' (i.e. low-order world cities) as the major focal points of this articulation. This extensive frontier is the true world periphery that supplies primarily raw materials and cheap labour to world city markets. Altogether absent from this picture, however, are large parts of the world that are barely integrated with the global economy, and where a very large part of the world's population still resides. We may want to call it the excluded *frontier of immiseration.*

178

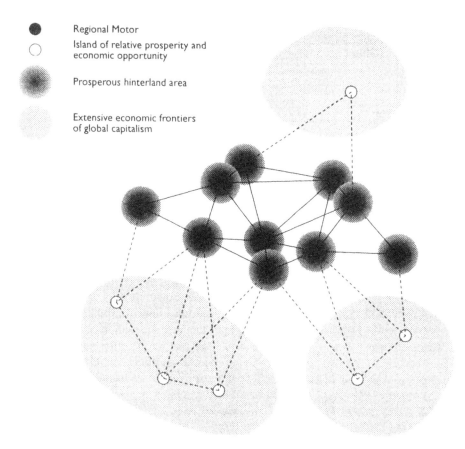

Regional Motor

Island of relative prosperity and economic opportunity

Prosperous hinterland area

Extensive economic frontiers of global capitalism

Figure 9.3   **A schematic representation of the contemporary geography of global capitalism**

The spatial dynamics of world city formation

Finally, and to conclude this rapid overview of the geography of global capitalism, I want to turn to what we may call the spatial dynamics of world city formation. For our hierarchy of cities is not in a stable equilibrium, and cities may rise or fall in their economic standing as 'basing points' and 'control centers' of global capital. I would like to highlight four major causes that can affect a city's future.

The first and perhaps most obvious cause is *changes in exogenous political circumstances*. Think, for example, of Vienna which also happens to be my native city. Following World War II, this former imperial capital of Austro-Hungary tried to safeguard its neutral position between East and West by attracting a large number of international organizations during the four decades of the Cold War era. With the collapse of communism in eastern Europe and the Soviet Union, Vienna hoped to revive its former glories as an imperial city by serving as 'broker' for the newly emerging capitalist economies on its doorstep. It wanted to become a multinational world city in *Mitteleuropa* (central Europe). But its hopes were dashed when it turned out that the newly elected democratic regime in Prague was more interested in being counted as a Western than a *Middle-European* state, when the Yugoslav Federation erupted in a brutal civil war whose end is not yet in sight, and when the neighboring Hungarians let it be known that they were quite happy to be on their own rather than under Austrian tutelage. And so, Vienna has been unable so far to translate its hope to be elevated to a higher position in the world city hierarchy into a concrete, realizable project.

Other examples come to mind. Johannesburg lost its preeminent position in southern Africa first because of a world-wide boycott to force South Africa to abandon its apartheid policies and then, with the coming to power of a democratic majority regime, because of continuing internal turmoil and political instability. Or Rio de Janeiro, which at one point in time could have risen to be a world city of significant rank, but lost the game in competition with São Paulo after the federal government changed its seat from Rio to the new capital, Brasilia. Rio's economy never recovered from this shock, and has been on a downward slide ever since. Similarly, Hong Kong's future remains somewhat uncertain with its reincorporation into the People's Republic of China. And what will be the effect of an eventual reunification of the two Koreas on Seoul? Similar questions could be asked of a number of major Asian cities that will be affected by political changes in the region.

A second force contributing to world city dynamics is *economic restructuring under global competitive conditions, coupled with a city's ability creatively to respond to exogenous change.* The most dramatic examples come from old industrial regions that rose to power on the strength of their production in the heavy smokestack industries of the late 19th and 20th century: iron and steel, metalworking, automobiles. The images of rusting factories, black rivers, and toxic soils are a familiar and heartbreaking sight in places like the British Midlands, the German Ruhr Valley, the Basque Country of Spain, and the northeastern industrial belt in the United States. Some, though far from all, of these regions have made successful comebacks, and the final verdict is still out. But clearly, the affected cities — Manchester, Essen, Bilbao, Detroit among them — have had to reinvent themselves at enormous financial and above all human cost. None of them have so far have been able to recover even their former position as proud 'workshops to the world' not to mention making a successful transition to a post-industrial era (Del Castillo, 1989; Kunzmann, 1996; IBA Emscher Park, 1996).

In Asia, one of a small number of 'rustbelt' cities is Shanghai which is now engaged in a major effort to raise itself to the level of a world city of regional rank. Vast new constructions are underway in Pudong, the eastern half of the city across the Huangpu River. Still, Shanghai continues to be a major industrial producer, though its heavy industries can survive internationally only because of extremely low wages and continuing heavy subsidies from the central government.

180

Although the economic restructuring of old industrial regions is forced upon regional economies by changes in technology and the power of capital to shift production from high-wage to low-wage parts of the world — in some cases, it is also an immediate consequence of political change, such as German reunification in 1989 which overnight laid waste to East Germany's industrial might — it can also be viewed as an 'internal' or endogenous process, as a regional economy evolves from labour-intensive to capital-intensive to brain-intensive production, making a series of transitions to world city status into the upper reaches of the global hierarchy. The cases of Singapore and Hong Kong come to mind in this regard, and Taipei seems poised to do the same. Here, it is clearly a matter of intelligent policies and their successful implementation which are the key to whether or not that endogenous restructuring process will be successful. I shall return to this question in the second half of this chapter.

A third causal factor in world city dynamics is undoubtedly *intercity competition*. The existence of competition among cities for a share of global capital is undisputed. Much of this competition is among cities within the same national territory. Thus, Los Angeles competes with San Francisco for primacy as a banking center; Australian city-states — Brisbane, Sydney, Melbourne, Adelaide — compete against one another, as in the infamous episode of the 'multi-function polis' (Spearritt, 1996); coastal cities in China have been given partial autonomy to negotiate directly for foreign investments; and so forth. In the longer term, however, this competition reaches beyond national borders. A good example is the recent competition among London, Paris, Brussels, Frankfurt, and Berlin to capture the headquarters of the new European Central Bank. In this instance, Frankfurt won the prize. Such competition can be extremely wasteful, however, as cities are likely to spend far more in the aggregate on, for example, transport infrastructure than a rational allocation of resources would have allowed. What appears to be an excessive construction fever of port and airport facilities in the Pearl River Delta of southern China is a relevant instance. I would like to return to this question later, arguing the case for intercity cooperation to balance a natural tendency towards 'out-of-control' competition which, in effect, leads cities to forfeit part of their future to transnational capital whose primary concern is, after all, nothing more ambitious than the prospect of super-profits.

The final cause of why cities may rise or fall in the world hierarchy is closely tied to the discussion on competition, and the nearsightedness of public policies that concentrate exclusively on economic issues. What I have in mind is the question of *socially and environmentally unsustainable growth*. An unspoken assumption among urban policy makers has been that economic growth as such is always a good thing, and that the more growth is generated, the greater will be the benefits for everyone. But many would contend that this assumption is wrong, both theoretically and empirically. It is theoretically wrong, because growth is always measured on private account, whereas sustainability can be captured only through a comprehensive social accounting system. In other words, increases in the gross regional product do not reflect the costs that growth imposes on third parties, the social and environmental costs. And it is empirically wrong because, as travellers to some of the famous names on any world city list can easily observe, life in these cities has become better for only a small minority of their population, and even these favoured few suffer from horrific air pollution, monumental traffic jams, and fear of crimes that range from kidnaping to car thefts and robberies, while the majority of the population can barely survive under conditions of enormous psychological and physical stress, beginning with insufficient housing and intolerable levels of environmental sanitation (ESCAP, 1993).

What if these third-party costs were to be subtracted from each year's increment of the gross regional product? Except for some World Bank studies on the productivity effects of pollution, the job has not been done, but we can safely assert that actual growth rates of regional income calculated would be very much less on a net basis than the reported figures. And where the reported figures are low to begin with — as they are, relative to Asian city regions in North America — the annual increments in the net regional product may actually turn out to be *negative*. The general sense in a world city like Los Angeles is that the conditions of life there, even for urban elites, have plummeted since the 1970s and continue to decline. Admittedly, the city is only now recovering from a long period of major restructuring, but the quality of life in Los Angeles has visibly declined over this twenty-year period.

My point is that the failure of urban economic policy to take the costs to third parties into account can undermine a city's ability to rise in the ranks of, or even to maintain its position in, the world hierarchy. Maximizing economic growth regardless of social and environmental costs is therefore not a sound policy, either at city-regional or national levels. Moreover, the get-rich mentality associated with it leads to a decline in public morality and may undermine such progress as has been made towards a more democratic social order (Heidenheimer, 1996). The present hyperurbanizing trend in Asia is not only beginning to yield the first hard evidence of corruption in high places (e.g. under the Marcos regime in the Philippines and, more recently also in Korea), it is leading to enormous increases in air and water pollution levels as well, many times greater than the already spectacular demographic growth. Reporting on Jakarta, Douglass has this observation (Douglass, 1996b, pp. 2-3):

A recent study by the World Bank cites figures showing that in terms of health effects of pollution in Jakarta, the economic costs of environmental degradation totaled $500 million in 1990 alone. Industrial and urban pollution is also threatening coastal fishing industries, and the loss of water to agriculture from the flushing of rivers in the dry season is also significant. Uncontrolled pollution from human and solid waste in tourist resorts is also presenting a potentially serious threat to the growth of tourism revenues, which totaled $3.2 billion in 1992. The report concludes that increasing pollution and congestion will work against Indonesia's efforts to remain internationally competitive for foreign investment, particularly in higher-technology industries, and, further, social resistance to the impacts of a projected ten-fold increase in industrial pollution may also arise.

182

Major policy issues confronting world city planners

Public policies can make a huge difference for urban outcomes. There are, to be sure, extraordinary events over which urban development planners and decision makers have little or no control, such as some of the changes in political conditions to which I have alluded. But the real question is how cities will respond to them. A point on which I would insist is that development planning is not just a matter of economics, and that economic infrastructure — building the world's biggest 24-hour airport, tallest office tower, or whatever — is by no means all that is needed, or even always the most important thing, to succeed in the process of world city formation. Cities are for the people who live in them, and a city's inhabitants must be assured a way of flourishing in the new economic order. Their life space must be defended against developments that tend to favour the few over the many; public services must be provided in adequate measure to everyone regardless of their ability to pay for them; and the conditions of the environment from city core to far periphery must be protected and enhanced. These are extraordinarily difficult but not impossible challenges. In the remainder of this chapter, I will address six major policy issues that confront planners concerned with placing their cities in the top rank of the world hierarchy: spatial organization, regional governance, social and environmental sustainability, migrant workers, the rise of civil society, and intercity networks. These six are not the only ones, but they seem to me to be among the more important.

Spatial organization

Earlier, I referred to the unprecedented scale of the new city regions of Asia in both population and area. And urban growth in both dimensions will undoubtedly continue for several more decades until most of the rural population excess has been shifted into urban occupations. Three policy issues arise from this simple and (as it seems to me) irreversible trend. First, can public policy guide the emerging urban form? Second, can land use planning be extended to the entire city region? And third, how can the region best be articulated through transportation?

Let me briefly consider the first of these questions. We are talking about agglomerations of five to 25 million people within a rapidly industrializing economy. What form should these city regions take in order to economize on travel, preserve fragile environments, and create a more liveable, more manageable city? We are dealing here with magnitudes that are unprecedented in human history and that approximate and even exceed some middle-sized countries, such as Australia or Canada (Ginsburg et al., 1991). Not all growth is beneficial, however, and some can be cancerous, destructive of the bases of human life. The physical form of cities can, in principle, be controlled even in market economies, through the wise use of planning instruments and infrastructure investments. Urban densities can be controlled to produce 'compact' cities. Multi-centric growth can be encouraged through New Town development schemes commensurate with the scale of the city-region as a whole. And high-density corridors can be promoted through rapid transit alignments. In this connection, it may be appropriate to recall a number of Asian inter-urban corridors that have already emerged, such as Tokyo-Osaka, Seoul-Pusan, Dalian-Shenyang, Tianjin-Beijing, Hong Kong-Guangzhou, and Taipei-Kaohsiung. Although it would be wrong to treat these as single entities, or linear 'cities', it is clear that both public and private investments will shape the future expansion of individual city regions at either end of the corridor, not to mention at intermediate points.

The second and related issue concerns regional land use planning. Existing land use planning techniques are barely adequate to function effectively at the regional scale or, for that matter, to reflect contemporary interest in sustainable development (McAllister, 1973). The region, large as it is compared to the old city cores, is still a very limited terrain and must therefore be treated as a precious resource that is not to be squandered. For millions of people, it is their life space, and for economic agents, it must also be a workable space. Furthermore, it is also a space that must preserve some of its natural characteristics as a human habitat. Some facilities, such as airports, are extremely space-demanding, while such modern 'landscapes of power' as research parks are typically found in park-like settings. Some European cities, such as Frankfurt, have made elaborate plans for 'green belts' and, although green belts are probably not suitable for most Asian cities, it is nevertheless important to preserve certain parts of the region from urban encroachments in order to protect watersheds, prevent floods, moderate climatic conditions, conserve unique landscape resources such as wetlands, ensure the nearby production of fresh vegetables, flowers, and small livestock, and create adequate environments for mass urban recreation. When all these uses are added up, they will amount to a very large — probably the major — portion of any city region. It is therefore obvious that land use planning on a regional scale is imperative. And yet, this can only be done if the region itself is defined in ways that allows for urban expansion without providing an incentive for environmentally destructive facilities to locate in less tightly controlled areas beyond its boundaries, and if land use planners are directly involved with major decisions intended to shape the form of the expanding city, such as airport location decisions, New Towns planning, major transportation corridors, etc. Jurisdictional conflicts over natural terrain — as between various government agencies charged with agriculture, forestry, water management, transportation, housing, and so forth — must also be avoided, by requiring a process of mutual consultation and regional planning review.

The third question relates to transportation planning as a way to articulate the evolving regional structure but also, and at the same time, help in shaping the form of the region. I have already had to introduce the subject of transportation planning in my discussion of both form and land use, showing that these questions are so connected that they cannot be meaningfully treated separately from practice. Let me therefore merely add an important proviso which I have not yet mentioned, and let me be plain-spoken about it. For an Asian city to replicate Los Angeles' love affair with freeways, because Los Angeles figures on most world city maps, is to commit collective suicide. As their income goes up, people will want to become motorized: first on bicycles with engines, then on motor bikes, and finally on cars. All of these

184

vehicles are extraordinarily polluting, however, and as experience has shown in cities from Tokyo to Bangkok, their proliferation chokes traffic in the city to the point of virtual standstill. Urban densities in Asia will require mass transit and stringent controls over the use of motor vehicles for private convenience. Singapore stands out as a shining example of how a large city can effectively control the private automobile and other motorized methods of individual transportation. The extended city region must similarly be controlled, partly by decentralizing into a multi-centric pattern so as not to overload the old city center and partly by investing heavily in high-speed bus lanes and rail transit. Limited access roads are probably unavoidable, if only to move goods quickly from one part of the region to another, but they must not be allowed to become — as they have in Los Angeles — the (almost) exclusive means of linking parts of the region to each other.

Regional governance

The preceding discussion has assumed some sort of capacity for government planning and implementation at the scale of the city region as a whole. This assumption must now be looked at more closely and become itself an object of public policy. For what is implied by regional land use planning, regional transportation planning, extending outwards the boundaries of city regions and moulding the emerging urban form to reflect a social purpose, is nothing less than a demand for a *new territorial division of powers*. This concept refers to a formal distribution of functions and authority among territorial units of government, from neighborhoods and urban districts to larger entities: cities, regions, states or provinces, the nation, and emerging multi-national territories. The existing division of powers is in most, and perhaps in all, cases insufficient to cope with the problems of urban growth on the scale and at the rates we are forced to take as given in Asian urbanization. On one hand, there is the danger of fragmentation to the point of ungovernability. This is the typical case of American cities, such as Los Angeles, with its hundreds of separate jurisdictions, autonomous single-function agencies (such as the Los Angeles Metropolitan Water district or the Los Angeles Air Quality Management district), and a toothless regional planning agency (the Southern California Council of Governments). The City of Los Angeles has a weak-Mayor-strong-Council form of government. Locally elected Council persons wield extraordinary influence within their own districts, while city government is encapsulated within a structure of County Government that is headed by a small but extremely powerful group of Commissioners. At the same time, Los Angeles must share decision-making powers with nearly ninety smaller cities, all of them within the County. This turns out to be a totally dysfunctional territorial division of powers that puts Los Angeles at a severe disadvantage in relation to many Asian and Pacific cities.

Australia, for example, has a very different structure of urban-metropolitan governance. In the Australian urban archipelago, where five major cities are the preeminent focal points of national urban life, it is the state governments of the federation — such as Queensland, New South Wales, Victoria, South Australia, and Western Australia — that have substantial planning powers over their respective city regions of Brisbane, Sydney, Melbourne, Adelaide, and Perth. Australian states, moreover, have considerable autonomy *vis-à-vis* the federal government sitting in Canberra and play a very active developmental role. In Asian cities, experience varies from the unitary city state of Singapore to different degrees of decision-making power in other leading cities, with continued high dependency on central resources and supervision. If United States practice errs on the side of fragmentation, Asian countries tend to err on the side of centralization. Moreover, actual powers of local government rarely, if ever, coincide with the expanding boundaries of city regions. A good illustration is Jabotabek which is a planning region without substantial executive powers and is already regarded by many as too small to encompass its actual growth dynamics. An optimum territorial division of powers can probably only be imagined. The tension between centralization and decentralization will probably never be resolved once and for all. Nevertheless, it is not a trivial question. If governance does not extend to the whole of the city region, and if local units of government are given insufficient powers, it is unlikely that other objectives vital to world city formation can be achieved. Regional overview questions must be resolved at the appropriate level. At the same time, the regional level should not become enmeshed in purely local matters which require a knowledge of details and capacity for conflict resolution which simply does not exist at the level of a region that is equivalent to a moderately sized country. Although a workable territorial division of powers capable of addressing the issues of world city growth will be difficult to achieve, a restructuring of territorial governance is nevertheless an essential part of any solution to the complex problems world cities face. Some observers have begun to speculate about the emergence of virtual city states in Asia and elsewhere (Taylor, 1995; Scott, 1996; see also Ohmae, 1995). Large Australian cities, for example, already have the characteristics of city statehood within a federal framework. It is perhaps not too fanciful to believe that substantial powers can be devolved from national states to regional quasi-city-states even in the unitary states of Asia, in order to endow critically important regions with the powers and resources they need to deal with their own affairs independent of national intervention.

The question of sustainability

For a number of years now, it has become virtually impossible to discuss development at whatever scale without adding the modifying adjective 'sustainable'. Efforts to give a precise meaning to this epithet have failed so far and will undoubtedly continue to do so in the foreseeable future. For most people, however, 'sustainable' suggests a quality of the natural environment or, to place it more firmly in the context of the human habitat, the *quality of people's life space*. A widely accepted implication of this understanding is that developments should not impair or, more optimistically, should actually lead to improvements in, the life spaces we inhabit, and that this should be done not only for all living generations but also with an eye to generations not yet born. There is no doubt that this demand is a tall order, not least because it is inherently a democratic one: the quality of life spaces should be maintained or improved *for all the people* and not just for the elites in power.

In practical terms, invoking 'suststainability' has more modest, but still daunting, implications: to ensure good air quality and make water drinkable, to protect unique and fragile environments such as wetlands against enroachments by urban uses, to cut down on noise and toxic fumes, to make streets easier to navigate and safer for pedestrians, to detoxify soils that have been poisoned, to dispose of solid wastes in ways not harmful to human life and amenities, objectives, in other words, that any city would almost certainly want to achieve and yet finds it immensely difficult to do. The actual trends, especially in hyperurbanizing Asia, seem to go in the opposite direction, and the results are measured in terms of sickness, death, energies drained, time lost, and a relentless assault on the senses. The problems are so well known that I do not wish to dwell on them (ESCAP, 1993; World Resource Institute, 1996). The steady deterioration of life spaces in many Asian cities is a result of the single-minded pursuit of economic growth to the exclusion of other considerations and reflects, at least partly, a failure of political will to make urban development 'sustainable'. Of course, there are those who would argue that countries and cities in the so-called developing world should 'grow now and improve later'. But I am not persuaded that generations must be sacrificed on the altar of prosperity for the few. The 'grow now, improve later' argument is identical with one that asserts increasing inequality of income as a necessary condition for capital accumulation, when even the World Bank has long ago abandoned this misguided doctrine. In the perspective of emerging world cities, the neglect of the physical environment is a particularly near-sighted strategy because, in the end, conditions may become so bad that international business interests will look for more amenable sites elsewhere, where lungs do not have to breathe leaded air, traffic can move at more than 5 km an hour, and clean water is not just what comes out of a bottle.

A less well-entrenched meaning of 'sustainable', and one I would like to speak to briefly now, is one that refers to an acceptable *quality of life* insofar as it is socially determined. Here I mean such things as housing, community infrastructure and public services (education, health, sport, security, communication, transportation, etc.), work at decent wages for all who seek it, and a robust, well-organized civil society. All these, except for the last, are typically subjects of public policy. Their coverage and quality, of course, are a matter of resources, but they are also one of distribution, fairness, and social justice. It has become part of everyday wisdom (assiduously promoted by international aid agencies), that the market should rule in these as well as other matters, and that the best policy for promoting the quality of life is to have no policy at all but to let the 'free market' decide. But consider the outcome of this doctrine. Those who have money will buy their way into a luxurious quality of life in their palatial homes (heavily guarded by private security services), send their children to exclusive private schools or abroad, be treated in private clinics, communicate with the world through computers, faxes, and cellular phones, drive private automobiles (on public roads, of course), and relax in country clubs whose golf courses (reserved exclusively for men) are kept immaculate and green while people in other parts of the city (nearly all of them women) stand in line for an intermittent supply of water dribbling out of a standpipe. Somewhere in all of this there must be a balance. Countries with extremely skewed income distributions — Brazil, Peru, Sri Lanka, and the Philippines come to mind — are stagnating, their political regimes unstable, their social fabric torn by civil war or serious social conflict and, for all these reasons, unable to establish even the minimum conditions that would permit them to flourish. And what holds for some countries holds for their cities as well. Somewhere there must be a balance, so that society does not polarize, the rich do not simply get richer and the poor poorer.

Migrant workers or citizens?

World cities — indeed, most cities — grow primarily through migration. If the natural rate of reproduction in the country is two percent and a city grows at six percent each year, it is safe to assume that the difference in rates is accounted for by migration. The hyperurbanizing cities of Asia are thus drawing on the so-called surplus population of rural and small town areas within their own country, although migrant workers are beginning to arrive in larger numbers also from abroad (Castles and Miller, 1993). What is striking about this situation is that migrant workers and their families are typically invisible. If they live in squatter areas, they do not appear on official maps; if they engage in small-scale trade or manufactures, academics theorize them as part of the 'informal sector' which means essentially that they are not monitored by the state and so are rendered officially invisible; if they are treated, as in China, as a 'floating' population, meaning that their official residence continues to be in the villages whence they came, they are again invisible: no provisions are made for them in the official plans for housing, education, health, and so forth; they are treated as non-persons.

Foreign workers fare worse. Their presence may or may not be known to the government — the number of illegal migrants is rising in Japan and elsewhere — but they are workers inherently without rights. They cannot join labour unions, they cannot buy housing, they are not expected to settle in the city where they work. Most would agree that they are among the least protected members of the workforce and often subject to brutal exploitation.

The invisibility of migrant workers is not unique to Asia; it is also present in Western countries, where foreign workers are made the scapegoat for economic stagnation and the decline of the blue-collar working class, and where recent legislative initiatives are specifically designed to exclude them from public services. The question I should like to pose now is this: are there alternatives to a situation that seems to be obviously unjust? Is making migrants visible the answer, if visibility is merely a code word for government surveillance? Or does it have something to do with what I shall call *citizen rights*? This issue strikes at the very heart of societal development. Migrant workers now form a sort of underclass that is deprived of virtually all rights, even of people's right to security of tenure on the land, which is the primordial condition for a stable family life and social reproduction. As things are at present, no matter how small they make themselves, they can be evicted from their shack dwellings or overcrowded living quarters at a moment's notice. And that is only the beginning of their rights deprivation. If they happen to work in sweatshops, they may not be paid for the work they do. When they complain, they are fired. When they take their case to the courts, no judge will listen to their story. And needless to say, they are excluded from all political processes.

We have inherited a concept that links citizenship to the nation state, even though, in its original meaning that goes back to ancient Greece, it designated a person with the right to participate in the political life of a city. A person had the city's identity as his or her highest civic good. Today, citizenship — which carries with it certain entitlements such as the right to vote, eligibility for social services, the right to a passport, the right to the protection of the law, along with certain duties, such as obedience to the law, military service for men, etc. — becomes increasingly difficult to define as a national monopoly. Dual citizenship is becoming an increasingly accepted practice, as more migrants become 'transnational' whose actual residence or work place is in two or more countries. And in light of this, we may ask why citizenship should be exclusive to the nation when, in fact, a person contributes with his/her work to the construction of a city and its wealth? Once the concept of multiple citizenship is accepted, as appears to be increasingly the case, cannot a person simultaneously be a citizen of Hong Kong, Bangkok, and Surabaya while carrying Chinese, Thai, Indonesian passports? And what would the entitlements be to go along with local citizenship?

In my view, entitlements would include the right to visibility, to equal treatment with long-term residents of the city, to equal protection under the law, to inclusion in plans for urban expansion, to eligibility for educational, health, and other social services on an equal basis and, above all, to secure housing. It would also involve a right to participate in local elections and to contribute with sweat equity to the construction and improvement of neighborhood communities. Proposals such as these have been made by political parties elsewhere, in Germany, for example (Friedmann and Lehrer, forthcoming). They are, it seems to me, preferable to the alternative, which is invisibility, social polarization, a burgeoning underclass, systematic deprivation of rights, and the growing lawlessness that characterize so many of our 'world class' cities today.

The rise of civil society

If you have followed my argument so far, you will be aware that I am giving a rather unusual twist to the usual story about world city formation. Instead of waxing enthusiastic about megaprojects — bridges, tunnels, airports, and the cold beauty of glass-enclosed skyscrapers — which so delight the heart of big-city mayors, I am talking about people, their habitat and quality of life, the claims of invisible migrant citizens, and now, in yet another turn, the concept of civil society.

Let me begin with a concrete fact. I shall quote from a recent paper by Douglass (1996b, pp. 16-17):

> For urban Indonesia, estimates of minimum housing demand are one million units per year, depending on what components are included. Within the current national planning period, about 40,000 hectares of densely populated slums in 125 urban settlements are estimated to be in need of upgrading. In the past, the for-profit private housing sector has supplied just a little more than one-tenth of urban housing and has responded principally to middle and upper income demand for housing. The public housing program, which provides another four percent of units, has principally served civil servants and other special groups. Thus, about 85 percent of urban housing in Indonesia is supplied by the people themselves mainly using household savings, self-help, and mutual aid efforts.

If we follow Douglass' account, civil society in Indonesia is everything covered by the last phrase in this quotation: "urban housing [...] is supplied by the people themselves [...] using household savings, self-help, and mutual aid efforts". This is a reference to agencies that are neither of the state nor of the corporate economy but that are acting on their own initiative, being so to speak *in* the market and state but not *of* it. Building their own housing and, along the way, their communities as well, people must organize, raise resources, make decisions, and carry them out in a responsible way. In this way, civil society engages in actions that are empowering (Friedmann, 1992).

But civil society is also a relational term, juxtaposed to state and corporate economy as a relation of (relative) power.[4] It is primarily in this sense that I speak of 'the rise of civil society' as a widely observed phenomenon throughout the world accompanying, whether you approve of it or not, the linked processes of economic growth, global market integration, and relentless urbanization. It is people who mobilize outside the state, asserting their claims. Many of these struggles take place over life space issues such as the ones I have discussed. Ultimately they are claims not only for social justice but for a broad spectrum of citizen rights, as people become aware that the state is not necessarily a benign institution acting in the best interests of the people as a whole. Their claims are as old as democracy itself. They are claims for inclusiveness, for accountability of those who hold public office, for transparency in the conduct on the public's business, for information that will allow people to form their own opinions and come to their own decisions, and for participatory processes whenever state actions are likely to affect people's life and livelihood.

The state can move to suppress civil society, keeping it under a tight lid. It can misinterpret simple claims for accountability as undermining the state's authority and move to repress all criticism. It can even resort to terror. But the long-term future of world cities cannot be imagined without a gradual process of democratization. Civil society will not be excluded from world city formation.

190

One of the illusions of economistic thinking is that market societies inserted into the global network can extract technology and capital without any of the institutions in which they are embedded. That is simply an unavailable option. Once a society is opened up to the outside world, you cannot restrict the incoming flows to disembodied capital and technology. You will have to make the state also more responsive to people's needs and more transparent in its operations. That is on the one hand. On the other, is the fact that in hyperurbanizing cities, people's needs cannot all be met without their active collaboration. That is the story of Indonesia with which I began this section. There is any number of ways that local governments can work collaboratively with people in the provision of basic necessities; Indonesia's famous *kampong* improvement programme is one such example. There are others.[5] The point is that world city formation is not a task for state and corporate interests alone but one that also involves organized civil society, especially at the level of the local community.

Intercity networks: from functional to strategic

To say that a city's economy is inserted into a globe-spanning system underscores the network character of its linkages or, as Manuel Castells would have it, its insertion into a global 'space of flows' involving money, goods and services, information, ideas, cultural practices, and not least also the worker-citizens who enable the economy to flourish. I call all of these *functional* relations, and although hard data are difficult to obtain, there can be no question about their existence. Of particular interest to us in the present context is the transnational 'space of flows' that connects city regions across national boundaries in a world-wide web of market relations.

Strictly speaking, of course, these transactions involve primarily economic agents such as corporations and banks located in cities and not the cities themselves as political entities, so that the reference to intercity networks should be taken in a metaphorical sense only. In a recent article, however, commenting on European intercity networks, Klaus Kunzmann defines, in addition to functional, a second category of *strategic* networks (Kunzmann, 1995). These are, above all, network linkages between and among cities as *political-administrative units*. Kunzmann also refers to them as *alliances* that exist between two or more cities. An early forerunner is the well-known sister-city arrangement which is intended primarily to promote cultural and ceremonial exchanges. Since the beginning of the nineties, however, strategic networks have become extremely popular in Europe. The most significant network so far is *Eurocities* (The European Association of Metropolitan Cities) with a membership of fifty-eight. *Eurocities* serves, among other things, as a powerful interest lobby in Brussels. With subventions of ECU 49 million, intercity networks are enthusiastically promoted by the European Council, presumably because it sees such networks as strengthening the European Union.

Strategic alliances among cities may come into being for a variety of reasons. Some, according to Kunzmann, promote *learning* about innovative city projects such as technology parks, job creation programmes, or the social integration of foreign migrants. Others lead to *collaboration* in undertaking challenging new projects, such as large-scale infrastructure investments (e.g. land reclamation schemes), while still others, such as *Eurocities, articulate and pursue common interests*, particularly in international forums.

Any such listing can be, at best, suggestive, but I would like to add to the three already mentioned, four others: joint city-marketing, especially as part of efforts to promote tourism; encouraging educational and scientific exchanges and research; joint financing of megaprojects, such as subways and port developments; and the extension of reciprocal local citizen rights. Europe's enthusiasm for strategic networking takes place against a historical background of city leagues that reaches far back to the late Middle Ages. One of the most important of these was the Hanseatic League in northern Europe, centred on the 'free city' of Lübeck. The Hansa cities initially banded together to promote and protect long-distance trade in a network that extended from London in the west to Riga and Novgorod in the east. Hanseatic outposts, such as Bergen (Norway), were used to 'capture' trade in strategic commodities, in Bergen's case herring, that were then shipped all over Europe through trading networks. According to the German historian Fritz Rörig (1971; orig. 1933), long-distance trade in the 13th and 14th centuries was more than marginally important; by creating the first world economy in the West, it was the lifeblood that enabled an increasingly prosperous urban economy to come into being and survive.[6] The Hanseatic League lasted until well into the 17th century (surviving miraculously for nearly 400 years); its definitive demise — it had been in decline for some time — came only with the rise of the national state after the Peace of Westphalia in 1648 which settled what came to be known to historians as the Thirty Years War, marked the end of the Holy Roman Empire as an effective institution, and inaugurated the modern state system with its centralizing, mercantilist policies.

I would like to suggest that the experience of strategic alliances, foreshadowed centuries ago in the cities of the Hanseatic League and currently enjoying a revival in Europe, also holds significance for actual and/or emerging world cities along the Pacific Rim. As the national state gradually retreats from micro-managing local development, is it utopian to suggest the possibility of an Asian Pacific League of Cities for the 21st century? The beginnings of strategic networks in Asia are already visible in the new transnational 'growth triangles' of which the best known is centred on Singapore and the most promising, in the longer view, is the northern 'triangle', centered on the Yellow Sea, that would link Seoul, Dalian, Shenyang, Tianjin, and Osaka-Kobe (Rimmer, 1994). At the dawn of the APEC era, trans-Pacific intercity networks can be similarly imagined.

Conclusions

I shall be brief in my conclusions. For many people, an era of transition such as the present induces high anxiety about the future. New ways of life and work are

192

emerging. The old order is dying and the new is not yet born. With the upheavals all around us, only a few things seem fairly clear. Just as the 20th century was the century of falling empires and waning national states, so the 21st promises to be one of trading cities and, consequently, an era as much of competition as of cooperation among them. Global forces will continue to be at work, providing the framework for urban policies. But to a large extent, the future of world cities will be determined by the vision, entrepreneurial daring, and skill of their political elites who will need to break loose from traditional habits and patterns of thought so that the brave new world may come into existence.

Notes

1. According to Paul L. Knox, "world cities are centres of transnational corporate headquarters, of their business services, of international finance, of transnational institutions, of telecommunications and information processing. They are basing points and control centers for the interdependent skein of financial and cultural flows which, together, support and sustain the globalization of industry." (Knox, 1995, p. 6) In another attempt at definition, he calls them "the pre-eminent centres of commercial innovation and corporate control, undisputed centres of taste-making, crucibles of consumer sensibility, and seedbeds of material culture" (Knox, 1995, p. 7).
2. To construct this map, a matrix was created of scheduled air services to and from 266 cities whose metropolitan populations exceeded one million. Only non-stop and direct flights between cities were captured. The global airline network was divided into seven regions, and the dominant cities in each region were analyzed and mapped. The data revealed twenty cities that dominate their respective regional hinterlands and function as major hubs in the global air network (Keeling, 1995, pp. 120-25).
3. The conceptual language here is a bit difficult to navigate. World cities are city regions, but also function as organizing and control centers for wider areas (which I also call here by that ever-useful but slippery term, 'region'). Global centers, such as Tokyo or New York, have the whole world as their *space of articulation*; other cities exert a strong (often decisive) economic influence over multinational or national economic 'region', and so forth. It is therefore necessary always to identify the scale to which the term 'region' is applied. All of this is to say that cities are not spatially disarticulated, and only a small number of world cities exert control at a global scale. *The global economy requires a functional network of cities in order to sustain its processes of accumulation.*
4. There is a rapidly expanding literature on civil society (Keane, 1988; Cohen and Arato, 1994). The concept itself has a long pedigree in Western political theory. For an interesting discussion of both civil society and citizenship from a legal perspective which also incorporates a number of Brazilian case studies, see De Sousa Santos (1995).

5. For a splendid attempt to develop a 'theory of community activation' which is relevant in the present context, see Douglass (1995).
6. For a fascinating account of intercity networks in Asia during the 12th and 13th centuries, see Abu-Lughod (1989, Part III).

References

Abu-Lughod, J.L. (1989), *Before European Hegemony. The World System A.D. 1250-1350*, Oxford University Press: New York.
Castles, S. and Miller, M.J. (1993), *The Age of Migration. International Population Movements in the Modern World*, Guilford Press: New York.
Cohen, J.L. and Arato, A. (1994), *Civil Society and Political Theory*, The MIT Press: Cambridge, MA.
De Sousa Santos, B. (1995), *Toward a New Common Sense. Law Science and Politics in the Paradigmatic Transition*, Routledge: New York.
Del Castillo, J. (ed) (1989), Regional Development Policies in Areas in Decline, *EADI-Book Series 9*, University of the Basque Country: Bilbao.
Douglass, M. (1995), 'Urban Environmental Management at the Grass Roots: Toward a Theory of Community Activation', *East-West Center Working Papers, Environment Series, No. 42*, East-West Center: Honolulu.
Douglass, M. (1996a), 'World City Formation, Poverty and the Environment on the Asia Pacific Rim: Reflections on the Work of John Friedmann', Paper prepared for a Conference on Planning and the Rise of Civil Society, University of California at Los Angeles, April.
Douglass, M. (1996b), 'Land Use Planning and Management Strategies for a Sustainable Greater Jabotabek', Paper prepared for the Seminar on Strategies for a Sustainable Greater Jabotabek, Jakarta, August.
ESCAP (1993), *State of Urbanization in Asia and the Pacific, 1993*. United Nations, Economic and Social Commission for Asia and the Pacific: New York.
Friedmann, J. (1986), 'The World City Hypothesis', *Development and Change*, Vol. 17, No. 1, pp. 69-84.
Friedmann, J. (1992), *Empowerment: The Politics of Alternative Development*, Blackwell: Cambridge, MA.
Friedmann, J. (1995), Where We Stand: A Decade of World City Research, in Knox, P. and Taylor, P. (eds), *World Cities in a World System*, Cambridge University Press: Cambridge.
Friedmann, J. and Lehrer, U. (forthcoming), 'Urban Policy Responses to Foreign In-Migration', *Journal of the American Planning Association*.
Friedmann, J. and Wolff, G. (1982), 'World City Formation. An Agenda for Research and Action', *International Journal of Urban and Regional Research*, Vol. 6, No. 3, pp. 309-44.
Ginsburg, N., Koppel, B. and McGee, T. (1991), *The Extended Metropolis: Settlement in Transition in Asia*, University of Hawaii Press: Honolulu.

Heidenheimer, A.J. (1996), 'The Topography of Corruption: Explorations in a Comparative Perspective', *International Social Science Journal*, No. 149, pp. 337-48.

IBA Emscher Park (1996), *The Emscher Park International Building Exhibition*, Internationale Bauaustellung Emscher Park: Gelsenkirchen.

Keane, J. (ed.) (1988), *Civil Society and the State. New European Perspectives*, Verso: London.

Keeling, D.J. (1995), 'Transport and the World City Paradigm', in Knox, P.L. and Taylor, P.J. (eds), *World Cities in a World System*, Cambridge University Press: Cambridge.

Knox, P.L. and Taylor, P.J. (eds) (1995), *World Cities in a World System*, Cambridge University Press: Cambridge.

Knox, P.L. (1995), 'World Cities in a World System', in Knox, P.L. and Taylor (eds), *World Cities in a World System*, Cambridge University Press: Cambridge.

Kunzmann, K.R. (1996), 'Das Ruhrgebiet: Alte Lasten und Neue Chancen', in Akademie für Raumforschung und Landesplanung (ed.), *Agglomeratsionsräume in Deutschland: Ansichten, Einsichten, Aussichten*, Forschungs- und Sitzungsberichte, Vol. 199.

Kunzmann, K.R. (1995), 'Strategische Städtenetze in Europa: Mode oder Chance?', in Karl, H. and Henrichsmeyer, W. (eds), *Regionalentwicklung im Prozess der Europäischen Integration*, Bonner Schriften zur Integration, Vol. 4. Europa Union Verlag.

Lo, F.C. and Yeung, Y.M. (eds) (1996), *Emerging World Cities in Pacific Asia*, United Nations University Press: Tokyo.

McAllister, D.M. (ed.) (1973), *Environment: A New Focus for Land-Use Planning*, National Science Foundation: Washington, D.C.

Ohmae, K. (1995), *The End of the Nation State. The Rise of Regional Economies*, The Free Press: New York.

Rimmer, P.J. (1994), 'Regional Economic Integration in Pacific Asia', *Environment and Planning A*, Vol. 26, pp. 1731-59.

Rörig, F. (1971; orig. 1933), 'Mittelalterliche Weltwirtschaft', in *Wirtschaftskräfte im Mittelalter*, Herman Böhl Nachf: Vienna.

Sassen, S. (1991), *The Global City: New York, London, Tokyo*, Princeton University Press: Princeton, NJ.

Sassen, S. (1994), *Cities in a World Economy*, Pine Forge Press: Thousand Oaks, CA.

Scott, A.J. (1996), 'Regional Motors of the Global Economy', *Futures*, Vol. 28, No. 5, pp. 391-411.

Spearritt, P. (1996), 'The Realisation of the Multi-Function Polis', in Walter, J. et al. (eds), *Changing Cities: Reflections on Britain and Australia*, Sir Robert Menzies Centre for Australian Studies, University of London: London.

Taylor, P.J. (1995), 'World Cities and Territorial States: The Rise and Fall of the Mutuality', in Knox, P.L. and Taylor, P.J. (eds.), *World Cities in a World System*, Cambridge University Press: Cambridge.

World Resource Institute (1996), *World Resources: A Guide to the Global Environment*, The Urban Environment. An official publication of HABITAT II, the

United Nations Conference on Human Settlements, Oxford University Press: New York.

10 Economic Integration or Interdependence?

The Nation State and the Changing Economic Landscape of Southeast Asia

Carl Grundy-Warr and Martin Perry

Introduction

A borderless world economy is widely claimed to be upon us. In this new world order, distinct national economies and their associated domestic economic strategies are assumed to be irrelevant, surviving only as relic features amongst states that seek to swim against the tide of globalizing forces. The world economy, it is argued, has moved beyond its former components of international trade and multinational enterprise to become dominated by uncontrollable market forces. The main agents of change being the growing population of truly transnational corporations, that owe allegiance to no nation state and locate wherever in the world that economic advantage is currently seen to reside.

This chapter takes up the proposition of declining national sovereignty and examines the status of the nation state in Southeast Asia. The starting point for this discussion is the view that a clear understanding of political processes needs to underpin claims about the advent of globalization. With this in mind, the chapter begins by outlining definitions of national sovereignty, integration and interdependence. The last-mentioned two terms might appear to be interchangeable, but closer review highlights the need for a precise description of the process through which national sovereignty might be changing.

Essential to an understanding of the political map is the relationship between territory, statehood and sovereignty. In a politico-legal framework, territory is divided into different 'sovereign state' areas, each of which is separated by the right, vested in the state, to exercise functions exclusive to that locality (see James, 1986).[1] Within its domain, state prerogative is protected by a 'set of global legal principles associated with the governance of space' (Herzog, 1990, p. 20). In other words, state and territorial sovereignty have little meaning except *in relation to* other states and their mutual recognition of each other's sovereignty reflected in the canons of international law and the rhetoric of state leaders (Murphy, 1994).

The acceptance of a transformation that is leading to the need to reconceptualize the notions of sovereignty and the significance of nation states depends partly on a view that many national economies have become 'increasingly complex, unmanageable, porous and fragile' mechanisms 'poorly suited to the exercise of state sovereignty' (Camilleri, 1990, pp. 33-4). Space-time shrinking technologies, the increased mobility of capital, transnational financial institutions and the more transient location of telephone and computer networks used for huge transfers of money (O'Brien, 1992); and other processes of 'global shift' related to the activities of transnational corporations (Dicken, 1992), have weakened the ability of nation states to exercise national economic management. This has led some writers to argue that the very notion of 'national' economies is becoming meaningless (Ohmae, 1990; 1995). It is clear that at the end of the twentieth century we have 'a global geography of economic activities not readily captured by state-territorial representatives of economic characteristics or performance' (Agnew & Corbridge, 1995, p. 89).

In order to interpret the changes taking place to our economic and political landscapes it is necessary to be precise about the terminology used. The terms 'international' and 'global' are not to be used synonymously. As Dicken (1994, p. 106) puts it:

Internationalization refers simply to the extension of activities across national boundaries; globalization involves more than this and is qualitatively different. It implies a degree of purposive functional integration among geographically dispersed activities.

Even this distinction is not without complications. For instance, Taylor (1995, p. 1) has pointed out that the term 'international as interstate is a product of the success of state-centred politics legitimating itself as national politics'. He has suggested alternative terms, such as 'interstateness' and 'interterritoriality', to sharpen the theorization of 'states in their multiplicity' in the world economy. 'Interstateness' refers to relations between 'a multiplicity of formally equal units' while 'interterritoriality' emphasizes how almost every section of occupied land across the world is the sovereign territory of some state (Taylor, 1995, p. 3).

It is therefore simplistic to characterize the changes taking place to political and economic maps with reference only to processes of globalization and internationalization. The term 'international' is misleading where it is used in the context of inter-state relations. There is also a need to recognize a distinction between 'inter' and 'trans' processes. Whereas *inter*-state processes rely on the continual existence of strong nation states and their associated exercise of sovereignty, *trans*-state processes rely on a weakening of this sovereignty and system of national-state jurisdictions. This is highly relevant to our discussion, for as Taylor (1995, p. 12) has stressed: "... our 'inter' concepts are set against our 'trans' concepts as polar opposites; the former defines processes reproducing states, nations and territories, the latter processes undermine them".

Whilst processes of internationalization make the boundaries between domestic-foreign spheres of activity increasingly blurred, they may simultaneously

198

strengthen some aspects of political sovereignty and inter-stateness (Taylor, 1995). We have tried to illustrate the fact that the notions of economic interdependence and integration will involve both 'inter' and 'trans' nation, state and territorial processes, although 'trans' processes are obviously dominant in the case of integration. Diagrammatically, the linking together of nation states is shown by overlapping spheres, where each sphere represents a zone of potential national sovereignty (figure 10.1). The term domestic is used to refer mainly to the business and regulatory environment which is presided over by national regulators and government. It could also be applied to 'the business conducted in the same market as the domicile of the firm or customer, for the most part being the place where taxes are paid and where the majority of ownership lies' (O'Brien, 1992, p. 4). In fact it is increasingly hard to justify a rigid domestic-foreign dichotomy in the 'international' political economy (Agnew & Corbridge, 1995, p. 100). This is particularly so in a world economy where nation states are involved in economic diplomacy with other states and with companies in hot competition for markets, trade and investment opportunities, which results in states themselves becoming internationalized (see Stopford & Strange, 1992; Dicken, 1994).

Clearly there is a need for careful application of terminology like international, global, integration and interdependence. Describing globalization as a process of functional integration may not be sufficient if there are both 'trans' and 'inter' state processes operating simultaneously. The revision of world trade rules, for example is partly a process of 'a political adaptation to globalization, a reinforcement of inter-stateness', and, partly a process involving 'capital restructuring with profound trans-state implications', leading to the conclusion that 'globalization in all its manifestations incorporates these two contrary processes and should therefore be understood as contradictory' (Taylor, 1995, p. 14).

A variety of possible degrees of interdependence and integration between nation states at both sub-regional (world region) and regional levels of analysis need to be distinguished. At the sub-regional level of economic cooperation between two or more nation states across 'international' boundaries, a truly 'integrated' borderlands exists where the economies of nation states have merged and movement of people, goods, capital and resources across political territories is unrestricted. This would involve each state willingly relinquishing 'its sovereignty to a significant degree for the sake of achieving mutual progress' (Martinez, 1994, p. 5). In this sense, there would be genuine trans-nationality, trans-territoriality and trans-stateness. In practice, it is more likely that states would cooperate to the extent that some forms of limited functional integration would make the boundary meaningless for only specified types of economic activity, movements of capital, goods and people.

'Interdependent borderlands' involve a mix of 'trans' and 'inter' state processes in which increased cross-border economic interaction, friendly and cooperative inter-state relations coexist alongside the continuance of two distinct political sovereignties, whilst economic linkages are strengthened.

The greater the flow of economic and human resources across the border, the more the two economies will be structurally bonded to each other. The end result will be the creation of a mutually beneficial economic system (Martinez, 1994, p. 4).

GLOBAL

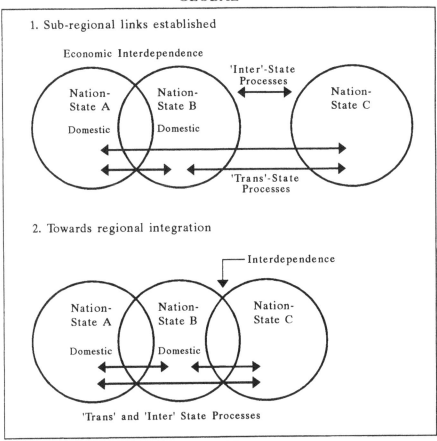

GLOBAL

Figure 10.1   **Diagrammatic representation of nation state links and spheres of national sovereignty**

Sources: Adapted from O'Brien (1992), Martinez (1994); aided by helpful definitions from Taylor (1995), Dicken (1992, 1994), and Milward & Sørensen (1993)

Greater economic interdependence, or even limited economic integration, may involve dilutions of state sovereignty, but they do not necessarily signal the beginning of the demise of nation states. Sovereignty is an elastic concept as 'the frontiers of national sovereignty' are being moved, modified or changed based on deliberately taken alterations in state policies and actions (Milward & Sørensen, 1993). This proposition is examined through the recent history of the Association of Southeast Asian Nations (ASEAN), including its promotion of regionalization amongst the nation states of Southeast Asia (refer to ch. 3 of this volume) and the development of sub-regional forms of cooperation amongst certain of ASEAN's member states.

ASEAN: towards integration or inter-dependence?

A number of broad-based changes are apparently tending towards greater economic co-operation within ASEAN[2], including between longstanding and new[3] member states in the late 1990s. For much of the period prior to the early 1990s ASEAN's record on economic cooperation between member states was fairly poor. Indeed, one astute observer of developments within the region argued that talk of an evolving regional market was one of the big myths of ASEAN.

> Although the grouping stresses economic co-operation it basically remains an instrument for discussions among essentially autocratic governments reluctant to surrender any power to regional institutions [...] The Asian business community knows that substantive economic integration lags far behind the rhetoric [...] Boasts about regional integration amount to a type of tailored trickery worthy of *The Emperor's New Clothes* (Clad, 1991, pp. 217 & 219).

Evidence of the lack of progress in economic integration is not hard to find. There was the failure of the ASEAN Financial Corporation, the tiny level of intra-regional trade, poor progress in electricity-sharing projects, and the ill-fated ASEAN Industrial Joint Ventures (AIJVs) (Clad, 1991).

Two reasons for the 'reluctant regionalism' were to do with the political make-up of ASEAN itself and the big vested interests within some of the economies of the Association. First, member states of ASEAN have been reluctant to cede any power to their collective entity so that, "All the 'integrative' exercises thus cannot disguise a stubbornly material bias in ASEAN [...] The truth is that no common institutions have emerged in Southeast Asia that have a scrap of independent life" (Clad, 1991 , p. 227).

Second, dominant business interest linked to the Indonesian, Malaysian and Philippine political leaderships were little interested in promoting genuine regional integration because it would 'upset too many comfortable monopolies and corned import agencies' (Clad, 1991, p. 226). There were also fears that dismantling intra-

ASEAN trade barriers would hurt 'infant industries', and mostly benefit foreign, particularly Japanese capital in league with non-indigenous retailing networks. Whatever the motivation of economic nationalists within ASEAN for their actions, it is clear that intra-regional linkages played only a minor role in the relatively high economic growth enjoyed by individual economies of ASEAN. This is partly related to the way these economies have been incorporated into the world economy either as suppliers of particular commodities or as export-oriented manufacturing bases for multinational capital.

In the early 1980s the region was in recession as a result of sharp falls in export prices for crude oil and primary commodities, which accounted for a large share of ASEAN exports. The general response was to intensify efforts to attract inward investment, partly by relaxing previous restrictions on foreign direct investment (FDI), such as low equity participation rules and licensing controls to restrict investment in specified sectors. Whatever the contribution of these policy innovations on the growth in FDI, two things are clear. First, all then members of ASEAN, except Philippines, achieved growth averaging 6 percent to 11 percent a year during the second half of the 1980s (see table 1, ch. 3). Second, FDI encouraged extra-regional rather than regional dependence.[4]

Intra-ASEAN trade integration remains low. As of 1990, trade within the region accounted for around 20 percent of total export value or less than 2 percent above the level of intra-regional trade at the time of ASEAN's formation in 1965. This is despite a variety of initiatives taken by ASEAN that have sought to promote the economic integration of the region. Following an ASEAN summit conference in 1976, for example, the World Bank encouraged attempts to establish large scale, multinational industrial projects that would otherwise be deterred by the limited size of individual national markets. By restricting the duplication of projects and through selective lowering of trade barriers, the intention was to assist the viability of investment by providing access to an enlarged market area. Whilst several projects were devised covering such products as fertilizer, pulp, and diesel engine manufacture, practical outcomes were few (Takeuchi, 1993). Each individual ASEAN member, although especially the larger countries, favoured economic self-reliance through a full range of industrial activity and was reluctant to participate in shared industrial projects and compromise their ambition. The ability to capture a substantial share of world FDI helped fuel this ambition.

Tentative integrative steps

The first regional integration initiative to bring results was the Brand-to-Brand Complementation scheme launched in 1988. This programme has more modest ambitions than the attempt to get collective support for industrial infrastructure. It focuses simply on encouraging firms to increase their regional purchasing of parts and materials, although even so Indonesia has not joined. This initiative targeted automotive parts and provided a 50 percent tariff discount on intra-ASEAN cross-border shipments of approved, locally-made parts. A number of Japanese companies are known to have participated (Fujita & Hill, 1995), but without extension to other sectors the overall impact of the programme is minor.

A significant step toward greater ASEAN economic integration was taken in January 1993 through a commitment to implement an ASEAN Free Trade Area (AFTA), which according to one self-proclaimed 'ASEANocrat' 'represents a quantum leap in the history of ASEAN economic co-operation' (Abad, Jr., 1996, p. 245). This project can be seen as a response to external and internal influences. Externally, the growth of regional trade arrangements, notably in North America (NAFTA) and the removal of internal customs barriers within the European Union raised concern. As well as the perceived threat to export growth arising from such agreements, ASEAN nations are concerned that China and Indochinese countries as well as Mexico have emerged as more attractive places of investment. Fear that investment flows into ASEAN will slow down, is prompting a new priority to regional cooperation. At the same time some of the previous impediments to regional cooperation have reduced through the geographical redistribution of FDI received by ASEAN.

Since 1986, a 'second-tier' of newly industrializing nations have emerged, comprising Indonesia, Malaysia and Thailand. This second tier was originally promoted by Japanese investment which accounted for at least a quarter of all FDI into Indonesia, Malaysia, Singapore and Thailand during 1986-1990. More recently, investment from the first wave of Asian newly industrialized economies (NIEs) has grown in importance to the second tier locations, particularly from Hong Kong, Taiwan and South Korea. These investment flows have deviated from past TNC activity by seeking greater regional integration of affiliate activity, in a move that has been interpreted as an outcome of 'global Toyotaism' (Fujita & Hill, 1995). A further investment trend, of some importance to ASEAN co-operation, is the growing strength of ASEAN TNCs.

With a view to raising the importance of regional trade, ASEAN commitment to implement the AFTA by the year 2008 was given in 1992 (later brought forward to 2003). The cornerstone of AFTA is a two-stage achievement of a Common Effective Preferential Tariff (CEPT). One is a fast track programme to reduce tariffs to 0-5 percent over 7-10 years; the second involves tariff reductions to similar levels over 10-15 years. Already, there are some encouraging signs of greater intra-regional economic activity. Following the adoption of the CEPT, intra-ASEAN trade expanded from US$79 billion in 1993 to US$111 billion in 1994 and to US$140 billion in 1995, which is about 25 percent of ASEAN's global trade (Daquila, 1997). As a consequence, intra-regional trade now exceeds the volume of trade between any one ASEAN state and its individual trading partners, although as a whole external trade continues to dominate. On the other hand, economic analysis has suggested that AFTA alone will have a limited impact on regional trade expansion: one estimate predicts that the share of regional trade will rise in a range of 2-4 percent for individual member states (Takeuchi, 1993).[5]

Even allowing for the localization strategies of Japanese investment, foreign companies still tend to emphasize the region as an export base to third countries or home territories, although there is a shift towards manufactures in the 'second-tier' Asian industrializing countries. Local exports from Thailand, Indonesia, the Philippines and Malaysia are chiefly natural resources and primary commodities. Even so, agricultural products, as well as services, are not included in AFTA, although there is some expectation that these items will be made part of the agreement. In addition, some manufactured items such as electronic parts, automotive components, plastics, and ceramics are on individual country exemption lists. It should also be noted that Singapore and Brunei entered AFTA with no significant tariff barriers while other ASEAN members had introduced tariff reduction programmes prior to the implementation of the CEPT.

There is little doubt that some progress has been made towards closer intra-regional cooperation. Even so, beyond improvements in intra-regional trade and certain efforts to promote sub-regional linkages (see later) there is still a long way to go before ASEAN is seen as a genuinely united and coherent economic grouping. Recently, Rafidah Aziz, the Malaysian Minister for Trade and Industry, called upon member states of ASEAN to consider pulling together the synergies of major corporations within the region so that they could compete on a more equal footing with multinationals. Commenting on this, Sofjan Wanadi, chief executive of Indonesia's Gemala Group, observed the lack of industrial policy cohesion at national levels, especially in Indonesia, and noted several examples of a lack of industrial cooperation between ASEAN members. He concluded that 'high-sounding talk about the potential power of ASEAN as a coordinated economic unit has yet to prove itself to be anything more than just that' (Wanandi, 1997, p. 68).

Enlargement of ASEAN

As well as TNC investment strategies, intra-regional trade and investments are benefiting from the end of ideological and military partitions. ASEAN-Indo-China cooperation has developed rapidly since the Cambodian peace accords were signed in Paris in 1991. The inclusion of Vietnam into ASEAN in 1995 (see Hoang, 1994) and further enlargement into an 'ASEAN-10' with the inclusion of Cambodia, Laos and Myanmar (Antolik, 1994; Paribatra, 1994) represents a pragmatic blend of economics and politics underlying regional security interests. It is argued that peaceful cooperation between former political foes in Southeast Asia is a prerequisite for accelerating economic development and growing prosperity (Endo, 1994).

Population growth plus new membership means that the ASEAN market has grown from 202 million in 1970 to around 491 million in 1996. ASEAN's combined population is about 113 million: this is bigger than that of NAFTA and 120 million bigger than the European Union-15. Assuming an ASEAN-10, its regional income presently stands at approximately US$600 billion, which according to some economic forecasts, is expected to double every eight years (Daquila, 1997, p. 4).

Underlying the new economic regionalism and expansion of ASEAN is the belief that the established and industrializing member states and home-grown businesses are in a position to both service and profit from the economic development of the so-called 'transitional economies' of Indo-China as they move away from dogmatic central planning and heavy state ownership towards more open market economies. As Chee Peng Lim (1995, p. 308) has put it,

> the transitional economies in Indo-China will be able to profit from the experiences of the ASEAN countries in mobilizing, and effective utilization of, domestic and external financial resources. [...] Subsequently, it may be possible to envisage the possibility of enhancing intra-subregional co-operation between the Indochinese and ASEAN organizations.

He goes on to argue that there will eventually be a 'convergence of perceptions of development objectives' based upon 'a shared view of the development process, which is pragmatic rather than ideological in nature' (Chee, 1995, pp. 310-11). As for the Indochinese states themselves, ASEAN is viewed as a valuable 'bridge' to huge export markets and as a source of advanced technology, investments and market know-how (Antolik, 1994; Hoang, 1994).

The growing economic links between the newly industrializing economies (NIEs) of Southeast Asia and the formerly closed 'transitional' economies of Indo-China is helping to boost intra-regional trade. The main beneficiaries appear to be investors from Singapore, Malaysia, Thailand and Indonesia who are sinking money into projects as diverse as building new roads, timber extraction, financial services and floating casinos (Tripathi, 1996). As a result the relatively poor resource-based economies of Laos and Cambodia are facing big development dilemmas relating to asymmetrical economic relations, rapid natural resource extraction, and inappropriate investments (Hirsch, 1995; Rigg, 1995). ASEAN's growing trade and investments with Myanmar are related to its on-going policy of 'constructive engagement'[6] which should not be divorced from broader economic objectives and regional security issues. In contrast, intra-regional trade links only form a relatively small proportion of Vietnam's total trade with the rest of the world, although the market and business implications of Vietnam's incorporation into ASEAN are very significant (Hoang, 1994). It should also be noted that there is an enormous volume of undocumented, 'unofficial' business across many of the borders of mainland Southeast Asia (see, for example, Mya Than, 1992, 1994; Phongpaichit, et al., 1996), which means that analysis of transboundary economic ties in this region should go beyond an analysis of formal intra-ASEAN and inter-state relations.

Alongside the physical and geopolitical enlargement of ASEAN, expectations that intra-regional competitiveness amongst Southeast Asian nations will continue are encouraging some ASEAN members to promote wider regional economic groupings (McIntyre, 1993, pp. 265). Two competing initiatives exist: the Asia-Pacific Economic Cooperation (APEC) forum and the East Asian Economic Caucus (EAEC). The latter is a Malaysian initiative designed to promote links between ASEAN, Japan and the Northeast Asian NICs. This grouping has even higher hurdles to overcome than ASEAN: intra-NIC trade (Singapore, Hong Kong, Taiwan and South Korea) was less than 10 percent throughout the 1980s and political issues prevent any official diplomatic ties between Taiwan and other prospective members of the EAEC. Unlike APEC, North America and Australasia would be excluded (as well as China) and as this has primarily been a consideration for Malaysia alone, APEC has made greater progress (Higgott, 1994). Advocates of APEC are working towards further institutionalization building on some already significant achievements: the establishment of a secretariat in Singapore, regular senior officials meetings and the creation of a range of work programmes.

The growth of intra-regional trade and cooperation to enlarge ASEAN undoubtedly mean the Emperor is no longer naked. Considerable political capital has been invested into the AFTA deliberations. In 1994, a meeting of ASEAN economic ministers agreed to bring forward full implementation to 2003. In August 1995, it was agreed to expand the range of 'fast-track' items and to bring services into the agreement and that further discussion would be held on a 2000 implementation date. The commitment to strengthen intra-ASEAN cooperation, as well as to expand the membership of the regional organization, relate to two primary motives. First, the end of Cold War geopolitical divisions that kept ASEAN 'united and purposeful' have made it all the more imperative for the Association 'to move economic cooperation and integration to centre stage' (Chia, 1995, p. 302).

Second, ASEAN needs to develop 'a viable basis for its external economic diplomacy', particularly, as noted above, with the emergence of major regional economic groupings in Europe and NAFTA (Soesastro, 1992, p. 3). According to Abad, Jr., (1996, p. 250) there is a concerted effort underway to 're-engineer' ASEAN into 'an inter-governmental organization promoting regional interests vis-à-vis the rest of the world' providing a multilateral framework for the pursuit of unilateral interests'. The aim of this transformation being to present a united front in external relations, particularly with those powers strategically engaged in the region. In this way ASEAN has become an Association representing member states and an outward-looking body participating in the ASEAN Regional Forum (ARF), the Asia-Pacific Economic Cooperation (APEC) forum, and in meetings with European Union officials.

Regionalism, sovereignty and security

An assessment of the impact of ASEAN's espousal of regionalism on national sovereignty is assisted by reference to our earlier definitions of integration and interdependence. As noted in the introductory section, integration, whether it is economic or political, must involve a concession of nation state power to 'supranational' or 'international' bodies. By contrast, interdependence requires adjustments to be made primarily within the national political system or within the existing bodies representing the interests of member nation states. It has been argued elsewhere, that even in the European Union where there has been considerable progress in terms of economic integration, the tendency has been for nation states to transfer sovereignty over specific policy areas to common institutions where this has been seen to be the most convenient and effective way of advancing national objectives (see Milward & Sørensen, 1993). While the costs of integration are higher, integration is sometimes favoured over interdependence to provide a framework that is less easily reversed, more exclusive (i.e. it is easier to discriminate against outsiders to the bargain), and legally enforceable (Milward & Sørensen, 1993, p. 19). Thus, integration may mean giving up some sovereignty in return for a more secure regional framework in which national policy objectives can be pursued in an increasingly inter-linked global economy.

Undoubtedly, the AFTA Agreement is 'a first step in the institutionalized process towards regional economic integration' (Soesastro, 1992, p. 6), but in some respects it represents a move that is based more on developing stronger regional inter-dependence than on far-reaching integration. For instance, under the CEPT programme of the AFTA Agreement of 1992, individual member states have retained the unilateral and discretionary prerogative without the aid of an objective criterion to determine whether or not products should be included or excluded from the programme (Santiago, 1995, p. 19). This 'AFTA loophole' gives legal sanction for each nation to protect their perceived interests. Whilst the exclusion of products to protect domestic industry on the basis of political patronage would violate the rule of *pacta sunt servanda* under the law of treaties[7], there is still scope for member states to produce excessively long exclusion lists for products which have the effect of undermining AFTA's objectives (Santiago, 1995, p. 20).

Another critical matter concerning the character of regional integration is that ASEAN member states have so far resisted the creation of independent organs 'that can issue decisions which are binding and enforceable against them and their instrumentalities' (Santiago, 1995, p. 21). The AFTA Agreement provides for the establishment of a ministerial-level Council comprising one nominee from each member state for the purpose of supervising, co-ordinating and reviewing the implementation of the articles therein. Differences of interpretation or application between member states may be submitted to the Council. However, the Council is not granted sufficient powers 'to make pronouncements on non-implementation by a member state', and the Council's composition makes it unlikely that it would do so (Santiago, 1995, p. 21). While some ASEAN member states have ratified treaties and conventions that have imposed stringent legal regimes diminishing aspects of state sovereignty[8], this has been strenuously resisted or viewed as unnecessary for the ASEAN structure itself. The re-engineering of ASEAN is unlikely to entail any moves towards the moulding of new supranational institutions, although it has entailed a strengthening of the ASEAN Secretariat which now recruits its officers through 'region-wide open competition' (Abad, Jr., 1996, p. 246).

The 'ASEAN way' seems to be an attempt to strengthen intra-regional links and enlarge collective responsibility without any loss of national resilience or political sovereignty on the part of member states. In a similar way, the enlargement of ASEAN is to be accomplished without threatening the territorial integrity and political sovereignty of member states, and without interference in domestic political affairs.

Regional togetherness within the 'family' of ASEAN is to be achieved in accordance with the fundamental principles of the Treaty of Amity and Co-operation (1976), which was initially promulgated to foster political stability in a non-communist bloc in the aftermath of sweeping communist victories in Indo-China in the mid-1970s. The Treaty sets out the principles for managing relations between ASEAN states. It strengthened regional cohesiveness by allowing common security positions to be reached through processes of consultation and consensus without any member-state 'losing face' (see Hoang, 1994). Similarly, officially sanctioned forms of economic cooperation such as the formalization of trade with new ASEAN states and different forms of intra-ASEAN sub-regional cooperation (see below) are used to promote regionalism without seriously weakening the sovereignty of individual member states.

Paradoxically, greater regional cohesion over common security and economic issues can actually serve to bolster the juridical and empirical sovereignty of weaker states.[9] An example of a 'weak state' (Buzan, 1983) that may be strengthened by intra-regional trade and diplomacy is Myanmar. Protracted state-societal conflict and ethnic conflicts in Myanmar have severely hindered empirical statehood. The ruling military regime, the State Law and Order Restoration Council (SLORC) has (since its clamp-down on pro-democracy demonstrations in 1988) managed to gain a firmer territorial and political grip over the diverse populations in the country's extensive border regions, which were previously under the *de facto* control of armed groups in opposition to the military regime (see Lintner, 1995; Grundy-Warr, 1993). Cross-border economic ties with Thailand, increasing revenues from trade and foreign direct investments from the US, some European companies, Japan and Asian neighbours, have provided a degree of economic legitimacy to SLORC.[10] Undoubtedly some of the revenue derived from trade and investments is filtered into the *tatmadaw*'s (Burmese Army) efforts to weaken, if not destroy, all armed resistance within Myanmar's internationally recognized boundaries. There is a resource and economic dimension to both state-centred and cross-border security (see Grundy-Warr & Rajah, in press).

We should not detach 'the pursuit of economic regionalism' from 'the regional political and security dynamic' (Acharya, 1995, p. 175). The end of the Cold War has provided new opportunities to raise the pace of intra- and extra-regional economic cooperation as a means to 'enhance regime legitimacy' by creating new avenues for capital accumulation for both public and private sector interests (Acharya, 1995, pp. 175-8). As Van Grunsven et al. (1995, p. 174) have observed:

> Regionalization and sub-regional economic integration should be seen against the background of not only the pressures of industrial restructuring but also the dramatic alterations over the past decade in the geopolitical situation in the region.

The above discussion emphasizes two critical issues in the analysis of economic regionalism. First, we should be as precise as possible in the way we apply terms such as 'integration' and 'inter-dependence' in the Southeast Asian context, or indeed in any part of the world. Second, as Acharya (1995, p. 175) has argued, 'the market-driven dynamic does not operate outside the constraints of state sovereignty and control'. Therefore, we should consider the politics and security aspects of different forms of economic agreement, cooperation and interaction between states. Hitherto, the discussion has emphasized broader regional linkages and the formal expansion of ASEAN, but it is also necessary to consider the emergence of new economic landscapes associated with different sub-regional initiatives.

ASEAN growth triangles: new forms of sub-regional economic development?

Foremost amongst the growth of sub-regional developments are the so-called ASEAN 'growth triangles' based on notions of economic complementarity, geographic proximity and existing infrastructure specializations (Perry, 1991; Chia & Lee, 1992; Toh & Low, 1993; Thant et al., 1994). The first such growth triangle involves cooperation between Singapore, the southern Malaysian state of Johor and the western Indonesian province of the Riau islands. The so-called SIJORI, or southern growth triangle, responds to development pressures on the Singapore economy and the Indonesian government's long-standing desire to link the development of the Riau islands to the city state's resource constraints (Esmara, 1975; Rice, 1989).

As well as organizational simplicity, growth triangle arrangements are seen as a way of gaining mutual advantage from the economic disparities existing across proximate national boundaries (Rodan, 1993; Tang & Thant, 1994). In the case of SIJORI, the economic complementarity is generally perceived in terms of a technical, sectoral and regional division of labour. From the perspective of Singapore, labour and land constraints require that low-value added and labour intensive activities are relocated to neighbouring territory. As well as enabling the region as a whole to grow, such localized decentralization is thought to offer other advantages. It does not threaten Singapore's advanced industrial activities or business service sectors as the neighbouring territory does not have the resources to accommodate such activity. At the same time, new investment can be attracted by marketing the region as an integrated production base combining low cost production with advanced managerial, logistic and operational networks. This potential is enhanced by appropriate infrastructure provision (for example, on the Riau island of Batam 'smart card' immigration facilities were provided to ease the daily commuting of business executives from Singapore) and possibly some regulatory innovation to ease movements across the border zone.

As well as the SIJORI triangle, other ASEAN sub-regions identified for similar cross-border cooperation are the northern ASEAN growth triangle, comprising the northern states of Malaysia and Sumatra and southern Thailand; and the east ASEAN growth triangle linking regions in the Philippines, Indonesia and Malaysia. As well as the SIJORI example, it has been suggested that the multiplication of growth triangle proposals is influenced by the perceived dynamism of the Hong Kong-Taiwan-Southern China region.

According to several scholars the growth triangles represent new forms of economic cooperation that express the 'inseparability of political and economic relations in the international arena' (Rodan, 1993, p. 223; Kumar & Siddique, 1994). The real extent of originality associated with these subregional initiatives may, however, be less than first thought. They are not new in the sense that there are already well-established examples of cross-border manufacturing and transnational economic integration in parts of western Europe (see, for example, Briner, 1986; Scott, 1993); in the form of the *maquiladoras* (since 1965) in the Mexico-US borderlands (see, for example, Herzog, 1990; Sklair, 1993); and in the substantial cross-border investments, trade and sub-contracting aided by pre-existing kinship and business ties in the Hong Kong-Zhujiang Delta region (see, for example, Leung, 1993; Sung et al., 1995).

Whilst the growth triangles are not radically new departures for the world economy, they do represent significant change in the intra-ASEAN approach to economic cooperation. Furthermore, the political and economic character of sub-regional change in ASEAN contrasts with that in other parts of the world (see Van Grunsven et al. 1995). Amongst some of the new features of ASEAN growth triangles are:

1. Cooperation without institutional innovation — Growth triangles involve few awkward institutional and legislative changes at state level whilst promoting greater transboundary economic activity, which, it has been suggested, is a response to particularly 'Asian' styles of government (see Abonyi, 1994; Thant et al., 1994). The argument runs that ASEAN is promoting forms of sub-regional cooperation that require a minimum of formal, legalistic decision-making processes and fit the 'ASEAN way' of doing deals through networking and consensus behind closed doors (Kumar & Siddique, 1994).

One can cite several mechanisms that have evolved in the ASEAN context which facilitate this consensus-seeking process. Perhaps the most important is the high priority assigned to networking. Familiarization tours, formal and informal contacts amongst counterparts, the constitution of *ad-hoc* problem-solving committees, and visits by ministerial delegations, all emphasize the establishment of interpersonal relationships at all levels of the national bureaucracies of ASEAN members, and, clearly, at the sub-regional growth triangle level as well (Kumar & Siddique, 1994, p. 55).

A unique feature of the growth triangles is that they can be initiated by senior politicians without the need for new institutional structures and without too many changes to 'national' regulatory frameworks (Abonyi, 1994).

2. National security-enhancing features — There are certain 'security-enhancing consequences of transnational production' for the states concerned (Acharya, 1995, p. 178). Growth triangle projects, to the extent that they strengthen bilateral ties between neighbours, can help to lessen political tensions without any great loss of political sovereignty.[11] The fact that economic cooperation can progress with existing institutions, whilst regulatory changes can be restricted to particular enclaved developments, helps to preserve national boundaries as protectors of state sovereignty but allows for greater economic transaction across political divides.

3. Incremental intra-regional cooperation — Participation in growth triangles may be viewed as a way of advancing the cause of broader intra-regional economic cooperation. This idea is expressed very well by Kumar & Siddique (1994, p. 53):

> growth triangles have become sub-regional groupings within an ASEAN context that promote intra-ASEAN linkages. Characterizing growth triangles as 'mini-AFTAs' (ASEAN Free Trade Areas) has provided a niche for them within the evolution of the loosely structured ASEAN framework. Indeed, it has been argued that providing a web of growth triangles covering the ASEAN area may be a critical element in the realization of AFTA over the next fifteen years.

Linking these three processes to subregional projects can give the impression of another step toward regional integration, but there are two problems with this interpretation. First, it overlooks the lack of any implementation in most of the areas proclaimed as growth triangles with the main exceptions of SIJORI and the Pearl River Delta, which in any case is outside Southeast Asia. Second the focus underpinning the projects vary, even in the case of the two well-developed examples. For both these reasons it is necessary to examine a little more closely the economic and political dynamics of these growth triangles in order to ascertain whether they really do represent 'coherent and integrated divisions of labour that transcend formal national political boundaries', as Rodan (1993, p. 223) has suggested, and are stepping-stones to further economic integration as suggested by Abonyi (1994) and Kumar and Siddique (1994).

Borderless economies or integrated borderlands?

There are two very contrasting perspectives of sub-regional economic development involving the creation of cross-boundary manufacturing zones. Whilst both perspectives discuss economic processes leading towards greater integration at local or 'sub-regional' levels, one gives primacy to transnational capital and consumer demand as the main agents of change, whereas the other perspective sees nation states as key agents in the processes of integration at local levels. Attempting to resolve these perspectives draws attention to the difficulty in distinguishing between 'global' and 'local' 'processes'. Arguably it is misleading to talk about borderless economies and integrated borderlands without specifying precisely what is 'borderless' and what is 'integrated' about them, as the discussion goes on to explain.

Ohmae's 'cartographic illusion'

Kenichi Ohmae is a high profile business consultant who zealously writes about the coming of a new age of borderless economies (Ohmae, 1990; 1993; 1995). Indeed, Ohmae has already announced confidently that nation states have become 'little more than bit actors' on the global stage (1995 , p. 12).

> The nation state has become an unnatural, even dysfunctional, unit for organizing human activity. It represents no genuine, shared community of economic interests; it defines no meaningful flows of economic activity. In fact, it overlooks the true linkages and synergies that exist among often disparate populations by combining measures of human activity at the wrong level of analysis (Ohmae, 1993 , p. 78).

In this new world order, distinct national economies and their associated domestic economic strategies are assumed to be irrelevant, surviving only as relic features amongst states that seek to swim against the tide of globalizing forces. The world economy, it is argued, has moved beyond its former components of international trade and multinational enterprise to become dominated by uncontrollable market forces. The main agents of change being the growing population of truly transnational corporations, that owe allegiance to no nation state and locate wherever in the world that economic advantage is currently seen to reside. Stateless corporations are now the prime movers in an inter-linked world economy dominated by the triad of North America, Europe and Japan (Ohmae, 1990). National governments cannot compete with the flexibility of resource flows within global corporations straddling the triad, and so, it is suggested, their intervention should be abandoned as it merely impedes the efficient allocation of resources and consumer choice. Interestingly in the Asian context, Ohmae (1995) claims further evidence of the erosion of national economic sovereignty in the formation of region states of which his examples include the Pearl River Delta and the SIJORI zone. These sub-nodes in the global economy comprise overlapping national economies, or part of national economies, that provide zones of border-hopping business. Although on a smaller scale to the triad, the same conclusion is drawn: national governments are best advised to step aside from the trade and investment flows across their border.

In a number of respects Ohmae's arguments about the nature of the so-called inter-linked global economy are very persuasive. In the late twentieth century many of the older patterns of inter-state interaction have begun to lose their dominance so much so that it is futile to try to map all the flows and linkages that transcend political borders because they have become so extensive. The very existence of complex 'production chains' and 'relational networks'[12] means that trying to specify the origin of a particular product or trying to attach a 'national' label to a product is either complicated or meaningless (Dicken, 1994). And it is certainly true that flows of economic activity measured in terms of trade statistics represent a tiny and steadily diminishing share of economic linkages between two countries (Ohmae, 1995, pp. 16-17). In these and other ways, the political map made up of a patchwork of nation states is indeed 'the cartographic illusion' Ohmae states it is.

Ohmae's analysis correctly calls into question the significance of territorial nation states as adequate units of economic analysis and originators of the real forces that are shaping economic change. This does not necessarily imply an 'end of geography' as the rising tide of forces related to globalization and greater economic inter-linkage engulf states, although this has become the prognosis for financial markets (see O'Brien, 1992). On the contrary, Ohmae is essentially saying that much of the economic data used to measure the performance of national economies and often referred to as measures of economic change are at best misleading, if not 'out-and-out falsehood' (Ohmae, 1995, p. 18). Indeed, Ohmae seems to be on the same wavelength as geographers who are warning us against 'the territorial trap' of reifying sovereign states (Agnew & Corbridge, 1995, ch. 4), by recognizing the simple crucial fact that nation states are not single economic entities, but are in fact made up of

> a motley combination of territories with vastly different needs and vastly different abilities to contribute (to the inter-linked global economy) (Ohmae, 1995, p. 12).

However, while the general context of Ohmae's argument bears scrutiny, investigation of his specific examples and the claims he builds upon then are more open to question. As noted above, Ohmae has picked out the examples of SIJORI and the Pearl River Delta to illustrate his arguments that such 'region states' are an important geographical manifestation of borderless economic processes undermining nation states. The distinguishing features of a region state being:

1   They represent 'natural economic zones' conforming more to flows of human economic activity than political bodies. The implication being that market linkages and investment flows are overcoming artificial political constraints at national levels and transcending political borders at international levels.
2   They may or may not fall within the geographic limits of a particular nation state. For instance, Ohmae cites the Silicon Valley/Bay Area in California, northern Italy and Japan's Kansai region (Osaka, Kobe and Kyoto) as examples that do; and SIJORI, Hong Kong-South China (although not after June 1997!), and San Diego-Tijuana, as examples that spill over political boundaries.
3   They possess, in one or another combination, the key ingredients for successful participation in the global economy. These include combinations of managerial skill, technology, infrastructure, professional services, labour and resources. Built into the notion of region state is the combining of resources to enable comparative advantages in international markets vis-à-vis less fortunate regions.
4   Their primary economic linkages are with the global economy and not with their host nations. In fact domestic legal, political and institutional constraints may frustrate region state participation in global markets.
5   They should have populations large enough to share certain economic and consumer interests but of adequate size to justify the infrastructure and services necessary to fully participate economically on a global scale.

Ohmae paints an exciting business perspective of newly emergent region states developing rapidly as a result of corporate expansions, cross-border private investments and consumer power; a potent combination of forces that is helping to reduce the barrier effects of different national rules and regulations. What the assortment of intra-state and cross-border zones Ohmae calls region states have in common is 'that they gladly sidestep the bunting and hoopla of sovereignty in return for the ability to harness the global I's (Investment, Industry, Information Technology, and Individual Consumers) to their own needs' (Ohmae, 1995, p. 81). The notion of region states incorporates several assumptions about the evolution of world economy. Ohmae's assumptions are worth reviewing in detail to undermine the difficulty in substantiating any sudden loss in national sovereignty.

Even a superficial examination of SIJORI should reveal that this is not a 'natural economic zone' as that Ohmae requires to meet his criteria of a region state. First, economic cooperation between Singapore and Indonesia has only been made possible by a big investment in political capital. Whilst both states have very different political systems there is one thing they have in common and that is the strong influence of centralized decision-making. The economic development of Batam, Bintan, Karimum and a few neighbouring Riau islands has involved joint state ventures for specific projects and substantial Singapore government-linked company investments and Indonesian state-fostered private sector investments.

Second, with regard to Ohmae's use of the term 'borderless' economies, the fact remains that all states of Southeast Asia are extremely sensitive about issues of national sovereignty. Sub-regional economic cooperation poses a dilemma, because the states involved 'have to reconcile the tension between statism and market forces, particularly those which have a tendency to create interdependence and in the process, undermine sovereignty' (Ganesan, 1993, p. 6). From the case of Singapore-Indonesia cooperation in the SIJORI triangle it can be seen that joint developments have been carefully restricted to self-contained projects, whether this is an industrial park, a golf course or recreational resort. There has been very little movement towards the creation of genuine transboundary institutions or towards a harmonizing of national laws in the sub-region. For instance, Indonesia's land laws are considered confusing to foreign investors and have deterred many from investing in property (Davidson, 1992). The national borders mark the limits of very different regulatory and enforcement environments for business and ordinary citizens, and the existence of pragmatic state-level economic cooperation has done little to reduce national differentiation within the sub-region itself. Certainly the willingness of Southeast Asian states and sub-state authorities to foster transnational institutionalization has so far been a good deal less than in parts of Europe (see Scott, 1993). Without the development of genuine transnational institutions and without a more complete harmonization of regulatory systems across boundaries it is difficult to talk of the sub-regional borderlands as being in any way 'integrated' in the sense discussed by Martinez (1994). Such developments would require political willingness to compromise over national sovereignty in a way that is not discussed in Ohmae's analysis of region states.

Global-local tensions, border regions as centres of production and the politics of sub-regional integration

From the foregoing, it is clear that we should analyze both the political and economic dimensions of changing economic landscapes in Southeast Asia (Van Grunsven et al. 1995; Acharya, 1995). Foreign policy and diplomacy is increasingly about raising economic wealth, capturing new market and investment opportunities, rather than about territorial possessions or traditional security concerns (Stopford & Strange, 1992). States are finding that external-orientation, forging strategic economic alliances (with corporations and with other states) and internationalizing state activities are becoming necessary for survival in the inter-linked global economy. Thus, the different types of sub-regional economic zones we now see in Southeast Asia are the 'spatial outcomes' of complex competitive and bargaining relationships between and within states, between and within firms, and between firms and states (Dicken, 1994). Globalization has not brought an end of geography, but there is a great variety of possible spatial outcomes, as both autonomous and state-induced forces of change 'are producing spaces which are increasingly diverse, in both geographical scale and structural characteristics' (Van Grunsven et al., p. 151). As one scholar has enthusiastically proclaimed:

The emergence of urban centres along international boundaries reflects a pattern of gradual integration of border territory into the financial and economic circuitry of the global political-economic system. Where once boundaries were seen as marginal spaces in a world that was largely organized around centrist nation states, the late twentieth century has seen the old system fade away: in the new global territorial order, boundary regions may become centres of production and urban life. Thus, a new form of city has evolved: the international border- or transfrontier-metropolis (Herzog, 1991, p. 520).

Studies of urban regional transformations alongside changes in economic structures in border regions help us to appreciate the global-local dynamics of cross-boundary interaction and integration (see, for example, Herzog, 1991; McGee & MacLeod, 1992; Van Grunsven, 1995).

Dicken (1994) has discussed numerous 'global-local tensions' arising from the organization and politics of production as both states and firms attempt to gain added wealth and to be competitive in the battle for market shares (see also, Stopford & Strange, 1992). By 'local' Dicken was mostly referring to the political context provided by nation states. Nevertheless, it is important to break the meaning of 'local' down to different spatial scales, to incorporate territories and localities at sub-nation state levels as well as borderlands. In fact, borderlands by nature are more than just dividing zones or passage zones between neighbouring nation states for they represent zones of considerable cultural intermingling, socio-economic interaction, trade, exchange and movement across political space (Strassoldo, 1982; Rumley & Minghi, 1991; Martinez, 1994). Whilst some of the local-level tensions are related to the internal dynamics of particular border regions, most are influenced or caused by broader processes of change at global, regional and national levels. It is useful to highlight some of the inherent conflicts and contradictions involved in forms of sub-regional economic development. For as Acharya (1995, p. 180) observed, 'growth triangles have the potential to aggravate cleavages along political, administrative/constitutional and ethnic lines'.

Issues of distribution, substitution and power — One area of possible conflict relates to the spreading of economic gains that result from transnational production. Any form of economic development has uneven social and spatial outcomes. Part of the problem relates to the fact that states (the political, military and bureaucratic elites) often tend to act for special interest groups, political parties or class elites, bureaucratic interests, big businesses, military interests or even on behalf of specific ethnic groups, and this can conflict with the interests of the broader population or at least with the weaker sections of that population. Rumley (1991) has argued that where there is a coincidence of political, economic, cultural and geographical core-periphery relations, there is a greater potential for conflict. Such is the case with many of the border regions of Myanmar (Lintner, 1995). The case of SIJORI cannot be properly understood without some understanding of federal politics in Malaysia as they relate to relations between the federal government and local state agencies and elites in Johore. Similarly, there is a need to consider centre-periphery political, administrative and economic structures in Indonesia. In other words, there is a need to understand how regional planning relates to structures of power and wealth and to the political organization of space (Slater, 1989).[13] It is also necessary to consider how social and economic processes produce particular spatial forms (Massey, 1994). Related to these issues are the ways in which states try to intervene to influence spatial outcomes. With regard to the SIJORI growth triangle, as Rodan (1993, p. 243) has put it:

> there is the multifaceted set of problems around the issues of equality and distribution between states which both Malaysian and Indonesian central governments have to address, but their counterparts are not troubled by the sovereign city-state. For one thing, the rapid industrialization of those Malaysian and Indonesian states within the triangle must demonstrably benefit citizens in other states and provinces in those nations. Conspicuously better standards of living in these states, especially where central governments have fostered the Growth Triangle, would be unsustainable politically.

We should not divorce questions of sub-regional development from issues of state power and legitimacy. Throughout Southeast Asia, state-induced spatial policies are not simply concerned about distributing economic development benefits to more localities, but are often directly associated with attempts to extend state power over people, resources and territory in peripheral areas (Rumley, 1991; De Koninck, 1996; Grundy-Warr & Rajah, in press).

The issues of substitution, that is where development in one place may displace development elsewhere, are closely related to those of distribution. For instance, there appear to be questions relating to the extent to which specific enclaved industrial developments in one locality, such as the Batam Industrial Park, will actually generate positive spillovers for the rest of the Riau province. Furthermore, the creation of a special bonded zone with special investment conditions, incentives and a regulatory framework that has been adjusted to favour foreign capital, has led to an influx of foreign direct investment that would be difficult to replicate in many localities dispersed throughout different parts of the vast archipelagic state of Indonesia.

Complementarity or competition — Many of the supposed economic benefits of sub-regional economic development are to come from the linking up of economies at different stages of development with differentials in economic structure, resources and costs that produce a complementarity that can help to generate new market opportunities, attract new foreign direct investments, as well as facilitate vertical specialization across borders (Lee, 1993; Thant et al. 1994).

The existence of substantial economic cooperation sanctioned by states does not, however, remove the potential for aggressive economic nationalism, particularly when there are perceived political advantages to be gained from this. For example, there is increasing competition between Malaysia and Singapore for information technology business, particularly with the development of Malaysia's Multimedia Super Corridor project (*Straits Times*, 12 March 1997, p. 34). Such competition is set to intensify in spite of the pre-existing extensive transboundary economic ties between Singapore and Malaysia. Furthermore, some writers have argued that 'the inherent dynamics of borderland integration are to transform previous economic partners into future economic competitors', a trend already noted in Guangdong Province *vis-à-vis* Hong Kong and in Johore in relation to Singapore (Ho & So, 1997, p. 257). In fact, given the diverse range of industries and economic activities found in these examples of sub-regional development, there is in fact likely to be a mix of competition and complementarity with core, intermediate and low value-added activities existing within close geographic proximity (see, for example, Van Grunsven, 1995).

In contrast other proposed ASEAN growth triangles, such as the northern triangle between northern peninsular Malaysia, northern Sumatra, Indonesia and southern Thailand (MIT), may have significant problems arising from too little complementarity between the component parts of the zone (Salleh, 1993; Hady, 1993; Ali, 1996).[14]

Social tensions — The nature of economic change and development arising from sub-regional cooperation may give rise to a wide range of actual or potential social problems. For instance, the rapid industrialization processes in Johore and Batam have led to considerable inflationary pressures, property speculation and conflicts over land-use development. Whilst Singapore and TNC subsidiaries from the Lion City have been one of the principal and largest investors in Johore since the mid-1980s (Van Grunsven, 1995)[15], and some 25,000 'day-trippers' cross the 1.2-kilometre causeway into Johore where they are the major consumers (Heibert, 1997, p. 64), such economic interdependence is not without its costs. Singaporean consumers have driven retail prices above levels found elsewhere in Malaysia, and Singaporeans and some of the 60,000 Malaysians who commute to work in Singapore, have contributed to property price hikes that are beyond the reach of many locals. This has prompted the government to introduce a MR100,000 levy on foreign buyers in late 1995 (Heibert, 1997, p. 65). There is also great sensitivity in Johore concerning perceived Singaporean aloofness and attitudes. Negative externalities associated with the speed and nature of economic development are also found in Batam. Many of these problems are associated with the daily influx into the island of undocumented migrants from other parts of Indonesia attracted by news of the 'Batam boom', and they include rising unemployment and underemployment, rising crime, prostitution, and numerous squatter settlements. There are frequent reports in the local press about insufficient housing, a lack of basic amenities and inadequate services for the majority of people now living in Batam (*Riau Pos*, 26 September 1996, p. 8). One of the biggest planning worries that threatens to compromise the quality of life on the island for many thousands of people is the shortfall in affordable and appropriate housing. Over-populated and make-shift squatter settlements (*ruli*) coexist alongside purpose-built executive housing estates with names like Shangri La Gardens and Palm Springs, which stand virtually empty. It is estimated that there are well over 20,000 units of squatter housing in and around 60-80 locations dotted throughout the island. Even a conservative estimate of 20,000 *ruli* units and an average of five persons per unit would mean that almost 100,000 people, or half of Batam's 1996 official population of 208,248, would be squatters.[16] In fact, the total population of the island is likely to be much higher due to the fact that most migrants do not have proper permits or residency status.

Political relations and national security issues — Earlier some of the security-enhancing aspects of regionalization and economic integration were mentioned. Even so, it is important to note that there may also be security-diminishing aspects (Acharya, 1995). Again this can be illustrated by drawing on the case of SIJORI. Undoubtedly, an important motive underlying Singapore's agreement to undertake joint development projects in the Riau islands with Indonesia was the city-state's need to lessen dependence on Malaysia for critical resources, particularly freshwater supply.[17] Speculation exists in Malaysia that Singapore is using its economic and security ties with Indonesia to act as a counterweight to Malaysia. For example, at a particular time when political tensions across the causeway were high in March 1997, *The Straits Times* (18 March 1997, p. 1) was confidently reporting that Singapore's relations with her southern neighbour were thriving and quoting President Suharto's reference to Singapore as 'our closest neighbour'.[18]

Clearly we need to consider the politics of sub-regional change very carefully. In all the ASEAN growth triangles there is currently a lack of strong transnational institutionalization to ensure the smooth operation of various bilateral or trilateral projects. As Acharya (1995, p. 182) has stated:

> While the various governments speak of the need to let the private sector take the lead in organizing the growth triangles, their lack of willingness to familiarize and institutionalize these triangles also ensures that the latter remain hostage to inter-state political relationships, which are vulnerable to periodic setbacks.

Many of the examples used in the latter half of this chapter have been drawn from the SIJORI case, which is still the most established of ASEAN's formal attempts to encourage the creation of cross-border economic zones. Even so, sub-regional development has become the buzz-word for planners, policy-makers, bureaucrats and investment brokers, such as the Asian Development Bank, throughout Southeast Asia. In each case of sub-regional development there is a need to ask what is the form of economic integration that is planned? Who are the main players, agencies or investors? Who are the beneficiaries likely to be? Where are the changes taking place? What are the likely externalities and costs involved? The fact remains that in the region there is still cautious coexistence between states rather than interdependence, and evidence of integration in some parts of mainland Southeast Asia relates much more to undocumented and illegal activity than to forms of formal cross-border linkage (see, for example, Grundy-Warr, 1993; Mya Than, 1994; Phongpaichit et al., 1996). Efforts to formalize transboundary trade and to incorporate these borderlands into regional and global markets are obviously going to have a great variety of social, economic, political and spatial outcomes that will occupy the minds of interested researchers for many years to come.

Conclusion

This chapter has assessed claims about the loss of national sovereignty and drift towards a globalized world economy in the context of regionalization initiatives promoted by or within ASEAN. The general concern has been to argue that claims about such a trend have tended indiscriminately to label processes producing different outcomes. Allegedly, the centrality of national institutions and their capacity to act are being undermined by the intensification of flows of goods, people, capital and information across borders. In practice, it is possible to encourage this form of economic integration without significant loss of sovereignty, as in the case of ASEAN. Greater economic regionalism, the formalization of trade and investment links between longstanding and new ASEAN states, and progress with AFTA, are strengthening intra-regional ties and inter-stateness. Detailed empirical research is needed, however, to examine the differentiated outcomes of these linkages, particularly in mainland Southeast Asia.

We have also examined some of the issues relating to economic change at sub-regional levels, particularly the creation of new cross-boundary zones for manufacturing activity. Hitherto, there have been relatively few intensive micro-level studies that focus on the complicated political, economic, social and spatial dynamics involved in cross-border interaction and regional change. Much of the existing literature for Southeast Asia focuses on the one operational growth triangle — SIJORI. Clearly within these zones, there are numerous global-local tensions and different 'inter' and 'trans' state processes at work worthy of further investigation. We have argued that the blanket application of terms such as 'interdependence', 'borderless economies', 'region states' and 'integrated borderlands' tends to mask the contradictions produced by globalization as well as the segmentation and internal differentiation that often exists in any territory, particularly borderlands. We have also suggested that whilst the sub-regional economic zones have certain 'transnational' characteristics, they are favoured forms of interaction precisely because levels of integration can be largely restricted to specific functions and activities. Furthermore, growth triangles involve little change in national and institutional arrangements and may even operate, as in the case of SIJORI, without formal treaties or changes in domestic regulations.

In addition, there are large parts of the region where questions relating to the significance of nation states in a rapidly changing world economy are largely redundant due to the large proportion of cross-border interaction and business that remains undocumented. Thus, more empirical and theoretical work is required if we are to understand better the different 'inter' and 'trans' processes at work where nation state presence is strong and where it is weak or even absent. We suggest that SIJORI represents a significant pioneering effort to create new and enhance old economic ties between neighbouring territories, but given its rather special circumstances, it is not necessarily a particularly applicable model for sub-regional change in other parts of Southeast Asia.

Acknowledgements
The authors would like to thank Elaine Wong Siew Yin for her efficient assistance in the preparation of this paper.

Notes

1. Alan James (1986) has noted that the term sovereignty is both an essential qualification for full membership of the international system of sovereign states and a fundamental organizing principle of the inter-state system. Even so, the United Nations Charter tells us little about sovereignty which is a prerequisite for membership of the international club of member states. James explains that the necessary prerequisite to be in the running for admission to international society, and for mutual recognition by other states, is constitutional independence.
2. The longstanding member states of the Association of South East Asian Nations (ASEAN) include Brunei, Indonesia, Malaysia, Philippines, Singapore, and Thailand.
3. The new member states of ASEAN are Laos, Myanmar and Vietnam.
4. During the 1980s, ASEAN attracted a quarter of all FDI into developing economies. In 1993, Singapore, Malaysia and Thailand were amongst the top ten developing country recipients of FDI, in a year when estimated flows of FDI to developing countries were equivalent to total world FDI in 1986. Consequently, although China has emerged as a significant competitor destination, the global expansion of FDI has continued to support the economic expansion of ASEAN member states.
5. Despite the adoption of Preferential Trading Arrangements (PTAs) in 1977, intra-ASEAN trade was around 15-20 percent of its global trade. The PTAs were of limited value because of the omission of so-called 'sensitive items', which meant that a decade after launching the PTAs only five percent of 12,000 offered items were actively traded by member countries. In contrast, the trade value covered by products in the AFTA Inclusion List was 85

percent of intra-regional trade in 1993 (see Abad, Jr., 1996, pp. 237-53). Other variables which adversely affected the expansion of intra-ASEAN trade under the PTA were (a) inclusion of products that had low trade content; (b) very low tariff reductions; (c) the nullifying effect of increased utilization of non-tariff barriers to compensate for the reduction of tariff rates. A number of measures are being recommended under AFTA to reduce the defects evident under the PTA.

6. Constructive engagement with Myanmar was largely initiated during the administration of General Chatchai Choonhavan of Thailand in 1988 as part of a Thai foreign policy initiative to generate better economic relations in order to gain access to valuable natural resources in Myanmar, such as natural gas, fisheries and forestry products. It slowly became part of the political lexicon of ASEAN as other member states adopted cordial economic links with their politically troubled neighbour. The term itself was borrowed from the same term utilized by the United States in its relations with South Africa during the *apartheid* era, and indeed, more recently with China. ASEAN states have argued that it is only through economic leverage and diplomatic contacts that they can help to moderate the excesses of the State Law and Order Restoration Council (SLORC) currently ruling Myanmar without popular mandate. It will be interesting to see if ASEAN's collective position will alter in any way following the US decision to impose an economic embargo on new US investments in Myanmar in late April 1997.

7. The rule of *pacta sunt servanda* is meant for the parties to adhere to an agreement to fulfil their obligations and to fulfil them in good faith (refer to O'Connor, 1991)

8. Santiago (1995) discusses ASEAN member states' experience on sovereignty diminution, particularly in regard to the obligations on states that are party to international treaties and agreements. For instance, he examines three agreements Southeast Asian states have been party to — World Trade Organization Agreement's Dispute Settlement Mechanism; the Convention on the Recognition and Enforcement of Foreign Arbitral Awards; and the Convention on the Settlement of Investment Disputes Between States and Nationals of Other States (ICSID Convention).

9. Juridical sovereignty refers to the international legal framework and the mutual acceptance of a state's sovereignty, whereas empirical sovereignty refers to the actual ability of a particular state to control people and resources throughout the whole of its territory. It is possible to lack empirical sovereignty but still receive international recognition of sovereign statehood with the benefits that it entails. For a full discussion of the significance of this distinction see, Jackson and Roseberg (1986, pp. 259-82).

10. The State Law and Order Restoration Council (SLORC) was established on 18 September 1988 by the armed forces as the national instrument of government following a continuous period of public disturbance and pro-democracy rallies throughout the country. SLORC continues to head the

military regime even though there was an overwhelming victory for the opposition National League for Democracy headed by Aung San Suu Kyi in May 1990. SLORC has refused to allow the People's Assembly to convene and the NLD to form a legitimate government.

11. The growth triangle projects are not the only ways to lessen inter-state tensions. Other developments that have helped improve relations include the willingness of states in the region to attempt peaceful settlements of thorny territorial and sovereignty disputes. A good example of this is the submission of documents by Singapore and Malaysia concerning the disputed sovereignty over the tiny island of Pedra Branca/Pulau Batu Puteh, to the International Court of Justice (ICJ).

12. According to Dicken (1994) 'production systems' should be 'thought of as a complex input-output system of linked production chains with vertical, horizontal, and diagonal links' (p. 103). There are also many kinds of networks consisting of 'a mix of intrafirm and interfirm structures' (p. 105). A very useful empirical study that shows how notions of production chains and linkages can be applied to sub-regional and regional analysis is Van Grunsven (1995).

13. David Slater's (1989) work on what he calls the regional problematic is potentially very applicable to issues of cross-border subregional development in the developing world, particularly in mainland Southeast Asia where questions of economic development cannot be separated from issues of protracted state-societal conflict, ethnic and minority problems and the on-going territorialization strategies of central states in peripheral territories..

14. It is important to stress that the mostly agricultural base of the three components of the IMT triangle, plus the fact that cost and wage differentials between the three are not so marked as in SIJORI zone, represent a potential drag on economic cooperation. Nevertheless, the IMT does have trade complementarities for some items, such as Northern Sumatra (fresh fish, oil and natural gas, fertilizers, low-end garments); Northern Malaysia (high skill manufactures from Penang, industrial chemicals, refined palm oil, iron and steel, processed wood); and Southern Thailand (fresh fruits, processed marine products, processed parawood furniture). For more details, see Ali (1996).

15. Singapore accounted for almost half of the manufacturing jobs in Johore in the early 1990s. The share of Singaporean investments in Johore, which accounted for 22.7 percent of approved investments for the 1981-90 period, was second after Japan (27 percent). Singapore government-linked companies and the subsidiaries of government statutory boards have also participated in the development of several of the 16 industrial estates in Johore. In 1996 alone, businessmen from Singapore captured 91 investment licences worth approximately MR3.2 billion (S$1.3 billion).

16. The official data comes from the Batam Industrial Development Authority (BIDA) which is the Indonesian agency with overall responsibility for the

island's Master Plan and economic development. Data on the squatter settlements was obtained from an unpublished report by Karen Joanne Peachey on existing and alternative planning approaches to informal housing on the island, which was submitted to Lembaga Ilmu Pengetahuan Indonesia (Indonesian Institute of Sciences), Jakarta, in 1996.

17. The importance of the water resource issue for Singapore should not be understated. In anticipation of increasing water consumption in Johore itself and in other states of Malaysia, Singapore's supplies from her northern neighbour are unlikely to expand, and the cost of existing supplies is likely to increase. Thus, the economic cooperation with Indonesia has provided Singapore with an opportunity to diversify its sources of water. In June 1991 there was a Singapore-Indonesia agreement for the supply of up to 1,000 million gallons (4.55 million m³) of water per day to Singapore. Subsequent to this the Public Utilities Board of Singapore incorporated a subsidiary company, Singapore Utilities International (SUI) specifically to participate in water resource development projects in Indonesia (PUB Annual Report, 1992). A further Memorandum of Understanding was signed in January 1993 allowing Singapore to tap the water resources from the Sungei Kampar Catchment in Sumatra. Earlier Singapore's joint development projects in Bintan, one of the Riau islands, included the development of water resources as an objective.

18. In mid-March 1997, the multi-million dollar Karimun Marine and Industrial Complex was launched on the Riau island of Karimun, which represents the latest phase in Singapore-Indonesia bilateral cooperation in the growth triangle. Hitherto, there has been a conspicuous absence of well-developed linkages between Malaysia and Indonesia in the southern (SIJORI) growth triangle, and it seems that the Malaysia authorities are more actively promoting their northern triangle with Indonesia and Thailand (MIT). The Karimun project involves the influential Sembawang Group, a Singapore government-linked company, which is building a shipyard and oil base in a S$1 billion joint venture with Jurong Environmental Engineering (Singapore) and the Salim Group of Indonesia. Karimun is to be a strategic base in the Malacca Straits for shipyards, fabrication works, oil storage facilities and heavy engineering industries. This is further emphasizing the functional specialisms of particular Riau islands involved in the growth triangle. President Suharto of Indonesia met with Prime Minister Goh Chok Tong of Singapore on Karimun to launch the project. He emphasized the complementarity and interdependence between the two countries, and he indicated the cooperative links would develop further in the future. PM Goh has stressed that 'the model of cooperation in the Riaus is also a good one for intra-ASEAN regional cooperation', see *The Straits Times* (18 March 1997, p. 20).

References

Abad, Jr., M.C. (1996), 'Re-engineering ASEAN', *Contemporary Southeast Asia*, Vol. 18, No. 3, pp. 237-53.

Abonyi, G. (1994), 'The Institutional Challenges of Growth Triangles in Southeast Asia', *MPP Working Paper Series*, No. 3, Public Policy Programme, National University of Singapore.

Acharya, A. (1995), 'Transnational Production and Security: Southeast Asia's 'Growth Triangle'', *Contemporary Southeast Asia*, Vol. 17, No. 2, pp. 173-86.

Agnew, J. and Corbridge, S. (1995), *Mastering Space. Hegemony, Territory and International Political Economy*, Routledge: London and New York.

Ali, H. (1996), 'Vanishing Borders: A Case of Indonesia, Malaysia, Thailand Growth Triangle', *Vanishing Borders: The New International Order of the 21ˢᵗ Century*, Commonwealth Geographical Bureau International Conference, Selangor, Malaysia, 19-23 August.

Antolik, M. (1994), 'The ASEAN Regional Forum: The Spirit of Constructive Engagement', *Contemporary Southeast Asia*, Vol. 16, No. 2, pp. 117-36.

Briner, H.J. (1986), 'Regional Planning and Transfrontier Cooperation: The Regio Basiliensis', in Martinez, O.J. (ed.), *Across Boundaries: Transborder Interaction in Comparative Perspective*, Texas Western Press: El Paso, pp. 45-56.

Buzan, B. (1983), *People, States and Fear: The National Security Problem in International Relations*, Wheatsheaf Books: Brighton.

Camilleri, J.A. (1990), 'Rethinking Sovereignty in a Shrinking Fragmented World', in Walker, R.B.J. and Mendlovitz, S.H. (eds), *Contending Sovereignties: Redefining Political Community*, Lynne Rienner: Boulder, pp. 13-44.

Chee, P.L. (1995), 'ASEAN-Indo-China Relations: Prospects and Scope for Enhanced Economic Co-operation', in Toshihiki Kawagoe and Sueto Sekiguchi (eds), *East Asian Economies: Transformation and Challenges*, ISEAS: Singapore, pp. 305-31.

Chia, S.Y. (1995), 'Progress and Issues in ASEAN Economic Integration', in Toshihiko Kawagoe and Sueto Sekiguchi (eds), *East Asian Economies: Transformation and Challenges*, ISEAS: Singapore, pp. 265-304.

Chia, S.Y. and Lee, T.Y. (1992), 'Subregional Economic Zones: A New Motive Force in the Asia-Pacific Region', Paper presented at the 20th Pacific Trade and Development Conference, Washington, D.C. 10-12 September.

Clad, J. (1991), *Behind the Myth. Business, Money and Power in Southeast Asia*, Grafton Books: London.

Daquila, T.C. (1997), 'At 30, ASEAN Looks Ahead with Optimism', *Trends*, No. 79, March 29-30, p. 4, The Business Times: Singapore.

Davidson, P. (1992), 'An Economic Law Perspective', Paper presented at the International Symposium on Regional Cooperation and Growth Triangles in ASEAN, National University of Singapore, 23-24 April.

225

De Koninck, R. (1996), 'The Peasantry as the Territorial Spearhead of the State in Southeast Asia: The Case of Vietnam', *Sojourn*, Vol. 11, No. 2, pp. 231-58.

Dicken, P. (1992), *Global Shift. The Internationalization of Economic Activity*, P. Chapman Publishing Ltd.: London.

Dicken, P. (1994), 'Global-Local Tensions: Firms and States in the Global Space-Economy', *Economic Geography*, Vol. 70, No. 2, pp. 101-28.

Endo, S. (1994), 'Issues of Security in East Asia in the Post-Cold War Era', *Caps Discussion Paper*, #5-13, Seiki University: Tokyo.

Esmara, H. (1975), 'An Economic Survey of Riau', *Bulletin of Indonesia Economic Studies*, Vol. 7, No. 1, pp. 41-57.

Fujita, K. and Hill, R. (1995), 'Global Toyotaism and Local Development', *International Journal of Urban and Regional Research*, Vol. 19, No. 1, pp. 7-22.

Ganesan, N. (1993), 'Conceptualising Regional Economic Cooperation: Perspectives from Political Science', in Toh, M.H. and Low, L. (eds), *Regional Cooperation and Growth Triangles in ASEAN*, Times Academic Press: Singapore, pp. 1-8.

Grundy-Warr, C. (1993), 'Co-existent Borderlands and Intra-State Conflicts in Mainland Southeast Asia', *Singapore Journal of Tropical Geography*, Vol. 14, No. 1, pp. 42-56.

Grundy-Warr, C. and Rajah, A. (forthcoming), 'Security, Resources and People in a Borderlands Environment: Myanmar-Thailand', in Blake, G.H., Chia, L.S., Grundy-Warr, C., Pratt, M.A. and Schofield, C.H. (eds), *International Boundaries and Environmental Security: Frameworks for Regional Cooperation*, Kluwer/Martinus Nijhoff: London.

Hady, H. (1993), 'The Northern Growth Triangles: An Indonesian Perspective', in Toh, M.H. and Low, L. (eds), *Regional Cooperation and Growth Triangles in ASEAN*, Times Academic Press: Singapore, pp. 75-91.

Herzog, L.A. (1990), *Where North Meets South: Cities, Space and Politics on the US-Mexico Border*, Center for Mexican American Studies, University of Texas: Austin.

Herzog, L.A. (1991), 'Cross-National Urban Structure in the Era of Global Cities: The US-Mexico Transfrontier Metropolis', *Urban Studies*, Vol. 28, No. 4, pp. 519-33.

Heibert, M. (1997), 'Being Neighbourly. Malaysia's Johor State Finds Singapore Too Close for Comfort', *Far Eastern Economic Review*, Vol. 160, No. 13, pp. 64-5.

Higgott, R. (1994), 'Ideas, Identity and Policy Coordination in the Asia-Pacific', *The Pacific Review*, Vol. 7, No. 4, pp. 367-79.

Hirsch, P. (1995), 'Thailand and The New Geopolitics of Southeast Asia: Resource and Environmental Issues', in Rigg, J. (ed.) *Counting the Costs: Economic Growth and Environmental Change in Thailand*, ISEAS: Singapore.

Ho, K.C. and So, A. (1997), 'Semi-Periphery and Borderland Integration: Singapore and Hong Kong Experiences', *Political Geography*, Vol. 16, No. 3, pp. 241-59.

Hoang, A.T. (1994), 'Vietnam's Membership of ASEAN: Economic, Political and Security Implications', *Contemporary Southeast Asia*, Vol. 16, No. 3, December, pp. 259-73.

Jackson, R.H. & Roseberg, C.G. (1986), 'Why Africa's Weak States Persist: The Empirical and the Juridical in Statehood', in Atul Kohli (ed.) *The State and Development in the Third World*, Princeton, NJ: Princeton University Press, pp. 259-82.

James, A. (1986), *Sovereign Statehood: The Basis of International Society*, Allen & Unwin: London.

Kumar, S. and Siddique, S. (1994), 'Beyond Economic Reality: New Thoughts on the Growth Triangle', *Southeast Asian Affairs*, ISEAS: Singapore.

Lee, T.Y. (1993), 'Sub-regional Economic Zones in the Asia-Pacific: An Overview', in Toh, M.H. and Low, L. (eds), *Regional Cooperation and Growth Triangles in ASEAN*, Times Academic Press: Singapore, pp. 9-58.

Leung, C.K. (1993), 'Personal Contacts, Subcontracting Linkages, and Development in the Hong Kong-Zhujiang Delta Region', *Annals of the Association of American Geographers*, Vol. 83, No. 2, pp. 272-302.

Lintner, B. (1995), 'Recent Developments on the Thai-Burma Border', *Boundary and Security Bulletin*, Vol. 3, No. 1, pp. 72-6.

Martinez, O.J. (1994), 'The Dynamics of Border Interaction. New Approaches to Border Analysis', in Schofield, C.H. (ed.), *World Boundaries, Vol. 1, Global Boundaries*, Routledge: London, pp. 1-15.

Massey, D. (1994), *Spatial Divisions of Labour: Social Structures and the Geography of Production*, Methuen: New York.

McGee, T. & MacLeod, S. (1992), 'Emerging Extended Metropolitan Regions in the Asia-Pacific Urban System: A Case Study of the Singapore-Johor-Riau Growth Triangle', Workshop on the Asia-Pacific Urban System Towards the 21st Century, Hong Kong, 11-13 February.

McIntyre, A. (1993), 'Indonesia, Thailand and the Northeast Asian Connection' in Higgott R., Leaver R. and Ravenhill, J. (eds.), *Pacific Economic Relations in the 1990s: Cooperation or Conflict?*, Allen & Unwin: Sydney, pp. 250-70.

Milward, A.S. and Sørensen, V. (1993), 'Interdependence or Integration? A National Choice', in Milward A.S., Lynch F.M.B., Romero F., Ranieri R., and Sørensen V. (eds), *The Frontier of National Sovereignty. History and Theory 1945-1992*, Routledge: London, pp. 1-33.

Murphy, A.B. (1994), 'International Law and the Sovereign State: Challenges to the Status Quo', in Demko, G.J. and Wood, W.B. (eds), *Reordering the World: Geopolitical Perspectives in the 21st Century*, Westview Press: Boulder, CO., pp. 209-55.

Mya Than (1992), *Myanmar's External Trade. An Overview in the Southeast Asian Context*, Institute of Southeast Asian Studies: Singapore.

Mya Than (1994), 'Border Trade in the Golden Quandrangle', Conference on Asia's New Growth Circles at The Chaiyong Limthongkul Foundation, Chiang

Mai, Thailand, 3-6 March.

O'Brien, R. (1992), *Global Financial Integration: The End of Geography*, Routledge: London.

O'Connor, J.F. (1991), *Good Faith in International Law*, Dartmouth Publishing Co.: Vermont.

Ohmae, K. (1990), *The Borderless World. Power and Strategy in the Global Market place*, Harper Collins: London.

Ohmae, K. (1993), 'The Rise of the Region State', *Foreign Affairs*, Spring.

Ohmae, K. (1995), *The End of the Nation State. The Rise of Regional Economies*, The Free Press: New York.

Paribatra, S. (1994), 'From ASEAN Six to ASEAN Ten: Issues and Prospects', *Contemporary Southeast Asia*, Vol. 16, No. 3, pp. 243-58.

Perry, M. (1991), 'The Singapore Growth Triangle: State, Capital and Labour at a New Frontier in the World Economy', *Singapore Journal of Tropical Geography*, Vol. 12, No. 2, pp. 138-51.

Phongpaichit, P., Piriyarangsan, S. and Treerat, N. (1996), 'Thailand's Illegal Economy Is Reeling Out of Control', Extract of a Research Report of the Political Economy Centre, Chulalongkorn University, Bangkok, published in *The Straits Times*, Singapore, December 5, p. 60.

Riau Pos, 'Tanpa Antisipasi Serius, Pendidikan di Batam akan Hadapi Problem Pelik', 26 September 1996, p. 8.

Rice, R. (1989), 'Riau and Jambi: Rapid Growth in Dualistic Natural Resource-Intensive Economies' in Hill, H. (ed.), *Unity and Diversity: Regional Economic Development in Indonesia since 1970*, Oxford University Press: Singapore, pp. 125-50.

Rigg, J. (1995), 'Managing Dependency in a Reforming Economy: The Lao PDR', *Contemporary Southeast Asia*, Vol. 17, No. 2, pp. 147-72.

Rodan, G. (1993), 'Reconstructing Divisions of Labour: Singapore's New Regional Emphasis', in Higgott, R., Leaver, R. and Ravenhill, J. (eds), *Pacific Economic Relations in the 1990s: Cooperation or Conflict?*, Allen & Unwin: Sydney, pp. 223-49.

Rumley, D. (1991), 'Society, State and Peripherality: The Case of the Thai-Malaysian Border Landscape', in Rumley, D. and Minghi J.V. (eds), *The Geography of Border Landscapes*, Routledge: London, pp. 129-51.

Rumley, D. & Minghi, J.V. (eds), *The Geography of Border Landscapes*, Routledge: London.

Salleh, I.M. (1993), 'Economic Cooperation in the Northern Triangle' in Toh, M.H. and Low, L. (eds), *Regional Cooperation and Growth Triangles in ASEAN*, Times Academic Press: Singapore, pp. 59-66.

Santiago, J.S.S. (1995), 'A Postscript to AFTA's False Start. The Loss of Sovereignty Issue', *ASEAN Economic Bulletin*, Vol. 12, No. 1, pp. 18-28.

Scott, J.W. (1993), 'The Institutionalization of Transboundary Cooperation in Europe: Recent Development on the Dutch-German Border', *Journal of Borderlands Studies*, Vol. VIII, No. 1, Spring, pp. 39-66.

Sklair, L. (1993), *Assembling for Development: The Maquila Industry in Mexico and the United States*, Center for US-Mexico Studies: San Diego.

Slater, D. (1989), 'Peripheral Capitalism and the Regional Problematic' in Peet, R. and Thrift, N. (eds), *New Models in Geography: The Political Economy Perspective*, Unwin Hyman: London, pp. 267-94.

Soesastro, H. (1992), 'The ASEAN Free Trade Area (AFTA) and the Future of Asian Dynamism', Centre for Strategic and International Studies: Jakarta.

Stopford, J. and Strange, S. with Henly, J.S. (1992), *Rival States, Rival Firms: Competition for World Market Shares*, Cambridge University Press: Cambridge.

Strassoldo, R. (1982), 'Boundaries in Sociological Theory: A Reassessment', in Strassoldo, R. and Delli Zotti, G. (eds.), *Cooperation and Conflict in Border Areas*, Angeli: Milan.

Sung, Y.W., Liu, P.W., Wong, Y.C.R and Lau, P.K. (1995), *The Fifth Dragon: The Emergence of the Pearl River Delta*, Addison Wesley Publishing Company: Singapore.

Takeuchi, J. (1993), 'Effect of AFTA on ASEAN Industrial Structure', *Pacific Business and Industries*, Vol. 1, pp. 10-41.

Tang, M. and Thant, M. (1994), 'Growth Triangles: Conceptual and Operational Considerations', in Thant, M., Tang, M. and Kakazu, H. (eds), *Growth Triangles in Asia*, Oxford University Press: Hong Kong.

Taylor, P.J. (1995), 'Beyond Containers: Internationality, Interstateness, Inter-territoriality', *Progress in Human Geography*, Vol. 19, pp. 1-15.

Thant, M., Tang, M. and Kazaku, H. (eds) (1994), *Growth Triangles in Asia. A New Approach to Regional Economic Cooperation*, Oxford University Press: Hong Kong.

The Straits Times, Singapore, 'IT Trade 'Enough for Both Singapore and Malaysia'', March 12, 1997, p. 34.

The Straits Times, Singapore, 'A New Milestone in Singapore-Indonesia Ties', March 18, 1997, p. 1.

Tripathi, S. (1996), 'The Good, the Bad and the Ugly. Malaysian Cowboy Capitalists Rushing in Where Others Fear to Tread: Cambodia', *Asia Inc.*, Vol. 5, No. 4, pp. 40-47.

Van Grunsven, L. (1995), 'Industrial Regionalization and Urban-Regional Transformation in Southeast Asia: The SIJORI Growth Triangle Considered', *The Malaysian Journal of Tropical Geography*, Vol. 26, pp. 47-65.

Van Grunsven, L., Wong, S.Y. and Kim, W.B. (1995), 'State, Investment and Territory: Regional Economic Zones and Emerging Industrial Landscapes', in Le Heron, R. and Park, S.O. (eds), *The Asian Pacific Rim and Globalization. Enterprise, Governance and Territoriality*, Avebury: Aldershot, pp. 151-77.

Wanandi, S. (1997), 'ASEAN Inc.? First, The Region Needs to Get Its Act Together', *Asiaweek*, Vol. 23, No. 15, pp. 68.

Index

230

236

For Product Safety Concerns and Information please contact our EU
representative GPSR@taylorandfrancis.com Taylor & Francis Verlag GmbH,
Kaufingerstraße 24, 80331 München, Germany

Printed and bound by CPI Group (UK) Ltd, Croydon, CR0 4YY
08/05/2025
01864370-0008